Praise for

CASCADES

In *Cascades*, Greg Satell delivers an essential guide to navigating and driving change in today's disruptive environment. I wish he had written it years ago. It would have reinforced our need not only to have the right strategy but to manage the entrenched forces working against it.

—John Antioco, former CEO of Blockbuster Video and Chairman of Red Mango

Greg Satell's *Cascades* is among the most useful, engaging, and well-crafted books ever written on how to start and sustain large-scale change. Satell does a masterful job of weaving cases, stories, and evidence to illustrate the nuances of his simple formula—small groups, loosely connected, and united by a common purpose—and to show when and how leaders can use these elements to spread ideas and change organizations for the better.

—Robert Sutton, Stanford Professor and bestselling author of *Good Boss, Bad Boss* and *Scaling Up Excellence*

One of the great puzzles of history is how enduring business, political, and social orders can crumble without warning, seemingly overnight. In *Cascades,* bestselling author Greg Satell lucidly combines insights from network science, historical case studies, and his own experience living through Ukraine's Orange Revolution in 2004 to deliver a thought-provoking account of this profound phenomenon. *Cascades* is essential reading for policy makers, business leaders, and social activists alike.

—Duncan J. Watts, author of *Six Degrees*

Greg Satell really understands movements—how they arise and what makes them succeed or fail. What makes him unique is his ability to show how the principles apply beyond the political sphere to organizations, industries, and society as a whole.

—Srdja Popović, Executive Director of the Centre for Applied Nonviolent Action and Strategies (CANVAS), Cofounder of Otpor!, and author of *Blueprint for Revolution*

The complex nature of modern-day counterterrorism taught us that defeating threat networks requires a hybrid structure of network and hierarchy. In *Cascades*, Satell walks us through the impacts that networks are having in other spaces, and shows us that it is often small groups with the ability to interoperate with other small groups that are the key to driving change. For those hoping to deepen their understanding of the current state of play, *Cascades* is a must-read!

—Chris Fussell, President of McChrystal Group and bestselling author of *One Mission* and *Team of Teams* (with General Stanley McChrystal)

In *Cascades*, you will learn how to create a successful movement, while avoiding pitfalls along the way. Throughout the book, Greg makes the case that the principles of great movements throughout history can empower you to create change in your own life, community, and company.

—Dan Schawbel, bestselling author of *Back to Human*, *Promote Yourself*, and *Me 2.0*

Creating change today requires more than a strategy, but a deep understanding of how information flows through networks and ecosystems to affect behavior. Greg Satell has a real talent for explaining the science behind networks and how it affects events in the real world in a way that is fun, engaging, and powerful.

—AnnaLee Saxenian, Dean and Professor at UC Berkeley School of Information and author of *Regional Advantage* and *The New Argonauts*

I wish I had this book when we started our movement to improve STEM education in America! *Cascades* promises to be an essential guide for anyone who wants to create meaningful change in the world.

—Talia Milgrom-Elcott, Executive Director
and Cofounder of 100Kin10

Cascades provides a powerful blueprint for corporate change that leverages lessons learned from social movements around the world and throughout history. This book will forever change your perception of change and how to make it happen.

—Stephen Shapiro, author of *Best Practices Are Stupid*

Ready to reboot your company culture? Create something new? Leaders in organizations large and small will find an important blueprint for how to fail at starting a movement and how to inspire the kind of change that makes history in Greg Satell's *Cascades*. A must-read for all innovators and daring organizers.

—Lu Ann Cahn, eight-time Emmy award
winner and author of *I Dare Me*

The test of an excellent book on a leadership topic is its ability to give profound insights on daily situations that help leaders to do their jobs better. I had many "aha!" moments reading this book, but my favorite idea is the notion of "keystone changes" (in Chapter 4). What a genius concept! I have tried this idea out with several work teams, and all of them have moved forward in their thinking and practice as a result. We are joining the ranks of Gandhi and the salt march, votes for women, and the same-sex marriage movement in finding a common cause that a diverse group of people can unite behind. The difference between tactics that work for social movements and tactics for contemporary organizations is actually not that great.

—Helen Bevan, Chief Transformation Officer at
NHS Horizons (National Health Service of England)

CASCADES

HOW TO CREATE A MOVEMENT THAT DRIVES TRANSFORMATIONAL CHANGE

GREG SATELL

McGraw Hill Education

New York Chicago San Francisco Athens London Madrid
Mexico City Milan New Delhi Singapore Sydney Toronto

1 2 3 4 5 6 7 8 9 LCR 24 23 22 21 20 19

ISBN 978-1-260-45401-7
MHID 1-260-45401-0

e-ISBN978-1-260-45402-4
e-MHID 1-260-45402-9

To all the friends I have met on my travels.
And to my wife, Liliana, and daughter, Ashley,
Who brought me home

CONTENTS

ACKNOWLEDGMENTS

Alfred Lord Tennyson wrote "I am a part of all that I have met," and that is doubly true for this book. A number of people contributed, in ways large and small, to developing and writing *Cascades*, and whatever it achieves is largely due to them. Any errors are, of course, my own.

Srdja Popović spent countless hours schooling me on the principles that led to the great successes of the Otpor movement and the Centre for Applied Nonviolent Action and Strategies (CANVAS). He was also generous to be frank and open with me about the failures along the way, how he and his colleagues learned from them and were able to adapt to changing contexts. Most of all, he became a dear friend, and for that I am truly grateful.

My friend and former colleague Vitaliy Sych, as well as Mustafa Nayyem and Vitaliy Shabunin, provided me with essential insights into what has transpired in Ukraine since I left in 2011. Each continues to play an important part in shaping the country for the better to this day.

Duncan Watts and Steven Strogatz, both through their work and through my personal interactions with them, helped me understand the dynamics of networks and the role they play in change movements. Over the years they have been incredibly generous with their time and insights. The conversations I have had with AnnaLee Saxenian shaped my thinking about how networks played a role in the rise of Silicon Valley and the reversals of fortune along Boston's "technology highway."

In a similar way, Bob Sutton has helped me understand how change happens within organizations and pointed me to others who could provide further assistance. Chris Fussell took the time to explain the work he has done with General Stanley McChrystal both in Iraq and at the McChrystal Group. John Antioco was also kind enough to speak to me candidly about his time at Blockbuster Video and helped correct some earlier misconceptions I had about the Blockbuster story.

Talia Milgrom-Elcott has shared her experiences at 100Kin10 with me, as have Maureen Bisognano and Joe McCannon regarding their efforts at the Institute for Healthcare Improvement. Irving Wladawsky-Berger has spent hours with me over the years helping me to understand IBM's historic turnaround in the 1990s.

Many people read through early drafts and provided helpful advice, including my mother, Penny Satell Berman, Anne Bockol, Todd Pruzan, Giles Anderson, Mark Bonchek, and Lu Ann Cahn. My publicists, Sarah Salbu and Eric Schmeltzer, were invaluable in helping to get the word out.

I would especially like to thank my friend Stephen Shapiro, who has provided constant help and encouragement over the past year. At critical junctures, he seemed to find exactly what needed fixing and was able to point the way forward. I am immensely grateful for it.

I would also like to thank my former colleagues at KP Media, with whom I experienced many of the events that inspired this book: Anya Dovgal, Olga Sych, Alexander Tismenetsky, Oksana Sohor, Vitaliy Gorduz, Herakliusz Lubomisrky, Magda Mazur, Svetlana Udod, Pavel Zhdanov, Elena Viter, Olga Shchur, Katya Vorapayeva, Alona Tokar, Maxim Tkachuk, Maxim Kulakov, Yuriy Ivashenko, Daria Ivashenko, and, of course, KP's founder, Jed Sunden, who made it all possible.

Finally, I'd like to thank my agent, Jill Marr at the Sandra Dijkstra Agency, as well as my editor, Cheryl Ringer, and the entire team at McGraw-Hill whose advice and guidance helped round off early flaws.

Most of all, I would like to thank my wife, Liliana, for being the partner of a lifetime. To my daughter Ashley, I apologize once again that this is not a children's book, but hope that one day, you will pick it up, read it, and understand what was keeping Daddy so busy.

PREFACE

One night in 2002, I had dinner with a man named Jed Sunden in Kyiv, Ukraine. I'd only recently arrived in town, but had been in the region for a number of years. Sunden, on the other hand, was already a legend in Ukrainian media circles. He had come in 1995 to work on a project to catalogue Jewish cemeteries and, sensing opportunity, launched the *Kyiv Post*, an English-language newspaper, with $8,000 he financed on his credit cards.

I had several reasons for setting up the meeting. First, I had been sent to Kyiv by a Swiss magazine publisher whose Ukrainian business unit was having some trouble, and it was clear that Sunden would be a valuable source of market information. Second, it was already well known that he was preparing to launch a Russian language newsweekly, *Korrespondent*, and the company I was representing had some interest, albeit not very serious interest, in investing in the venture. Third, I wanted to take the measure of the man and see what he was about.

I found Jed to be immediately likeable and wickedly smart. He seemed to know everyone and everything that went on in the post-Soviet media world. For his part, he seemed to be intrigued by my knowledge and contacts in the Western media world. It was an interesting discussion that lasted for hours and ended only when we started getting dirty looks from the waiters wanting to close up.

Eventually, the conversation turned to the launch of his upcoming magazine. I knew that Jed had been declared "persona non grata" by the Ukrainian government for running a hard-hitting journalistic operation in English at the *Kyiv Post*.

Introducing a more comprehensive version in Russian seemed like a gutsy move, and I told him so. He looked at me lucidly and said, "Maybe . . . but I just think that the Ukrainian people deserve a reliable news source in their own language."

That's what hooked me on Jed Sunden.

Over the next few years, we established a friendship and eventually became partners in a billboard venture. A few months after we had started working together, he asked me if I could help him with *Korrespondent*, the magazine we had discussed during that first dinner. It was doing well editorially but struggled financially. He also wanted my assistance with a women's fashion magazine that was in a similar position. Before I knew it, I was spending more time with Jed's business, KP Media, than on our joint venture. Eventually, we sold the billboard business and I went to work full-time managing KP Media.

The most formative experience I had in Ukraine was the Orange Revolution, and *Korrespondent* was at the center of it all. It was incredibly exciting, but also terribly confusing. Events seemed to happen with no rhyme or reason. Thousands of people who would ordinarily be doing different things would all of a sudden stop, then start doing something else entirely, in unison, guided by some mysterious force that neither I nor anybody else could seem to identify.

A few years later, in 2006, I was in California, taking a summer publishing course at Stanford University, and everybody in Silicon Valley was talking about a new online phenomenon called social networks. Between the online version of *Korrespondent* and the web portal Bigmir, essentially Ukraine's version of Yahoo!, KP Media had a commanding position in digital media and it seemed like it was important for me to understand what social networks were and how they functioned.

So I began to research network theory and, to my great surprise, what I found was a mathematical description of exactly what I saw unfold in the Orange Revolution. As the years went by and my interest continued, I learned that others found essentially the same thing in vastly different contexts. AnnaLee Saxenian, a professor at Cal Berkeley, saw similar effects in the formation of Silicon Valley. General Stanley McChrystal found the understanding of networks essential to defeating Al Qaeda in Iraq. After he left the military, he established a successful consultancy teaching businesses to harness many of the same network forces. I would later find that the same principles applied to turnarounds at companies like IBM and Alcoa, as well as movements to promote evidence-based quality practices in medicine, to recruit and train STEM teachers for schools, and even to shift the global giant Experian from a traditional to a cloud infrastructure. Finally, I got to know Srdja Popović, who leads CANVAS, the organization that trained the activists in Ukraine as well as in many other countries around the world. It seemed that everywhere I looked, whenever transformative change took place, networks were central to making it happen.

Today, as I write this, it's been more than 15 years since I began my journey at that dinner in Kyiv with Jed Sunden. What follows is what I've learned along the way.

INTRODUCTION

A Shift from Hierarchies to Networks

Power is easier to get and harder to use or keep.

—MOISÉS NAÍM

Nobody really knows exactly how or why everything erupted so suddenly. Most probably, it was a confluence of factors, events, and contexts. Clearly, though, when protestors began flooding into Zuccotti Park on September 17, 2011, it was the start of something big. The activists obviously touched a nerve that ran deeply throughout the populace and, almost immediately, "Occupy Wall Street" became a household name.

The most proximate cause was a campaign initiated by *Adbusters*, a pro-environment, anti-consumerist magazine based in Vancouver, Canada. Asking, "Are you ready for a Tahrir moment?"[1] and distributing posters with a ballerina perched atop Wall Street's famous bull statue,[2] those seemingly small sparks quickly grew to bonfire-sized proportions. "We basically floated the idea in mid-July into our [email list] and it was spontaneously taken up by all the people of the world," remembered *Adbusters* senior editor Micah White. "It just kind of snowballed from there."[3]

Others point to earlier precursors, such as a meeting held at 16 Beaver Street, an artists' collective in lower Manhattan, which had been discussing occupations for some time. Or the "New York General Assembly," which helped organize the "Bloombergville" protests that took place earlier that summer to decry budget cuts that would result in mass layoffs of teachers and firefighters.[4] Clearly, those earlier actions laid important groundwork.

Most likely, the embers had been stoking for some time and the call from *Adbusters* merely helped channel the anger that had been brewing since the financial crisis and had been slowly growing through the work of various activist groups. What is clear, though, is that nobody was quite ready for what followed. Thousands of protestors descended on Zuccotti Park, bringing tents, sleeping bags, and provisions. They were prepared to stay as long as it took to achieve their vision. "We are the 99%," they declared, and as far as they were concerned, it was time for the reign of the "1%" to end.

The movement spread like wildfire, and before you knew it, similar protests were popping up everywhere. In nearly 1,000 cities across more than 80 countries,[5] ordinary citizens took to the streets to rise up against those who wielded power. It was time for their voice to be heard, and they were determined to make sure it was.

Yet within a few months, the streets and parks were cleared. The protestors went home, and nothing much changed. Occupy was, to paraphrase Shakespeare, full of sound and fury, signifying nothing. It may have attracted attention and brought certain issues to the fore, but little more than that. Certainly, nothing tangible was accomplished, as Micah White himself admitted in a 2017 column in the newspaper *The Guardian*.[6]

Now consider the Serbian resistance movement called Otpor that succeeded brilliantly where Occupy failed so completely. Unlike *Adbusters* and the other groups that spawned Occupy, the founders of Otpor weren't very ideologically driven. They were, for the most part, just students who'd grown fed up with the incompetence and corruption of the Milošević regime that ruled their country with an iron hand. They also had very different ideas about how to move forward than the Occupy protestors. Otpor had no desire to sleep on the streets or ask anyone else to do so, but were, at heart, a fun-loving bunch. "Our product is a lifestyle," Ivan Marović, a cofounder of Otpor, would explain. "The movement isn't about the issues. It's about identity. We're trying to make politics sexy."[7]

The contrasts don't end there, either. While the Occupy protestors were adamantly anti-corporate and anti-consumerist, the founders of Otpor considered the branding strategies of corporate giants like Coca-Cola to be a model to emulate. One of their first acts was to create a logo—a clenched fist with the text "Otpor!" ("Resist!" in Serbian)—and spray-paint it throughout Belgrade. Compared to the dedicated activists of Occupy, it seems like a childish and futile act.

But the founders of Otpor were different from most activists. Growing up, they had been far less interested in politics than they were in going to rock concerts and having fun. Their heroes weren't civil rights leaders or revolutionaries, but the British comedy group Monty Python. Srdja Popović, a bass guitarist and a founding member of Otpor, would later write in his memoir, *Blueprint for Revolution*, "It's common for people launching nonviolent movements to cite Gandhi, say, or Martin Luther King, Jr., as their inspiration, but those guys, for all their many, many virtues, simply weren't that hilarious."[8]

In my own conversations with Srdja, he exudes the same easygoing spirit. At 46 years old, he still looks the part of a bass guitarist in a rock band. His easygoing smile hardly ever leaves his face, even when the subject of discussion is him getting brutally beaten in a police station and having a gun stuck in his mouth. When our conversation turns to current movements that seem unable to get results, he often points to their lack of a sense of humor as a key weakness.

So perhaps not surprisingly, Otpor's weapon of choice was street pranks. One of the earliest and best known involved a barrel with a picture of Slobodan Milošević's face drawn on it. They painted a big sign that read, "smash his face for just a dinar" (worth about two cents at the time) and placed it, the barrel, and a long wooden stick on a street called Knez Mihailova, which was famous for its fashionable boutiques and cafes. At first passersby were reticent, but eventually one dropped a coin in the barrel and took a swing. Soon there was a long line of patrons waiting for their turn to beat the brutal dictator's face with a bat.[9]

Soon the police showed up and were at a loss for what to do. There was no law against hitting a barrel with a wooden stick, and arresting pedestrians on the street would have caused an outrage. They couldn't arrest the members of Otpor either, who were sitting out of sight at a nearby café drinking coffee and smoking cigarettes, watching the scene with the utmost amusement. Out of options, the officers decided to arrest the filthy, rusted-out barrel. The next day a photograph of the burly men in uniform struggling to fit the thing in the back of their squad car made the papers. They looked ridiculous. A dictator can afford many things, but looking ridiculous in front of his people isn't one of them.

In another exploit, Otpor activists in the city of Kragujevac took white flowers, much like the ones Milošević's wife wore, and stuck them onto the heads of turkeys, which they then let loose in the streets. Now, a turkey is just about the worst thing you can call a woman in Serbia, so this was an outrageous insult to the first lady of the country. But what could the police do except to arrest the turkeys? The citizens of the city were then treated to the farce of out-of-shape police officers chasing turkeys all over town. Once again, journalists were there to take photos and published them in the next day's papers, another embarrassment for the seemingly all-powerful regime.[10]

Although these pranks earned Otpor admirers, its membership grew slowly at first. By March of 1999, a year after its founding, it had maybe 300 members,[11] nothing compared to the massive numbers that attended Occupy's protests. But eventually the movement hit a tipping point and its membership swelled to over 70,000 activists. By October 2000, things came to a head and Slobodan Milošević was voted out of power. He tried to annul the election's result, but by this time, even the police and the army would no longer obey his orders. The dictator died in his prison cell at The Hague six years later.

After their victory in their home country, some key members of Otpor would later form the Centre for Applied Nonviolent Action and Strategies (CANVAS) and train activists in other countries. One by one, regimes began to fall. In Georgia, Ukraine, Lebanon, Maldives, Egypt, Burma, and other countries, activists using Otpor's methods overcame seemingly insurmountable odds to create transformational change in their societies. To date, CANVAS has been active in almost 50 countries. Somehow, the party-loving pranksters developed a repeatable model that worked.

So we are left with a puzzle. How could a fun-loving band of students succeed so completely, while the hardened professional activists behind Occupy fail so miserably?

John Antioco's rise to the highest echelons of corporate America began in the humblest of fashions. The son of a milkman from a working-class neighborhood in Brooklyn, he started out as a management trainee at 7-Eleven. Smart and ambitious, he worked his way up quickly, becoming a district manager responsible for 35 stores by the age of 25. Antioco made the most of the opportunity, turning his region into one of the most profitable in the country. He then went on to become northeast division manager, then national marketing manager, and finally a senior vice president of the company.

As a fast-rising executive, Antioco got noticed and was recruited to turn around the struggling Circle K convenience store chain. He took the company private in a $400 million leveraged buyout, improved its operations, and three years later it was worth $1 billion. His next assignment was PepsiCo's Taco Bell chain, known unaffectionately to many as "Taco Hell." There, he introduced a new menu and a new ad campaign, and revamped the franchising strategy. Once again, it only took Antioco three years to work wonders. Years of declining sales were magically transformed into steady growth, and soon Taco Bell was humming again.[12]

When Antioco was named CEO of Blockbuster Video in 1997, he was, by all accounts, ideally suited to lead the 800-pound gorilla of the video rental industry. For his part, he saw a great opportunity to transform the business. At the time, video rental operations had to pay movie studios up front for the latest hits and needed to rent each one 30 times before they could make a profit. The model not only involved the rental chain taking all the risk, it tied up a lot of cash that could be more productively deployed elsewhere, such as for marketing new releases.

"It seemed crazy to me," Antioco would later remember. "I myself had stopped going to Blockbuster on Friday and Saturday nights because they never had the movies I wanted. So I went to the studios to ask them to enter into a revenue-sharing agreement. They would sell us each video for as little as a dollar, but then we would share 40 percent of the rental revenues with them."[13] He expected them to agree to a six-month pilot program, so he was surprised when the studios were so enthusiastic about the plan that they agreed to multiyear contracts. It turned out to be a win-win arrangement. Blockbuster reduced its risk and improved its capital position, while the studios got a recurring revenue stream.

It also allowed Blockbuster to guarantee availability of hot new titles. After all, the videocassettes themselves were cheap; it was the intellectual property that was valuable. As long as the studios were getting a 40 percent cut of the rental proceeds, they were more than happy to send Antioco and Blockbuster as many copies as he wanted. Also, with more cash on hand,

Antioco was able to boost his advertising budget by 30 percent, increasing profits for both his company and the studios. The strategy was nothing less than a stroke of genius.[14]

Yet in putting the plan into place, he encountered stiff resistance. "The experienced video executives were skeptical," Antioco told me. "In fact, they thought that the revenue-sharing agreement would kill the company. But throughout my career, I had learned that whenever you set out to do anything big, some people aren't going to like it. I'd been successful by defying the status quo at important junctures, and that's what I thought had to be done in this case."[15]

This time, it took only two years for Antioco to work his magic. In 1999, Blockbuster's parent company, Viacom, raised funds in an initial public offering that valued the company at $2.6 billion (it would spin off Blockbuster entirely in 2004). Once again, Antioco had transformed a struggling business into a well-oiled machine. Yet he would soon find that all of the acumen he acquired throughout his storied career had not equipped him for the challenges to come.

It started with a simple meeting with a fairly insignificant startup called Netflix.[16] Antioco's schedule was probably hectic that day and he wasn't able to attend, but if he had, it's likely he wouldn't have taken much notice. Netflix was still in its embryonic stage. The start-up proposed to run Blockbuster's brand online much like the deal Toys "R" Us signed with Amazon. That arrangement turned out to be a disaster for the toy retailer, and Antioco didn't see how it would benefit his company.[17]

Netflix would eventually develop an innovative subscription model for renting videos online. Rather than charging for each title, the company let customers pay a low monthly subscription fee for access to all the movies they wanted by mail. The fledgling company would grow quickly to rival Blockbuster. That, however, was years in the future. In 2000, when the meeting took place, the young start-up was much like the "Bloombergville" protests that preceded Occupy, fairly insignificant and easy to miss.

Yet Blockbuster's model had a weakness that wasn't clear at the time. It earned an enormous amount of money by charging its customers late fees, which had become an important part of the video rental giant's revenue model. Blockbuster was, in fact, a business largely dependent on penalizing its patrons. That's never a good sign.

And while Netflix was still just a small start-up that had yet to turn a profit (in fact, it was hemorrhaging money at the time), it had certain advantages that also weren't immediately obvious. By eschewing retail locations, it lowered costs and could afford to offer its customers far greater variety. Also, the monthly subscription model it would develop made the annoying late fees unnecessary. Customers could keep a video for as long as they wanted or return it and get a new one. In effect, Netflix was what Harvard's Clayton Christensen calls a *disruptive innovation.* Blockbuster would have to alter its business model—and diminish its profitability—in order to compete with it effectively.

Customers loved the subscription service, and the idea began to spread. People raved about Netflix and encouraged their friends to give it a try. Some were reluctant at first—they actually liked being able to browse movies at the store and pick one up at a moment's notice—but others jumped right in. As the holdouts heard more and more of their friends heap praise on Netflix, they tried it too, loved it, and convinced others to give it a go. Much like a social movement, there seemed to be a powerful force drawing people in.

While the story of Blockbuster and Netflix is often portrayed as a clever, nimble start-up running circles around dull corporate executives who were blind to the changes swirling around them, nothing could be further from the truth. In 2004, after Blockbuster's spinoff from Viacom was complete, Antioco felt he had much more freedom to address the Netflix threat head-on and formulated a plan to meet the challenge. He dropped the late fees that turned off customers[18] and invested in an online platform, which surprised industry observers with its user-friendly design. Before long, it began to gain traction.

In 2006, he instituted a hybrid plan, called "Total Access," which allowed customers to rent from either a physical store or online for one low subscription price. Customers were also saved the trouble of mailing movies back because they could return them to a local retail location. It proved to be an enormous success, and soon Blockbuster was adding online customers even faster than Netflix was.[19] The company's COO, Nick Shepherd, had also begun taking serious steps toward launching a streaming service, although that was still in the future.[20] Once again, it seemed that Antioco had come up with a brilliant plan to meet a thorny challenge.

Alas, it was not to be. While Antioco's handling of the Netflix threat was a textbook case of good strategic management in which he identified clear objectives, formulated a plan to address them, and deployed resources intelligently, there were other forces brewing that would undermine his cleverly crafted strategy.

First, there were the franchisees who had invested in Blockbuster retail outlets. For them, the new plan meant the demise of the businesses they had worked hard to build and, although they only accounted for 20 percent of stores, they could make their displeasure felt. The company's shareholders didn't measure success in terms of online subscribers but profits, and they didn't like the costs associated with the shift—about $200 million to abandon late fees and another $200 million to launch Blockbuster Online.[21] Much as in the case of the revenue-sharing agreement with the studios, Antioco understood their concerns but felt it was necessary to push forward.

Things came to a head when the Blockbuster CEO found himself in a compensation dispute with the company's largest shareholder, Carl Icahn. "I was at a point, both personally and financially, that I had little desire to fight it out anymore," Antioco told me. He left the company, and his successor, Jim Keyes, reduced investment in the digital platform, reinstated late fees, and refocused the company on the retail stores.

Where Occupy let its networks spin out of control and undermined its ability to effect change, Antioco was unable to align his network of stakeholders around the change needed to secure Blockbuster's future. In both cases, the result was the same—failure. Blockbuster went bankrupt in 2010.

Like John Antioco, Stanley McChrystal showed early promise and enjoyed a stellar career. The fourth child of an Army general, he enrolled at West Point in 1972. When he entered service as a young lieutenant in 1976, he gained a reputation for extraordinary discipline and quickly moved up through the ranks. McChrystal completed his Special Forces training in 1979, becoming an elite Ranger instructor and then a Fellow at Harvard's John F. Kennedy School of Government. He was, by all accounts, a model officer with an impeccable record both in and out of combat.[22] But like Antioco, nothing in his experience would prepare him for the challenge he faced leading US Special Forces in Iraq.

As a commander McChrystal led what was perhaps the greatest military machine ever built. Not only were his Special Forces operators among the world's most elite and highly trained soldiers, they had cutting-edge technology that could link up to an extensive network of satellites, manned aircraft, and unmanned drones. In an instant, they could access live video to surveil the battlefield, locate a target, and launch an attack. They also "owned the night," having the ability to move swiftly and silently under the cover of darkness, achieve an objective, and return to base before anyone knew they were there. Their outstanding fighting skills made them almost unbeatable in battle.

Yet still, they were somehow losing the war. As McChrystal would later write, "The world had outpaced us. In the time it took us to move a plan from creation to approval, the battlefield for which the plan had been devised would have changed. By the time it had been implemented, the plan—however ingenious in its initial design—was often irrelevant."[23]

The similarities between the situation he faced and that of Antioco and Blockbuster Video are striking. A well-led, well-resourced, and highly efficient organization was faced with a disruptive challenge by a smaller, less powerful, but far more nimble enemy. The usual metrics of success, such as the number of videos rented in Blockbuster's case or the number of enemy combatants killed in McChrystal's, were not only useless, but misleading. When Antioco's successor shifted the focus back onto the traditional retail model, it killed the company. Now McChrystal's forces were facing a similar fate, only literally instead of figuratively.

The problem, as McChrystal came to realize, was not of resources or capability, but of agility and interoperability. The individual units were operating at a high level, but the links between them were broken. Commandos would capture valuable intelligence on a raid, but then documents and hard drives would sit in a closet for days or even weeks before they could be translated and analyzed. The intelligence officers were highly adept, but without timely material, their analyses were of limited use to the soldiers. Perhaps not surprisingly, mistrust was endemic. It seemed to the Special Forces operators that the intelligence teams were blissfully ignorant about on-the-ground realities of war, while the analysts felt that the brawny soldiers were too dim to grasp the larger picture.[24]

Another problem involved how information flowed. Intelligence analysts could turn raw data into actionable insights, but by protocol they passed that information up the chain of command. Military planners would then develop strategies for the troops on the ground, which created further lags. "I began to reconsider the nature of my role as a leader," McChrystal remembered. "The wait for my approval was *not* resulting in any better decisions, and our priority should be reaching the best possible decision that could be made *in a time frame that allowed it to be relevant*."[25]

Yet the crucial difference between Antioco and McChrystal was that the general recognized that he had to fundamentally change how his organization functioned on a visceral level. His forces could not win by utilizing conventional notions of strategy, planning, and execution. As noted above, his teams were already performing well, but the links between them ceased to function effectively. So he dedicated himself to forging them anew. "It takes a network to defeat a network,"[26] he declared and set out to make his organization become one.

So McChrystal began to forge links wherever he could. He started embedding intelligence analysts into commando teams and vice versa. Liaison officer positions, traditionally given to marginal performers or those nearing retirement, were now earmarked for the very best operators. Moves like these slowed down the individual teams—commandos in business suits placed at embassies don't kill many terrorists—but that wasn't the point, building networks of trust and interoperability was. "We began to make progress when we started looking at these relationships as just that: relationships—parts of a network, not cogs in a machine or outputs and inputs," McChrystal would remember.[27]

This was a radical change in culture as well as practice. Traditionally, in a military enterprise, subordinates provide information and leaders make plans and give orders. Yet he saw that had to be reversed, with leaders providing information, connectivity, and context so that subordinates could act.[28] "I needed to shift my focus from moving pieces on the board to shaping the ecosystem," he would later write.[29]

Not all of his decisions were popular. In the military, people are trained to attain objectives with relentless efficiency, and creating those connections between teams could be something of an encumbrance. Commando teams need to depend on one another, and being saddled with an embedded intelligence analyst was a burden. The analysts, for their part, didn't welcome the Special Forces personnel with their bulging biceps, either. And nobody liked losing a top operative from their team to a liaison post in some far-off embassy. Nevertheless, the diverse teams learned to trust each other and work together. They became, to paraphrase McChrystal, not a collection of teams but a "team of teams."

The moves paid off. Although his actions may have decreased the efficiency of the individual units, overall operational efficiency *increased by a factor of seventeen.*[30] The tide of the war soon shifted, and the forces under his command would achieve their major objectives. The barbarians were no longer at the gate, but on the run.

Ironically, the strategies of General McChrystal in Iraq and the Otpor activists in Serbia were surprisingly similar. Both focused on weaving networks that were resilient, adaptable, and based on shared values. Once that was achieved, the specific tactics employed, to a large extent, took care of themselves.

As AnnaLee Saxenian explains in *Regional Advantage*, in the 1970s Boston was at the center of the technology industry. With some of the top research institutions in the world, such as MIT and Harvard, as well as a strong business and financial community, it had an almost unparalleled combination of brains, money, and acumen. It had also benefitted from having Vannevar Bush, a former MIT professor, as head of the Office for Scientific Research and Development (OSRD) during World War II. Perhaps not surprisingly, a disproportionate number of grants flowed to local institutions to develop radar and other key technologies for the war effort. Those funds, in turn, helped create the foundations that led to the region's technological prowess.[31]

Boston got a second boost when a number of its high-profile citizens, including Karl Compton, MIT's president and Vannevar Bush's former colleague at the OSRD, formed the American Research and Development Corporation (ARD). It was essentially the country's first venture capital fund, and its focus was to invest in commercializing technologies developed at local institutions. ARD's most successful investment was in a young company headed up by MIT graduate Ken Olsen. It was called Digital Equipment Corporation (DEC).[32]

In the 1960s, DEC pioneered a new technology called minicomputers. These were far smaller than the mainframes that dominated the industry at the time, but still fast and powerful enough to be incredibly useful. Before long, DEC grew into a major enterprise and led the way for other local technology companies, such as Data General and Wang Laboratories, which began to populate along Route 128 outside Boston.

Throughout the 1970s and 1980s, the region flourished in an economic revival often referred to as the Massachusetts Miracle. As the minicomputer industry continued to take market share from mainframes, the Route 128 companies created 100,000 new jobs[33] and helped the region reduce unemployment from 12 percent to less than 3 percent.[34] Yet by the 1990s, Boston's technology giants had been surpassed by Silicon Valley. And as Route 128 descended into obscurity, the Bay Area rose to even greater heights. Today, Silicon Valley has become so unparalleled in its leadership of information technology that it has become synonymous with the industry itself.

Much like Occupy and Otpor, to an outside observer the two regions seem so eerily similar that it's something of a puzzle why one succeeded brilliantly and the other just seemed to peter out. Like Boston's Route 128, Silicon Valley's rise was fueled by local universities and military contracts. Also, much like Boston, the initial success of a few local companies, Fairchild Semiconductor and Hewlett-Packard in the case of Silicon Valley, helped form the industrial base for a regional economy based on technology.

But look a little more closely, and the contrasts become clearer. First, while Boston's high-tech companies were rooted in traditional Eastern establishment practices, Silicon Valley was much more freewheeling, with lots of mixing between companies. Also, while the Route 128 stalwarts like DEC and Data General focused on vertical integration to dominate their industry's value chain, Silicon Valley firms were highly interdependent. Cooperation and competition flourished simultaneously. Another stark difference was in job mobility. In Boston, few people job-hopped, and those who did leave their company were treated as pariahs. Once an employee left there was no option of return. But in California someone leaving for greener pastures was seen as an asset who could be a valuable source of market intelligence and new business opportunities.[35] While the Boston firms built barriers to protect themselves, Silicon Valley thrived on connection.

Most of all, while the Route 128 companies saw themselves as a collection of self-sufficient firms competing for the same customers, Silicon Valley firms saw themselves as an ecosystem. Much like McChrystal's forces in Iraq, they came to see interdependencies as essential for creating shared purpose and shared consciousness. While captains of industry in Boston lobbied for tax breaks and sweetheart deals to benefit their companies, the Silicon Valley entrepreneurs worked to improve regional transportation, technical programs at community colleges, and other qualitative factors that would help the region prosper.[36]

In the final analysis, what made the difference was not one of resources, but of vision and perspective. The Route 128 companies, much like McChrystal's elite forces before he began their transformation, were so focused on winning battles that they failed to recognize that the war had changed. By insulating themselves they became incapable of understanding the forces that would lead to their downfall. As nascent technologies continued to render their products obsolete, they increasingly found themselves cut off from the changes swirling around them. In a fashion uncannily similar to the situation in Iraq, upstart companies that seemed to spring from nowhere would regularly thwart their well-laid strategic plans. Essentially, the Route 128 firms ceased to be cutting-edge firms and became champions of the dying minicomputer industry. When it ceased to exist, their own demise was just a matter of time.

Once again, we see similar principles at work. The Boston firms, much like the Occupy protestors and John Antioco at Blockbuster, failed to manage networks and, in fact, seemed scarcely aware that networks would play a role in their success or failure. The Silicon Valley firms, on the other hand, thrived on connection as much as the Otpor activists and McChrystal did.

THE END OF POWER?

Otpor, McChrystal's forces in Iraq, and the Silicon Valley firms all created transformational change, albeit in vastly different contexts and for very different purposes, because of their ability to connect and form networks. Whether you are an activist advocating for social and political change, a manager leading an organization, or a leader looking to shape an entire society, the need to create interconnectivity and interdependence remains essential.

These principles aren't new. As we will see later in the book, they played a part in successful movements throughout history. Yet today, they have become far more salient because the connectivity that drives networks has become predominant. We can now initiate, build, and maintain relationships with far greater velocity and at far greater distances. That has changed the nature of power, shifting it from being a function of hierarchies to one of networks.

Since ancient Rome, institutions have ruled the world. Throughout the march of history, hierarchies became increasingly elaborate. Better-organized societies were able to collect ample tax revenues, raise armies, and provide services more efficiently. Well-run bureaucracies could keep accurate records, organize the flow of information, and cut down on waste. Through the more efficient use of resources, societies could gain power by acquiring military assets, territory, raw materials, and other advantages that would further enhance their power.

By the mid-nineteenth century, the industrial revolution had brought a new level of organization to private enterprise. Large factories required resources, and men like Vanderbilt, Carnegie, Rockefeller, and Ford built powerful corporations by devising methods for managing assets efficiently. In the mid-twentieth century, Alfred Sloan built the first modern corporation at General Motors and it became the largest private organization the world had ever seen.

This principle of efficient hierarchies has held true in just about every realm and field of endeavor. In religion, charity, and labor, organizations like the Catholic Church, The United Way, and the AFL-CIO have used hierarchical organization to achieve greater efficiency, allowing for the accumulation of more resources with which an enterprise could compete on a superior basis. They then used those assets to crush or absorb rival entities and gain more power still.

While specifics would vary, success generally followed a clear, linear path: increase efficiency, acquire more resources, and wield your ever-greater power to keep down those who would try to usurp it. The objective was always the same: the power to shape the environment and determine one's own destiny. That's what allowed successful organizations and institutions to influence the actions of others and define the game for themselves.

Perhaps not surprisingly, over the years a number of scholars have attempted to define power and the correct way to use it. For example, in 1977, Ray S. Cline, a top official at the CIA during the 1960s and 1970s, defined the power of a nation as the sum of population, territory, economy, and military multiplied by strategy and will.[37] Theories about power in the private sector have followed in a similar vein. Nobel prize-winning economist Ronald Coase argued that enterprises derived their power from managing two countervailing forces: transaction costs (including informational and search costs) and organizational costs.[38] Harvard Business School professor Michael Porter built on Coase's idea, explaining how firms could use scale to build sustainable competitive advantage through the optimization of *value chains*. By controlling more of the process by which raw materials were transformed into finished products and delivered to customers, enterprises could continually tilt the playing field in their favor.[39]

Yet today, these notions have become largely obsolete. In Serbia, Milošević controlled all of the traditional levers of power, but was still unable to forestall the uprising that Otpor—a ragtag bunch of kids—engineered. John Antioco at Blockbuster was a paragon of effective strategy and planning, but was unable to bring investors and franchisees on board. He left the company in frustration and it descended into bankruptcy. The technology companies along Boston's Route 128 were widely recognized for their good management and business acumen, but were soon surpassed by the network of freewheeling Silicon Valley upstarts.

This phenomenon of falling giants is far from anecdotal. Moisés Naím, author of *The End of Power*, which was, incidentally, the first book that Facebook founder Mark Zuckerberg chose for his book club,[40] argues that it is even more widespread than it would first appear. He notes that everyone from chess masters to CEOs retain their status for far shorter periods than they did a generation ago. A study by the consulting firm Innosight found that the average lifespan for a company on the S&P 500 has declined from 33 years in 1964 to a mere 24 years in 2016, and it estimates that it will shrink to just 12 years by 2027.[41] Mark Perry, an economist at the University of Michigan, has calculated that of all the companies on the first Fortune 500 list in 1955, 87 percent no longer exist.[42] Everywhere you look, the great and mighty are continually being upended. Armies, religions, and even charities are being thwarted by far smaller adversaries who, in turn, later face similarly disruptive challengers.[43] As Naím puts it, "Power is easier to get and harder to use or keep."[44]

Yet the truth is that power itself remains, but has shifted from the top of hierarchies to the center of networks, and that's essential to understanding how to effect change in the modern world. Today, digital technology helps connections to form with blazing speed, upending the traditional forces that drove power in the twentieth century. We no longer need bureaucracies to carry a message, or even, strictly speaking, to organize work. In fact, traditional institutions are finding that conventional hierarchies are often too slow and cumbersome to function in the world today. To paraphrase General McChrystal, in order to compete with networks, they need to become networks themselves.

CREATING TRANSFORMATIVE CHANGE

This is a book about transformative change and the movements that create it. As we have seen, not all movements are successful. Some begin in a blaze of glory, make a lot of noise, and then fizzle out without achieving much at all. But others perpetuate and create a lasting legacy. This isn't random or by chance. There are reasons that some movements succeed and others fail—notice how CANVAS has been able to repeat its success across the globe—and if we want to effect change in this world we need to understand them. As you will learn in the pages ahead, successful movements combine two aspects:

The first aspect, which successful movements often share with unsuccessful ones, is network cascades. Hundreds of consumers standing in line at your local Apple store, thousands of protestors rushing to flood the streets of Cairo, Istanbul, or Washington, D.C. Countless fireflies blinking on and off in complete unison to light up entire forests. As individual entities or even small groups, each is negligible. However, when they connect and synchronize their collective behavior, they become immensely powerful cascades. An industry is remade, a country overthrown, the preceding order is no more, and the world is transformed.

This simple formula—*small groups, loosely connected, but united by a common purpose*—is one we will see continually throughout the pages ahead. Anytime an idea goes viral and becomes a cascade, we will see those three components. That's why movements tend to start slowly (sometimes taking years or even decades to gather strength) but grow as the density of connections between small clusters increases, eventually hit a critical mass, and finally explode (or percolate, to use a more technically accurate term) to create the potential for transformational change.

Sometimes, cascades can be spontaneous, like when enthusiastic fans do "the wave" at a stadium, with little or no planning or forethought. As we have already seen, the longtime activists behind the Occupy movement had been organizing protests for years—in some cases, decades—but nothing had caught fire before quite like their takeover of Zuccotti Park. It was an unusual confluence of forces, including the financial crisis, the political environment, and social media, that made theirs the right message at the right time. Successful movements, however, don't merely wait for lightning to strike, but develop clear strategies to gain support long before circumstances trigger a window of opportunity.

Otpor saw that even a supremely powerful dictator relied on others to impose his will and that by winning those people over to their cause, the regime's authority would crumble under its own weight. So the activists designed their tactics to appeal not just to fellow travelers, but also to everyone else. They were funny, engaging, and, above all, clear about what they intended to achieve: the downfall of the Milošević regime. As they built connections throughout Serbian society, their movement cascaded to victory.

General McChrystal saw that commanding the most powerful forces on earth was of little use if he couldn't make them interoperable. He recognized that having greater resources can actually be a disadvantage because as you expand the nodes in your organization, the links increase at an almost exponential rate.[45] So he set out to widen and deepen linkages between individual units in order to create a "team of teams." In doing so, he fundamentally changed the way his organization functioned, allowing information cascades to help his forces determine where they would strike next, instead of waiting for orders from centralized commanders.

The technology companies in Silicon Valley, taken individually, weren't all that different from their Route 128 counterparts. Yet by understanding the importance of the links between enterprises as well as those firms' connections to the communities in the region, they created a cascade that led to a technological movement that has no equal anywhere in the world.

The evidence is clear. In a world pervaded by digital technology, power no longer resides at the top of hierarchies, but at the center of networks. Movements become successful by expanding out, always seeking to widen their appeal. Those that continue to play to a narrow constituency of stakeholders eventually find themselves stuck on the periphery. This principle holds true whether you are seeking change in an organization, an industry, or throughout society as a whole.

In Part One of this book, we will learn how cascades work through understanding the new science of networks. In the late 1990s, researchers began to understand how real-world networks create order from chaos. We will meet some of these pathbreaking scientists and learn how the principles they uncovered can guide us as we seek to create positive change around us.

The second aspect, seemingly antithetical to the first, is planning, organization, and discipline, without which a cascading movement will spin out of control. It was Otpor's superior planning and discipline that empowered it to inspire fellow citizens and topple a dictator. And it was Occupy's lack of discipline that turned off many who may have sympathized with its message about economic inequality, but were reluctant to throw in with activists who often seemed extreme, disorganized, and vulgar.

Where Occupy hurled insults at police, Otpor saw every interaction, even arrests, as an opportunity to win converts. Otpor also trained its activists to defend police against violent protestors so that they wouldn't turn off the people they needed to help them effect change. They had more than passion, but a plan to identify pillars of support, win allies within the mainstream populace, and undermine their foes. It is not the passion and fervor of zealots that creates change, but it is when everyone else joins the cause that a movement gains power. Students and activists can protest, but it is only when everybody else starts taking to the streets that a true revolution can begin to take place.

In a similar vein, Al Qaeda's brutal tactics were able to make the populace tremble in fear, but its inability to provide even a modicum of governance to meet people's needs made it possible for McChrystal's forces to not only defeat it on the battlefield, but also in the hearts and minds of ordinary Iraqis. It was the "Sunni uprising," as much as anything else, that led to Al Qaeda's defeat in Iraq. It was also the Route 128 firms' inability to see beyond the boundaries of their own organizations that led to their irrelevance. On the other hand, it was the Silicon Valley entrepreneurs' efforts to build a regional ecosystem that helped create a global phenomenon. The reality of today's world is that connection wins and isolation loses.

As we will see, these principles do not just apply to the examples discussed above, but were also utilized by successful movements throughout history, such as those led by Gandhi, Martin Luther King Jr., and those who struggled to win LGBT rights. Their salience is not confined to political revolutions, either, but can be applied to transformational change in any context. Corporate revolutionaries, such as Lou Gerstner at IBM and Paul O'Neill at Alcoa, as well as other leaders, like Rick Warren of the Saddleback Church, applied many of the same precepts, as did the Institute for Healthcare Improvement, a movement to decrease preventable deaths in hospitals, and 100Kin10, a movement to recruit and train 100,000 STEM teachers in 10 years.

Part Two of this book will explain how to apply the concepts of planning, organization, and discipline to harness the power of network cascades to create your own brand of transformational change. We will see how creating clear purpose and values, and devising a plan to win over converts in the populace as well as within institutions, can help you make a positive difference in the world.

If you want to create change—real change, not just make noise—you will find these principles invaluable. They will be your playbook for making a true difference in the things you care deeply about. But before we get into the specifics of how transformational change is created, let's first take a look inside a true revolution. This is my personal story of how I first came to understand the power of network cascades and the movements they spawn.

It starts in the fall of 2004 in Kyiv, Ukraine, when I woke up one morning to find that my world had completely, unalterably changed.

PART ONE

THE ANATOMY OF A CASCADE

CHAPTER 1

What a Revolution Looks Like from the Inside

I ask you, people who care about the soul of Ukraine, those who want to preserve the heart, the spirit and the faith of our country for future generations, to please defend it.

—**YULIA TYMOSHENKO,** former Prime Minister of Ukraine

For 15 years, a significant portion of my adult life, I lived in post–Soviet Bloc countries in Eastern Europe, where I managed media companies and observed events from the fairly unusual position of being not quite an outsider, but not really a local either.

When President Clinton invited Poland into NATO, I was there, sitting just a few rows behind former Polish President Lech Walesa and U.S. Secretary of State Madeleine Albright (both are shorter than you'd think). I was in Moscow on my way to work when the Chechens were blowing up metro trains, and I happened to be traveling in the northern Georgian Republic and observed some of the early troop movements before Russia invaded South Ossetia and Abkhazia. Yet in all my life, I don't think I'll ever again experience anything quite like the events that occurred in Kyiv, Ukraine, in 2004—in what is now known as the Orange Revolution.[1]

Revolutions are remarkable things, because they do the opposite of what nature predicts. They upend an existing order, which has power and inertia on its side. And they do it with almost unthinkable speed. You wake up in the morning, and the world has changed overnight. No transition period, no forewarning. It's as if someone flipped a switch somewhere, and poof! The world begins anew.

That's what it was like when I awoke one morning in the fall of 2004 to see my fiancée wrapping a bright orange bandana around her neck as she prepared to go out. It seemed particularly early for a Saturday.

"Where are you going?" I asked.

"I'm going out to a demonstration," she replied.

"I thought you didn't care about politics," I said, now confused.

"I didn't, but we've had enough, and it's time to do something about it."

And indeed they did. Just like that, things had changed. Ukraine was about to join the wave of popular uprisings that came to be known as the "color revolutions," which swept across Eastern Europe in the first decade of the twenty-first century. They included Serbia, the Republic of Georgia, and, of course, Ukraine.

At the dawn of the new century, the work left unfinished by the 1989 revolutions and the fall of the Berlin Wall would begin again as post-Soviet dictatorships fell one by one. Later, another wave of political unrest erupted, this time in the Middle East, when a Tunisian street vendor set himself on fire in front of a governor's office, touching off a wave of protests that would soon engulf the whole region. It came to be known as the Arab Spring.

Political disruptions are, of course, nothing new, but the Orange Revolution is where I began to understand the power of cascades. I became intensely interested about why some movements succeed and others just seem to flame out. Why do some technologies, like VHS, become standards and others, like Betamax, fail? Why do start-ups like Google and Facebook become billion-dollar enterprises seemingly overnight, while well-established companies like Kodak and Blockbuster disappear almost as fast? Why do markets crash? Why do some Hollywood movies with the biggest budgets, the hottest stars, and the most accomplished directors bomb right out of the gate, while silly Internet memes like "LOLCats" and "Gangnam Style" enter the zeitgeist as runaway hits?

Each of these scenarios seems eerily familiar to what I experienced that morning I first encountered the Orange Revolution in my home. Through years of research, I have found that the similarities are far more than superficial. In fact, all point to basic truths that underlie the mysterious forces that create disruption in our lives and allow us to start anew.

So let's take a closer look at what happened in the fall of 2004 in Ukraine.

THE ORANGE REVOLUTION

Even among the sordid histories of Eastern Europe, Ukraine is particularly tragic. Over the centuries, Ukraine was ruled by the Mongols, the Duchy of Lithuania, and the Kingdom of Poland before it was overtaken by the Russian Empire during the eighteenth century. It endured the Holodomor, forced starvation under Stalin, in the thirties, and bore the brunt of Hitler's armies in World War II.[2] Somehow, through it all, it maintained a national culture, language, and identity.

Ukraine became independent when the Soviet Union disintegrated in 1991, then endured eight years of turmoil culminating in the currency crises of 1998. It finally began to gain traction in 1999, when President Leonid Kuchma appointed Viktor Yushchenko, the technocratic former head of the national bank, as prime minister, and Yulia Tymoshenko a former businesswoman known in some circles as "the gas princess," as his deputy prime minister for energy.[3] Despite her oligarchic background, Tymoshenko proved an effective shepherd of industry magnates, and tax collections ballooned under her tenure.

The next few years were unusually prosperous for Ukraine, with GDP growing 6 percent in 2000, 9 percent in 2001, 5 percent in 2002, 9 percent in 2003, and an astounding 12 percent in 2004. Unemployment fell; savings and investment increased.[4] While problems remained, it appeared that Ukraine was finally turning the corner.

Still, even amidst the unusual period of prosperity, the public was restless. There was a palpable feeling that the country had fallen far behind its neighbors to the west, most notably the Visegrad countries of Poland, the Czech Republic, and Hungary but also the Baltic states of Lithuania, Latvia, and Estonia. While those countries had enjoyed the political stability and legitimacy that came with NATO and EU membership, Ukraine was still considered a backwater, ruled by criminal oligarchs.

Then there were the scandals. First came the murder of Heorhiy Gongadze, cofounder of the country's second-largest news site, Ukrainska Pravda (Ukrainian Truth),[5] who disappeared in September 2000. His body was found beheaded and mutilated in a forest several months later. Shortly after that came Kuchmagate.[6] The head of the Socialist party, Oleksandr Moroz, announced that he had more than a thousand hours of tapes surreptitiously recorded by President Kuchma's bodyguard that caught the president ordering the assassination of Gongadze.

My friend and colleague Jed Sunden, founder and publisher of the English-language weekly *Kyiv Post*, was the subject of one tape. Sunden, returning from a business trip one day, learned he had been declared *persona non grata* and was denied entry to the country. Luckily, events conspired in his favor. Madeleine Albright was scheduled to visit Ukraine to encourage reforms two days later.[7] Sunden made a call to an acquaintance on her staff, and Albright intervened. Kuchma could be heard on the tapes dressing down his subordinates about the incident, chiding them for making a public spectacle when they could have just raised Sunden's rent.

Stories like these were plentiful. The tapes revealed a regime that was not only brutal and Machiavellian, but also almost comically inept. They reinforced the feeling that the country was ruled not by enlightened leaders, but by thuggish mafiosi. For the first time, widespread opposition broke out, led by Moroz and Tymoshenko, who had established herself as a charismatic opposition leader. Yushchenko rode the fence.

In a power grab, Kuchma fired Yushchenko and Tymoshenko from his administration (and subsequently had Tymoshenko arrested, at the behest of the powerful business interests that now despised her). The once-reticent Yushchenko became the de facto leader of the opposition, and his party, Nasha Ukraina (Our Ukraine), made significant gains in the parliamentary elections of 2002, as did Moroz's Socialists and Tymoshenko's eponymous party. The alliance of the three parties was quickly becoming a formidable political power in its own right.

Three other forces were converging at the time that would lead to what would be called the Orange Revolution. First, the "color revolutions" had begun, with the overthrow of Serbian strongman Slobodan Milošević in 2000 and of Eduard Shevardnadze in Georgia in 2003. So along with the recent EU ascensions of Poland, the Czech Republic, Hungary, Romania, and the Baltic States to the immediate west of Ukraine, a feeling of change was already in the air.

The second was a youth movement called Pora! (It's Time!). Trained, like the Kmara in Georgia, by Srdja Popović and his friends from Otpor, it was determined to see democracy thrive in Ukraine. This younger generation of Ukrainians was the first with little or no memory of Soviet rule, and its denizens yearned for a more stable, just, and prosperous country. Faced with the Kuchma regime's domination of the media, they would, in a foreshadowing of Barack Obama's campaign four years later, organize their supporters on the Internet and through mobile phones.

The third was a greatly weakened President Kuchma. Now thoroughly unpopular, Kuchma formed an alliance with the powerful Party of Regions and appointed Viktor Yanukovych, its leader and the governor of the Donetsk region, as his prime minister and handpicked successor. Yanukovych, a thuggish brute and twice-convicted felon, almost uniquely personified the grievances that had riled up the public in the first place. In that sense, he would prove a perfect adversary for the opposition.

The stage was now set for the presidential election of 2004. The Russian-leaning eastern third of the country would support Yanukovych. The Ukrainian-speaking western third would support Yushchenko. The mixed-language middle region—where the capital city of Kyiv is situated—would determine the fate of the country.

And it was about to explode.

A Ground's-Eye View of the Revolution

In truth, I was really more of an observer than a participant in the Orange Revolution. Although I had been in the region since 1997, I was still a newcomer to Ukraine. I had been in Kyiv for six months in 2002, but only came to live there permanently at the beginning of 2004, after a stint working in Moscow.

Over the summer, Jed Sunden and I became partners in a billboard business, and in the fall, he asked me to help him with his company, KP Media, where I would eventually become Co-CEO. Jed was a serial entrepreneur who had come to Ukraine in 1995 and founded the *Kyiv Post*, an English-language newspaper. In 2000, he launched Bigmir.net, which would become Ukraine's largest Internet portal. In 2002, he started *Korrespondent*, a Russian-language newsmagazine, which would play a major part in the Orange Revolution. So, although I was a relative newcomer, I worked closely with many of the country's top journalists and had a bird's-eye view of the events.

Nevertheless, I was genuinely surprised on that fall morning when my wife-to-be donned her orange bandana and set out for a political rally. My experience with Ukrainian political life up to that point could be summed up in one word: docile. While other countries in the region, such as Poland (where I had previously lived for six years) were extremely active politically, Ukrainians seemed mostly resigned to their fate. Fabulously wealthy oligarchs could take what they wanted, state-owned assets could be sold at a fraction of their worth, opposition politicians could be thrown in jail with no just cause, and everybody tried not to notice. They didn't exactly like it, but there was little they could do. So why worry or complain? It was better to focus on your own life—your family, your friends, your job, and maybe saving enough money each year to go on a nice vacation.

Even the journalists were different. Others in the region were typified by Adam Michnik, the legendary, famously combative, and chain-smoking editor of Poland's national daily newspaper, *Gazeta Wyborcza* (who we will meet again in Chapter 8). His Ukrainian counterpart, *Korrespondent*'s editor in chief Vitaliy Sych, on the other hand, was one of the calmest, most well-adjusted people I've ever met. Although we formed a close friendship over the years and spent countless hours drinking whiskey and talking about everything under the sun, I can't recall a single incident when he raised his voice. Other prominent journalists that I knew and worked with were similarly agreeable.

So, while I don't think I was particularly obtuse, I really had little idea that anything was afoot for most of 2004. Sure, there were things going on that would be considered outrageous in most places, but Ukrainians, at least in my experience, tended to take them in stride. They focused on what was close to them. Politics was just not something anybody ever got involved in or excited about.

Nonetheless, a fever *was* brewing that fall. My fiancée and her friends were going to more and more demonstrations. Politics became an active subject of conversation—and an increasing source of contention—in the workplace. Although the regime controlled most media outlets, a new cable news channel, Channel 5, owned by the relatively liberal chocolate magnate Petro Poroshenko, appeared and ran reports friendly to the opposition. The circulation of *Korrespondent* was picking up briskly, as was the activity on its website, Korrespondent.net.

By November, it was clear that the election would be hotly contested, and the atmosphere in the country became highly charged. On November 20, the eve of the runoff election, people started gathering around a platform at Maidan Nezalezhnosti (Independence Square), in the center of Kyiv. Then a tent city popped up on Kreshchatyk, Kyiv's main thoroughfare, filled with protestors gearing up for a protracted battle.

Although exit polls showed the opposition candidate, Viktor Yushchenko, winning by 11 percent, the Central Election Commission of Ukraine saw things differently. It gave the victory to Yanukovych by a margin of 3 percent.[8]

The Orange Revolution had begun.

SELF-ORGANIZING CASCADES

One word sums up the atmosphere of the Orange Revolution: confusion. Nobody seemed to know what was going on: not the diplomats I ran into at expat hangouts, the other business leaders I met with regularly, the government officials I chatted with each morning at the gym, or the journalists I talked with at work. Events took on a life of their own. We all just did our best to follow along.

In other words, we were all very much like Blockbuster CEO John Antioco in 2000, when Netflix came calling, General McChrystal before he realized he was facing a new type of enemy, and the Route 128 companies in the seventies and eighties. We were mostly oblivious to the forces swirling around us. In retrospect, all of the signs were there—the previous revolutions, the scandals, and the growing opposition—but we had also seen much of it before. Those who were hoping for change had already been disappointed many times, and those who preferred continuity had seen previous challenges to authority crushed in due time. Inertia can be a powerful force, even more powerful than hope or fear. It was hard to believe that this time could be different, no matter which side you were on. Nevertheless, it *was* very different.

It's often hard to discern a passing fad from a historic moment or why some events spark a cascade while others just seem to fall flat. If we are to understand cascades, and learn to operate within their context, we need to be able to recognize some telltale signs. I noticed them in 2004, but to be honest, didn't fully grasp their significance until years later.

Let's move along to the epicenter of the Orange Revolution, Independence Square, or as the locals know it, the Maidan. Tens of thousands gathered there every night to hear speeches from opposition leaders like Yushchenko and Tymoshenko. There were celebrities, too, like the champion heavyweight boxers Vitaliy and Volodymyr Klitschko, Eurovision star Ruslana, and pop singer Slava Vakarchuk.

But all that happened for just a few hours each night. The true power of the revolution emanated from an area just a few hundred yards away, in the tent city that had sprouted up on Kreshchatyk, the city's main thoroughfare. Hundreds of protestors stayed there for weeks in the bitter cold. Supporters brought food and warm clothing to sustain them. In offices around Kyiv, people worked in shifts: half of the workforce was out on the streets protesting or living in the tent city while the other half worked. Then they would switch places. At the office of our billboard company near Kreshchatyk, we would invite protestors into our conference room in groups of a dozen or so to drink tea, have something to eat, and get warm. Many other small businesses did the same. People from all over Ukraine came to Kyiv to join the protests, and when they did, they found perfect strangers willing to take them into their homes to sleep and get some warm food. Almost everybody we knew housed protest boarders. It was just something you did—although at any other time that type of thing would have seemed strange, even crazy, during the revolution it seemed perfectly normal and natural.

The atmosphere was electric, and that gave rise to unusual activity that you wouldn't normally expect to see. For instance, there was a no-drinking rule. As in most Eastern European countries, alcohol plays a large role in the culture of Ukraine. Vodka, cognac, beer, and champagne are present at every gathering. (Russian champagne is surprisingly good and costs just a few dollars a bottle.) It's not uncommon to drink beer at lunch during the workday, or to see someone walking down the street with an open bottle of vodka (although drinking from an open container in public is often frowned upon in more polite company).

So, in a strange way, one of the most impressive things about the revolution was that no alcohol was present at the protests. If someone were to be seen carrying a beer, they would be politely asked to throw it away. I never saw anyone refuse. There was no edict, nor were there any authorities (besides the occasional disapproving babushka) enforcing this rule. Somehow, word got around, and social pressure kept people in line. With the future of the country in the balance, everybody wanted to do their part, and the no-alcohol policy, although counter to cultural norms, was widely respected.

Another example was the horn protest outside the Central Election Commission. No one knows for certain how it started, but it's not hard to imagine. When the news of the fraudulent election results came over the radio, somebody honked their horn in anger. Others joined in, then others, until nearly everybody passing the building was leaning on their horn. This was done for only a few seconds by each car, but resulted in a long, unending drone for those working in the building. It continued unabated, 24 hours a day, for weeks and didn't ebb until the revolution was complete.

Eventually, to drown out the noise, Election Commission officials set up loudspeakers and blasted old Russian folk songs.

It wasn't much of an improvement, and it proved to be in vain. It takes more to drown out massive collective action than a few loudspeakers and some bad music.

One of the most interesting viral memes during the Orange Revolution was the chant "*Razom nas bahato, nas ne podalaty*" ("Together we are many, we won't be overcome.") Within a few days, it could be heard everywhere in Kyiv. The pop band GreenJolly set the chant to music. In 2005, after the revolution was over, the song became Ukraine's entry into the Eurovision song contest, an event viewed by 500 million people. GreenJolly didn't invent "Razom nas bahato," nor did the band make it popular. The chant spread widely weeks before the band recorded it. Much like most things in the Orange Revolution, it just sprang up and quickly became highly contagious.

That's what the Orange Revolution was like for those of us that were there. While Yushchenko and the other officials at the Maidan were the focal point, they weren't directing the action. There were, in fact, no truly identifiable leaders. The crowd had taken over. All conventional notions of power had become defunct.

THE AFTERMATH

On December 3, 2004, Ukraine's Supreme Court ruled that the election had indeed been fraudulent and ordered a revote to take place later that month. This time, Yushchenko emerged victorious, and he was sworn in as president on January 23. As unlikely as it had seemed just a short time before, democracy, in the end, prevailed. We had won, or so it seemed.

But before long, the new government was at war with itself. The Yushchenko and Tymoshenko camps, united during the drama of the revolution, fell into infighting amidst mutual recriminations. Both accused the other of betraying the ideals of the revolution, although to be honest, it was never exactly clear what those were. Pora, the grassroots activists who had spearheaded the protests, attempted to form a political party, but gained little traction. On September 8, Yushchenko dismissed Tymoshenko from her post as prime minister and ordered the formation of a new government for the first, but not the last, time during his term in office.

What followed was a disintegration of the political powers into three distinct camps, President Yushchenko's Our Ukraine party, the Yulia Tymoshenko bloc, and the Party of Regions. The latter was led by Viktor Yanukovych, who, to widespread amazement, still carried legitimacy in the eastern part of the country. Corruption remained rampant, and although Yushchenko was never accused of any personal wrongdoing, he proved to be an ineffective leader.

As Mustafa Nayyem, who would later provide the spark that led to the Euromaidan protests in 2013, told me, "In 2005, we had only one goal, for Yushchenko to be president. We had hope he would change everything. It was not so much about social mobilization or about political mobilization."[9] The vision was centered on personalities rather than values. When those particular people failed to deliver, the revolution died.

The financial crisis in 2008 and 2009 hit Ukraine especially hard, and the economy plummeted by 15 percent. The national currency dropped by nearly 40 percent against the dollar, and bank controls were instituted to prevent a further decline. The country was now in a full-scale crisis, and whatever legitimacy Yushchenko still had was lost for good. In the meantime, Yanukovych, the villain of the Orange Revolution, was polishing his image. Coached by Western political consultants, including Paul Manafort, who would later perform a similar service for Donald Trump, he was able to position himself as the champion of traditional working people against the elites in the rising middle class. In 2010, Yanukovych rose to the presidency in an election that international observers judged to be legitimate. The economic crisis proved to be a trigger, but the network of disappointment had been building for some time.

Yanukovych quickly moved to consolidate his power, first jailing Tymoshenko on trumped-up corruption charges, then orchestrating a fraudulent parliamentary election in 2012. The Ukrainian constitution was changed to put more powers in the hands of the presidency, a crackdown on the media commenced, and his fiscal governance was deemed so poor that the IMF suspended its relief program. Although expectations were exceedingly low to start with, the Yanukovych regime proved to be even worse than feared.

The corruption was, even by Ukrainian standards, mind-blowing. The president's son Oleksandr, a dentist by profession, quickly became one of the richest men in the country, amassing a fortune of hundreds of millions of dollars in just a few short years. A group dubbed "The Family," a network of friends and relations close to the regime, emerged from obscurity to control vast swaths of industry and real estate. Estimates of the looting run as high as $100 billion, nearly equal to Ukraine's GDP in 2017.[10]

It appeared as if our efforts had been made in vain. While we took to the streets to bring about the dream of a new day for Ukraine, what we woke up to was even worse than before. Ukraine was poorer, more corrupt, and even more poorly governed than ever. Even Kuchma, for all of his shortcomings, had gotten some things done. Under Yanukovych, however, even the most modest standards of competency—not to mention decency—would not be met.

Under the Yanukovych regime, corruption and cynicism had reached new heights, and there had been a series of incidents involving officials and their children.[11] Ukrainians came to expect violence and terror to be connected to the members of the regime that drove their luxury cars at high speed on city streets and made scenes at nightclubs and restaurants. Anybody who questioned their right to do so was intimidated and beaten. If someone was hurt or even killed, the worst that would happen was a suspended sentence. While there was some outcry, Ukrainians mostly took the incidents in stride. After all, what could they expect from a president who was himself twice convicted of violent crimes?

Yet the networks that had given rise to the Orange Revolution remained. They were dormant and hardly noticeable, but they were still there. Yes, the tent cities had long left Kreshchatyk, but they hadn't really disappeared, only dispersed. And when they found a purpose around which to coalesce, they could prove to be very powerful indeed.

One particular event involving a young woman, Oksana Makar, whose attackers were set free due to political connections, was so unimaginably brutal and cold-blooded that it shook the populace out of their complacence. Videos on YouTube, of both Oksana in her hospital bed and a leaked video of one of her attackers' chilling confession, as well as a variety of social media pages and websites decrying the incident, flooded the Internet and incited widespread protests. Eventually, the uproar became so intense that even President Yanukovych felt compelled to have the local prosecutor fired and publicly call for justice to be meted out.

There was, underneath the corruption and tacit acquiescence, a network of civil activity. From social media groups to more formal organizations like the women's rights group FEMEN, some semblance of protest remained. So when, 18 months after the Oksana Makar incident, President Yanukovych backed out of an EU trade agreement, the cascades began again. A Facebook post by the journalist and activist Mustafa Nayyem called his fellow citizens to return once again to the Maidan. Before long, Ukrainians were pouring into the streets to protest in numbers not seen since the Orange Revolution, nearly 10 years before.

Yet this time, the matter would not be settled by firing a prosecutor and throwing a few miscreants in prison. Despite the regime's seemingly complete hold on power, the networks formed during the Orange Revolution awakened from their vegetative state, and a new movement, this time called Euromaidan, was soon in full swing. Within the space of a few months, Viktor Yanukovych would go from despot to pariah to, finally, fugitive. The Ukrainian Parliament voted overwhelmingly to remove him from power, and he fled the country. He remains in exile to this day.

ARE CASCADES THE NEW NORMAL?

As I noted at the beginning of this chapter, revolutions are remarkable things because they upend the existing order, which has power and inertia on its side. In effect, they make farces out of the conventions of normalcy that have become ingrained in our minds. But, what if our conventional notions of how the world works are flawed? What if there are natural forces at work that make cascading movements not only possible, but inevitable?

It certainly seems that way. As we have already seen, the Orange Revolution and the Euromaidan protests, although incredible turns of events, weren't exactly unusual. In fact, they were part and parcel of a series of similar uprisings that began with the Otpor movement in Serbia. Even before that, there were earlier antecedents, such as the women's suffrage movement, Gandhi's Satyagraha in India, and the struggle for civil rights in America. More recently, the movement for LGBT rights, Black Lives Matter, and the "March for Our Lives" movement that arose out of the school shooting in Parkland, Florida, follow the same patterns. Despite their long history, movements such as these do seem to happen with increasing frequency.

An eerily similar trend can be observed in the business world. Consider technology. Microsoft was founded in 1975, Apple in 1976, and the personal computer revolution took hold in the 1980s. The next major disruption was the creation of the World Wide Web in 1989, more than a decade later. Then came the launch of Netscape Navigator, the first consumer browser, in 1995. That gave rise to new corporate titans such as Yahoo! and Amazon. Google was incorporated at the end of 1998; by the time of its IPO in 2004 six years later, it was a $23 billion company. Facebook's rise was even faster. A new breed of technology companies, known as "unicorns," often achieve massive scale in a matter of not years, but months.

And while viral cascades are most conspicuous in the technology sector, it's a mistake to dismiss them as a purely technological phenomenon. Moisés Naím has observed that similar disruptions occur in many other facets of modern life: military affairs, religion, and business. It's hard to think of anything that's been left untouched.

Many leaders and scholars have noticed this shift and have even come up with an acronym for it: VUCA (volatility, uncertainty, complexity, and ambiguity). Some say that leaders need to become more enlightened, to be more agile and open, to embrace flexibility and "join the conversation." Yet while it's tempting to see those who are taken by surprise by nascent movements as a bunch of feckless, self-important dullards with their heads in the sand, that's far too facile an explanation.

In retrospect, it may seem clear that Ukraine was ripe for revolution in 2004, but it was far from obvious to anyone who was there at the time. Despite my experience in Eastern Europe and deep connection to events, I didn't see the Orange Revolution coming, nor did the journalists I worked with or the business and political leaders that I knew. The leaders of the Route 128 companies outside Boston were no buffoons either, but super successful entrepreneurs who had once been considered visionaries. Still, they never saw the rise of Silicon Valley coming until it was too late.

At the same time, the seemingly enlightened leaders who bring powerful movements about often lack the planning, discipline, and organization to create change that lasts. As we have already seen, the coalition formed during the Orange Revolution broke down within months as the various factions fell to infighting. The Arab Spring has had a similarly spotty record. Egypt descended into chaos within two years after Hosni Mubarak was deposed and his successor, Mohamed Morsi, suffered a similar fate. Barack Obama made sweeping changes to America, but his successor has worked to reverse every single one of them.

Even Al Qaeda has been disrupted from within. As political expert Thomas Rid noted in *The Wilson Quarterly*, the interests of local and global jihadi elements diverged over time.[12] In America, so-called wave elections are usually followed by a countermovement. The massive support for Barack Obama in 2008 helped inspire the Tea Party victories in 2010. Many of those trends, however, were reversed again in 2012. And all of this was just a prologue to the unlikely rise of Donald Trump in 2016 and the reversal of his political fortunes in the midterm elections two years later, in 2018. As Moisés Naím has noted, power has become easier to gain and harder to use or keep.

And even when leaders recognize the danger, they are often powerless to effect the change needed to counter it. For example, after John Antioco of Blockbuster addressed the danger that Netflix posed to his company, his plans encountered strong opposition within his organization. Carl Icahn, a business icon renowned for his vision and acumen, replaced Antioco with Jim Keyes, who reinstated late fees and refocused the company's strategy on brick-and-mortar stores. Investment in the online platform was decreased.[13] Within three years Blockbuster was bankrupt.

Our existing mental model is that strong governance drives change. Wise leaders who sit atop hierarchal organizations recognize the need for a shift and make it happen. They confer with advisors, formulate plans, and execute them. Many of us were raised to believe in the "great man" theory of history, that movements succeed only when a charismatic leader like Martin Luther King Jr. or Gandhi inspires them. Clearly, that model will continue to fail us in this new age in which cascades increasingly drive events.

Cascading movements don't follow the "great man" script. If there were great leaders driving the Orange Revolution and the Arab Spring, what happened to them in the aftermath?

What happened to the Pora activists of the Orange Revolution? Why were they powerless in the aftermath? Why was it Mustafa Nayyem, a relatively unknown journalist and activist, who sparked the Euromaidan protests and not some greater personage? The charisma of Barack Obama seemed to inspire as much backlash as it did devotion. His successor, Donald Trump, seems even more divisive.

One of the important differences between watching a revolution on CNN and actually being there is that the significance of self-organizing cascades becomes abundantly clear when you are on the ground. While during the Orange Revolution in Ukraine the eyes of the world were fixed on the celebrities gracing the stage at the Maidan, it was obvious to those of us who were there that the true power lay in the tent cities, in the homes of those who housed protestors from across the country, and in the myriad communications that buzzed around new forms of electronic media and old-fashioned word of mouth.

The truth was that no one was in control. There were no marching orders or chains of command. Someone you knew received information through an online bulletin board or a text message about, say, a protest in front of Parliament or the Council of Ministers, and off you went. The no-drinking rule, the horn protests, and the chants of "Razom nas bahato" weren't the results of orders from a prevailing authority. Instead, people did the things they did because other people were doing them. Joining in was an act of membership in a collective, rather than one of obedience to authority.

Today's reality is that hierarchies have lost their power not because they have suddenly become illegitimate, but because they are slow and the world has become fast. In a world pervaded by digital technology, connections form much faster than we can keep track of them, much less plan their formation. We now live in a world where networks trump hierarchies and cascades form whether we want them to or not.

And the ramifications of cascades are profound. A generation ago, we would expect a dominant model in an industry to last an entire career, whereas today, we can't depend on a business model lasting even a decade. In the future, we can expect little respite. In fact, if history is any guide, disruptive cascades will become far more frequent, intense, and far-reaching.

In witnessing the events of 2004 and 2005 in Ukraine firsthand, from the almost unique vantage point of the country's leading news organization, I found myself confused more than anything else. How was it that so many people, who would ordinarily be doing so many different things, could all of a sudden stop what they were doing and start all doing the same thing at once? What were these mysterious forces that seemed to drive everything? I admit, I hadn't a clue.

I remember two prevailing thoughts I had at the time. The first was awe and respect for the courage and discipline of the protestors, who not only overcame overwhelming odds, but did so with dignity and restraint. The second was far more selfish. I wondered how I could bottle the mysterious forces I had witnessed and put them to some useful purpose. Leading a media company, I often wished I could get people to stop doing certain things and start doing something else. I wanted employees to embrace new initiatives, for customers to stop buying competing products and start buying ours. I wanted other stakeholders, such as advertisers and investors, to embrace where we wanted to take the company. If I could mobilize just a small fraction of the forces of change I saw on the Maidan, I felt I could do wonderful things, but I had no idea how to make that happen.

Yet as I have learned in the years since those heady days in Kyiv, we can harness those forces to create transformational change and make a positive impact on the world. We can learn to understand how networks function and how they give rise to cascades. There are reasons why some ideas become movements and others sputter out, just as there are concrete principles we can apply to increase the likelihood of a cascade forming or to prevent one from harming us. But to uncover them, we need to leave the tumult and turmoil of Ukraine in 2004 and 2005 and go back to 1998 in Ithaca, New York, where a young graduate student in mathematics had become fixated on the chirping of snowy tree crickets.

CHAPTER 2

Fireflies, Snowy Tree Crickets, and the New Science of Networks

I read somewhere that everybody on this planet is separated by only six other people. Six degrees of separation between us and everyone else on this planet.

—**JOHN GUARE,** ***Six Degrees of Separation***

When Steven Strogatz arrived at Cornell University in 1994, he was already an accomplished mathematician. A former Marshall Scholar, he wrote the standard introductory textbook on chaos theory, won a prestigious award from the National Science Foundation, and was even awarded MIT's highest teaching prize. He also had an unusual penchant for plucking interesting mathematical problems from everyday life. When he was a student at Princeton, he wrote a paper on the mathematics of love, based on Romeo and Juliet. Decades later, it became the basis for a subplot for an entire season of the hit TV series *Numbers.*

One of Strogatz's primary research topics was a strange phenomenon called coupled oscillation, which occurs when a disparate group of entities act in unison, such as when pacemaker cells synchronize to make our hearts beat. It happens about once a second for our entire lives. A more spectacular form of coupled oscillation comes in the form of various species of fireflies native to Thailand, Malaysia, and other parts of Southeast Asia, where it coordinates their behavior to make entire jungles blink on and off as if populated by Christmas lights. Many species of crickets can coordinate their chirping in a similar way, providing a pleasant backdrop to summer barbecues.

Coupled oscillation is important to our story about cascades as well. When you think about it, fireflies and crickets synchronizing their behavior is very much like the crowds of protestors chanting "Razom Nas Bahato" on the streets of Kyiv, drivers honking their horns as they passed the Central Election Commission, and ordinarily indulgent Ukrainians adhering to a no-drinking rule. Somehow people, just like fireflies and crickets, can coordinate their behavior across vast collectives.

Yet it's not just people in a political movement that can synchronize their behavior in a viral cascade. Sometimes, it's people deciding to share the same cat video on social media. Other times, as in the case of Netflix and Blockbuster, they switch ingrained habits. When that happens, markets are transformed and businesses rise and fall. We see long lines at Apple stores and sold-out movie theaters. Cascades tend to feed on themselves because they never stay localized. You may have no interest in buying a new iPhone or seeing the latest hit film, but you'll notice the cascade that forms around them and, more likely than not, it will arouse your interest and you'll be more likely to join in.

As we will see in Part Two of this book, understanding the building blocks out of which cascades arise is key to creating transformational change. Whether you are trying to turn around a big company like IBM or Alcoa, cut down on deadly medical errors by improving procedures in hospitals, or even implementing lean manufacturing techniques at a major pharmaceutical firm, you need people to synchronize their behavior. In effect, you need to transform them into something much like those thousands of fireflies blinking on and off in unison. Perhaps most importantly, trying to force that kind of collective action is futile—people need to decide to do it by themselves. The role of leaders is no longer to coerce action, but to inspire and empower belief.

So, you can see why Strogatz was so intrigued by coupled oscillators. There are very few natural phenomena that are both so widespread and still, at least at the time, so poorly understood. While scientists had been aware of the effect for centuries—Christiaan Huygens first observed it in 1665—no one could figure out how it worked. It remained a mystery.

Soon after Strogatz began his tenure at Cornell, he passed by a graduate student's office door and couldn't help but notice a picture of the young man hanging by his fingertips on the face of a cliff 70 meters above the sea in Australia. To Strogatz, the image was a perfect metaphor for how he liked to do mathematics, and as he was already on the lookout for young talent to help him with his research, he was determined to learn more about the young adventurer.[1]

The student's name was Duncan Watts, and he was quite unconventional himself. A six-foot-two-inch former Australian naval officer with sandy hair, a wide smile, and an enthusiasm for extreme sports, Watts looked more like a California surfer than a brilliant mathematician. As luck would have it, Watts was looking for a thesis advisor, and Strogatz immediately agreed to take him on. Although neither of them knew it then, the partnership would not only make scientific history, but also help shed light on our story about cascades, such as those I witnessed during the Orange Revolution.

In his role as Strogatz's research assistant, Watts found himself spending his evenings climbing trees in search of a coupled oscillator indigenous to Cornell's location of Ithaca, New York:

the snowy tree cricket. During the day, Watts attempted to classify the insect's behavior by translating the synchronized chirps into mathematical formulas.

However, he soon became distracted by a series of questions. How were the crickets connected to each other? If they were each reacting to the behavior of others, maybe the structure of their relationships could explain how individual behavior scales up to collective behavior. Obviously, they were influencing each other somehow, but exactly how wasn't clear. Was there a leadership structure? Was there some sort of conductor cricket, coordinating the orchestra? Or maybe some complicated web of influence?

Watts looked for answers in the library and pored over all the literature he could find about coupled oscillators. His search didn't yield much, but while chatting with his father back home he stumbled across a topic nobody had apparently seen fit to investigate—an urban legend about everybody in the world being separated by only six handshakes. Although he didn't realize it yet, he had not only found a subject suitable for his PhD thesis, but one that would resonate throughout the scientific community.[2]

Popularly known as "six degrees of separation," the legend asserted that in just six steps, you could connect any individual on the planet to any other: a bus driver in Tokyo, a Turkish kebab vendor in Germany, a Hollywood star, or even the American president. The idea stuck in Watts's head. Then, in a sudden flash of intuition, he wondered if the synchronized behavior of the snowy tree crickets and the six-degrees phenomenon could be related. Maybe, he thought, the same type of invisible bond that connected people also connected fireflies and crickets, and that's what was behind the mysterious synchronizations of coupled oscillation.

In the course of his journey to understand the six-degrees idea and its relationship to the crickets' strange ability to coordinate their behavior, Watts came across the remarkable career of Stanley Milgram.

STANLEY MILGRAM AND THE SMALL-WORLD PHENOMENON

Milgram was an innovative experimental psychologist who gained fame and notoriety in 1963, at age 30, when he conducted his "obedience to authority" experiments.[3] The design was deceptively simple. The study involved three people: an administrator, a "teacher" who was the subject of the experiment, and a "student" who, unbeknownst to the "teacher," was part of the study. The teacher and student were placed in separate rooms where they could hear but not see each other. The teacher would test the student, administering progressively higher voltages of electric shocks for wrong answers.

The shocks were a hoax (prerecorded screams were played when the supposed shocks were delivered). Inevitably, the subjects playing the role of teacher would begin to protest after a few shocks, and the administrator would respond with a sequence of prearranged prods:

1. "Please continue" or "Please go on."
2. "The experiment requires that you continue."
3. "It is absolutely essential that you continue."
4. "You have no other choice: you must go on."

The results were chilling. None of the subjects refused to "shock" the students until they had "administered" 19 shocks of increasing intensity, up to the dangerous level of 300 volts. Nearly two-thirds of the subjects didn't refuse even at the maximum level of 450 volts. Despite hearing the screams and the sounds of the "student" banging on the wall in apparent agony, the subjects would comply with authority, even when compliance meant torturing an innocent person.

This type of clever unmasking of human behavior became Milgram's hallmark. Intensely interested in the psychological aspects of everyday human relationships, he studied real-world scenarios, such as whether people would mail a lost letter or give up a seat on a New York subway.[4] (They would, but it caused considerable stress among those who asked.)

In 1967, Milgram focused his formidable talents on the small-world phenomenon: the relatively common situation of meeting a stranger at a cocktail party and discovering you have a close friend in common. ("Wow, what a small world!") Much like obedience to authority, it's something that happens to all of us, but we rarely stop to think about it much. That made it exactly the type of thing Milgram loved to study.

Milgram investigated the small-world phenomenon by asking randomly selected people in Wichita, Kansas, and Omaha, Nebraska, to get a letter to a stockbroker in Boston entirely through their personal social networks. They were given no information except the broker's name and occupation, and they were only allowed to send the letter to people they knew on a first-name basis. On average, the letters got to their destination in six steps.[5] More recent experiments with e-mail messages have confirmed Milgram's findings.[6]

Milgram's results demonstrate that "six degrees of separation" isn't just an urban myth, but an empirical result. If people so widely dispersed are so closely connected, then it seems reasonable that they can synchronize their behavior. Yet Watts was looking to establish more than conjecture, but to find a mathematical structure to explain the small-world phenomenon. His journey to solve that problem would take him far afield—first to St. Petersburg, Russia, where a mathematical genius encountered a strange puzzle and decided that he needed to create a new branch of mathematics to solve it.

A BRIEF HISTORY OF NETWORKS

Leonhard Euler was considered the greatest mathematician of the eighteenth century and the most prolific in history. In fact, he produced a body of work that runs to 73 volumes. Although he was blind for the last 12 years of his life, he continued to publish at a furious pace. Dictating his work from memory, he completed a textbook on algebra, a 775-page treatise on the moon's orbit, and a three-volume study of integral calculus, as well as a paper every week for the journal of the St. Petersburg Academy.

In 1736, while still a young man, Euler turned his formidable talents to a mathematical curiosity that had become something of a craze among learned men. The puzzle involved the seven bridges in Königsberg (Figure 2.1), then a great city in the Prussian Empire (known today as Kaliningrad, Russia).

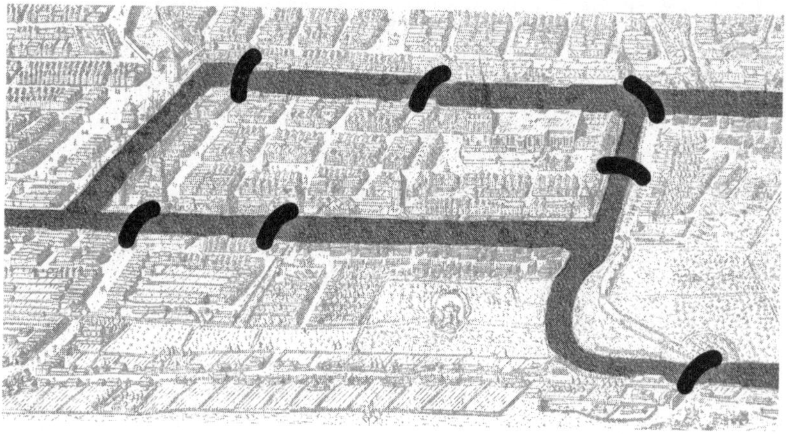

FIGURE 2.1 The Bridges of Königsberg

The question was simple: Could someone cross each bridge once without crossing any of them twice? While it seemed like a childish riddle, none of the great mathematical minds of the day could prove an answer to be correct. Euler, however, was an unusually creative thinker. To solve the puzzle of seven bridges in Königsberg, he constructed a branch of mathematics called graph theory: the analysis of links and nodes in a system.

Once Euler had framed the question in terms of a network, it became intuitively obvious that any system with an odd number of links cannot be continuous but must have a starting point and an end point (Figure 2.2). This rule is now known as the first theorem of graph theory.[7] Eventually, an eighth bridge was built and residents of Kaliningrad today can travel a continuous route across all eight bridges without repeating any, just as Euler said they could.

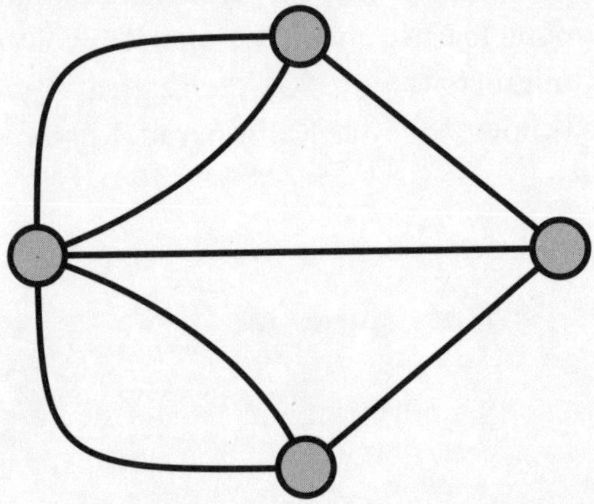

FIGURE 2.2 A Graphical Exposition of Euler's First Theorem of Graph Theory

Over the next two centuries, graph theory became a widely studied topic for ordered systems, from chess strategies to the atomic structure of crystals. Mathematicians today continue to use graph theory to study networks of connections. However, in the 1950s, graph theory took on a new life with the study of random networks, thanks to a Hungarian-born mathematician named Paul Erdős (pronounced "Erdish").

Erdős was almost a purely mathematical being, and one of the few mathematicians in history almost as prolific as Euler: he published no fewer than 1,500 papers before his death at 83 in 1996.[8] He often said that he considered mathematicians to be machines who turn coffee into theorems, and his caffeine-fueled working sessions sometimes lasted as long as 20 hours a day. When one of his (usually considerably younger) collaborators succumbed to exhaustion, he would call another on the phone and announce: "My brain is open."

Incidentally, Erdős's incredibly prolific work led him to become an exhibit in network theory himself. Even today, more than 20 years after his death, many mathematicians rate themselves based on their "Erdős number." Those who collaborated directly with the legendary genius earned themselves an Erdős number of one. Those who worked with those collaborators receive an Erdős number of two, and so on.

Erdős was as famous for his outlandish personality as for his genius. A citizen of the world, he lived mostly out of worn suitcases and off the hospitality of friendly mathematicians. He would arrive at their houses, usually unannounced, declare, "My brain is open," and then stay for a few days, or a few weeks. His unwitting hosts would have to compensate for his inability to do almost any activity a normal person performs in the course of daily life. Erdős couldn't cook, drive, or even tie his own shoes. Stories of Erdős are legion. One mathematician recalled:

> Erdős came to my twins' bar mitzvah, notebook in hand. He also brought gifts for my children—he loved kids—and behaved himself very well. But my mother-in-law tried to throw him out. She thought he was some guy who wandered off the street, in a rumpled suit, carrying a pad under his arm. It is entirely possible that he proved a theorem or two during the ceremony.[9]

To understand what Erdős and his Hungarian friend Alfréd Rényi discovered about random networks, imagine throwing a party for a hundred complete strangers. After a short while, the partygoers break off into small groups of two or three, chatting away. And there's some mingling at your party, too—every five minutes, two people from different groups swap their places.

Amidst the pleasant cocktail conversation, you whisper to one guest that you have a nice bottle of single-malt scotch, and you'll serve him a few fingers—as long as he tells no one else. But of course, the scotch loosens his tongue a little, and he mentions the prized bottle to one random person he meets in passing. Erdős and Rényi proved three things about this scenario:

First, your excellent scotch will be gone in record time: if each person passes the secret on to only one additional person in a different group, the chain will soon envelop everyone at the party. Those invisible ties, once connected, will allow information to transfer among the previously disparate group, causing its behavior to synchronize.

Second, even if the links were completely random and undirected, the party guests would be connected through remarkably few clusters, because not every grouping would need to be directly connected to each other. Many guests, in fact, would be connected through intermediate groups. Nevertheless, a single chain would connect them all.

Finally, and this is a crucial point, the groups in the room will not connect gradually: they will go from being relatively dispersed to being entirely connected in one step. This phenomenon is known as an *instantaneous phase transition*, and it explains why cascades take off so suddenly, like when my fiancée suddenly starting going to political demonstrations at the same time everyone else did. However, it takes a little thinking to understand how it works.

First, some math: The Erdős-Rényi theorem holds that if there are 40 groups in the room, generating 780 potential links amongst them all only takes 72 links to guarantee a continuous chain.[10] So, if every group in the room makes a connection to another group by exchanging a member every five minutes, then 60 links would have been created after 15 minutes. Yet because the links between groups form randomly, those 60 links will be unevenly distributed, leaving some groups tightly clustered while many others remain completely unconnected. In the next five-minute shift of mixing, however, the 72-link threshold will have been met and the entire party will have formed a continuous chain. A complete phase transition will have taken place in that one step.

A particularly vivid example of this phenomenon is the LOLCats videos that exploded on the web with no apparent origin. Seemingly all at once, they were traveling virally at breakneck speed as millions of people in offices and dorm rooms passed them back and forth. In actuality, there was nothing sudden about the LOLCats meme. It had been incubating for months on an online community called 4Chan, whose members occasionally sent them to friends outside the group. Eventually, the system tipped and LOLCats seemed to explode on the general consciousness all at once.[11]

A similar process took place on that morning in November 2004, when I woke up to find that the entire country of Ukraine had changed. It had been, of course, brewing for months, but I only really noticed it when people close to me got involved, despite the fact that I was working in a news office every day. Once the people that I knew started going to demonstrations, I joined in just like everyone else.

The Erdős-Rényi theorem also explains how Netflix transformed itself from a niche service into an overnight sensation. While the number of Netflix customers was small, they were connected to many others. As their enthusiasm for the service convinced people they knew to try it, the market for Netflix grew like wildfire. In much the same way, it explains how Silicon Valley overtook Route 128. Because the tech entrepreneurs on the West Coast regularly mixed with former colleagues and those outside Boston didn't, new technologies were able to spread faster, build scale, and dominate their more traditional rivals.

What we often miss when we look at nascent trends in the early stages is that diverse groups tend to intersperse and connect. These connections don't form in an organized, gradual manner, but exponentially. So while one minute you see a disperse assortment of unaffiliated people, the next minute there is one long, connected chain acting in concert. It is, as I noted earlier about my personal experience in the Orange Revolution, like someone flips a switch. Just like that, the world changes.

In effect, Erdős and Rényi showed how groups of millions of fireflies—or protestors, or consumers—could be connected with extreme efficiency through random links. For Duncan

Watts, the phenomenon of phase transition, much like Milgram's small-world phenomenon, suggested that he was onto something important.

However, it was clear to Watts that, in the real world, things don't link randomly. If we go out for a few beers with friends, it's unlikely we met them at random. They're probably people we met at work or school or who live in our neighborhood. If our relationships were truly random, we would be just as likely to meet people from across the world as from across the street. Experience, intuition, and common sense tell us that's simply not how relationships function.

As it turned out, about 10 years before Erdős and Rényi proved their theorem about random networks, another mathematician, Anatol Rapoport, studying an altogether different problem, found a similarly efficient network structure that was not random.

Rapoport, a Russian émigré to the United States, had an unusually expansive career.[12] Originally he had studied to be a concert pianist, but he switched to mathematics in his twenties and earned his PhD at the age of 30, in 1941, from the University of Chicago. Throughout a prodigious career, he made important contributions to mathematical biology, game theory, and network theory.

In the 1950s, Rapoport was studying how epidemics spread, and he began to realize that, as relationships develop, they tend to become more clustered. If you have two friends who don't know each other, there is a high probability that they will eventually meet through you and form their own relationship. Rapoport called this concept *triadic closure*.[13] The idea intrigued him, and in 1961 he collaborated with William Horvath to study junior high school students in Ann Arbor, Michigan. Rapoport and Horvath asked more than 800 students to list eight friends in order of the strength of the relationship: the best friend is listed first, the next best friend second, and so on.[14]

The mathematicians then attempted to map out the relationships according to the top two friends on each list. They didn't get very far. Only a small fraction of the student body was connected this way. However, when they mapped the relationships by using the bottom two names on the students' lists, showing the weakest relationships rather than the strongest, they found that almost the entire school was connected—much like the scotch-drinking cocktail party guests in the random-networks scenario. What Rapoport and Horvath learned was that information spreads not through best friends but casual acquaintances.[15]

Mark Granovetter, a sociologist who knew both Milgram's and Rapoport's work, decided to research the matter further. In the late 1960s and early 1970s, he studied how people found jobs in communities around Boston. He soon found that successful job searches revolved around a strange combination of acquaintance and chance.

In a book describing his research, Granovetter cited three examples. In the first, a salesman who was earning poor commissions started driving a cab to supplement his income. One day, he ran across an old friend while dropping off a passenger. His friend, surprised to see him driving a taxi, offered him a job as his company's labor relations manager. In the second example, a man named Edward had recently been discharged from the military. At a local playground, he met an older friend from the neighborhood who was working for an engineering firm and told Edward about an entry-level opening. Edward applied for the job and started a career in engineering. In the third example, Franklin, a stockbroker in Philadelphia, had received an offer from a firm in Boston. Before he accepted the job, he happened to go to Boston on a business trip with another member of his firm. During the trip, Franklin's friend suggested that they have a casual lunch with Robert, an acquaintance of the friend. When Robert found out that Franklin was considering relocating to Boston, he later contacted him privately and made him a better offer.[16]

These examples seem unexceptional. Still, when you think about it, choosing a job is a major decision. It's strange that career paths are so often determined by casual encounters. Granovetter found that more than 80 percent of the people in his study who found a job through a contact did not have a close relationship with the person who lined up the offer. In seeking an explanation, he cited Rapoport and Horvath's Michigan study.[17]

The phenomenon reminded Granovetter of something he had learned in a chemistry class about water. Besides the strong bonds between hydrogen and oxygen, there are also weak bonds between the water molecules themselves, which causes the molecules to cluster, forming raindrops. The similarity between the weak bonds of water molecules and human relationships was striking, which inspired Granovetter to brand his idea "the strength of weak ties."[18]

In some very important ways, human relationships do resemble molecules floating around in a liquid. While we have a few close relationships, we have many more casual ones, and those relationships form connections to an even larger and more disparate group. Moreover, those who are closest to us tend to come across the same information we do. If you're searching for a job, or if you want to coordinate activity across a large group, you'll most likely do it not through close friends, but through the casual acquaintances of second- and third-degree links that connect you to the greater world.

DISCOVERING SMALL-WORLD NETWORKS

So for more than 200 years before Duncan Watts attacked the problem of coupled oscillation, there had been scattered pockets of insight. Euler showed that arrangements of links and nodes could be a fertile mathematical area. Erdős and Rényi proved that even random arrangements of links can be incredibly efficient. Rapoport highlighted that real-life networks that were neither random nor directed, but biased toward clustering, were just as potent as random networks. Granovetter showed that these clusters could be very effective in transmitting information through second- and third-degree relationships.

Each breakthrough formed a piece of the small-world "six degrees of separation" phenomenon Milgram had exposed in his landmark experiment. However, no one had put them all together. In network terms, the information remained unconnected. It was Watts, under Strogatz's direction, who would show that information naturally forms a particular kind of network that accounts for the amazing behavior of pacemaker cells, fireflies, snowy tree crickets, and, more important to our story about cascades, protestors in a political revolution, consumers in a marketplace, terrorists on a battlefield, independent units in a large organization, and many other things.

Like many scientists, Watts was a fan of science fiction, and he had another idea for researching networks, based on two Isaac Asimov books he had read as a child. He didn't know it when he started his research, but hidden in the imagination of that famous author he was about to find the final piece to a puzzle that had baffled scientists for a very long time.[19]

One book, *Caves of Steel*, is about a future planet where everybody lives in underground caves. There is very little interaction between the caves, so if you lived in one, you would only know the people in your cave and nobody else. Moreover, in the close confines of the cave, the people you know also know each other. In the other book, *The Naked Sun*, the situation was at the other end of the communications spectrum. The novel is set on a planet called Solaria, where everybody lives on huge plantations and communicates remotely. Nobody's acquaintances know one another.

Watts decided to set up a mathematical model that would take into account both extremes and everything in between. He called his first attempt the alpha model, which examined the likelihood that two people would connect as a function of the number of mutual friends they had.

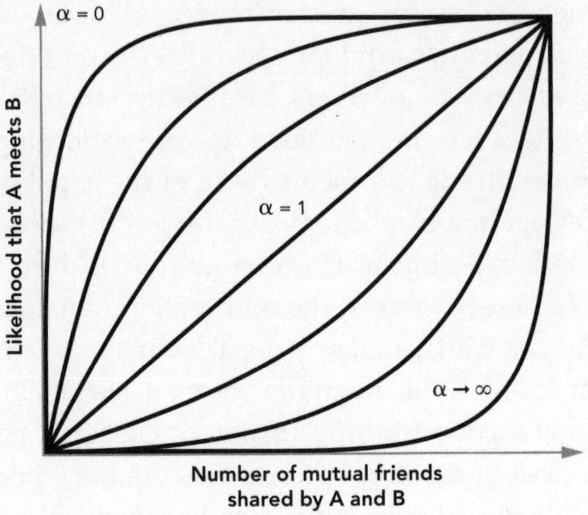

FIGURE 2.3 Likelihood of Meeting as a Function of Number of Friends

A graphic description of the model can be seen in Figure 2.3. The very top line represents the "caveman" world. As soon as two people have a mutual friend, they immediately meet each other. If they had no mutual friends, that would indicate they were in different caves and would never meet. The bottom line represented the "spaceman" extreme, where mutual friendships don't increase the likelihood of meeting at all.

What Watts was most interested in, however, was all of the possibilities in between.

The Alpha Model

Although he didn't immediately realize it, Watts had found a model very similar to Rapoport's random-biased nets. The more friends you have in common with someone else, the more likely you and that person are to become friends. However, unlike Rapoport, Watts had access to powerful computers, so he could explore the idea further by using the "alpha" metric to run simulations of systems with different attributes.

Armed with this mathematical representation of Rapoport's random-biased nets concept, Watts set out to see what would happen to the degrees of separation (technically called *path lengths*) as you increased the alpha metric. What he found amazed him so much that at first, he thought he had done something wrong. As alpha increased, in effect connecting caves or tent cities, path lengths increased (Figure 2.4). In other words, Watts found that it took *more* steps to connect one person to another. But then, alpha reached a critical value, and suddenly they crashed down to very low path lengths again.[20]

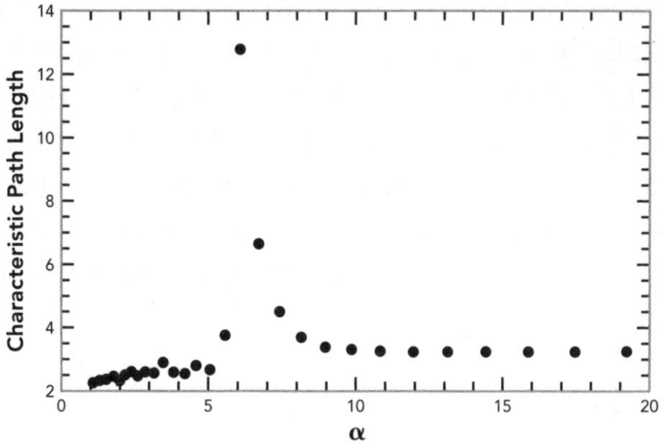

FIGURE 2.4 Change in Path Length as Alpha Increases

While this model is highly counterintuitive, it does make sense. Imagine you're living in a cave world, and an opening in your cave allows you to start meeting people in another cave. At first, the social distance for the combined communities is larger than when you started, because most people in the caves remain unconnected. Yet as time passes and the new reality of the connected caves sets in, more connections are built, and eventually the connected caves start to behave like one big community. We see an almost instantaneous phase transition where we might expect to see gradual change.

When groups first connect, there is always a period of awkward distance. Much like a dance at summer camp, where the boys and girls start on opposite sides of the room, the first connections are slow to happen. But eventually, two camp counselors start dancing, then a few campers, and then everybody. It's also precisely what I saw happen in the Orange Revolution in Ukraine. At first, the activity was dispersed around Ukraine. Then one morning, I woke up, and my fiancée was going out in her orange bandana to protest. Before I knew it, it seemed that everyone in Ukraine was attending protests and rallies. The world had changed, almost literally overnight. It was like someone had just flipped a switch.

Put into a real world context, the alpha variable translates roughly into the difference between living on campus in college (high alpha) and living off-campus (low alpha). The problem with the alpha model, however, is that it is very hard to understand what the alpha metric actually represents. It makes sense as a mathematical variable but explains little about the real world. So Watts began to work on a more intuitive version he called the beta model.[21]

The Beta Model

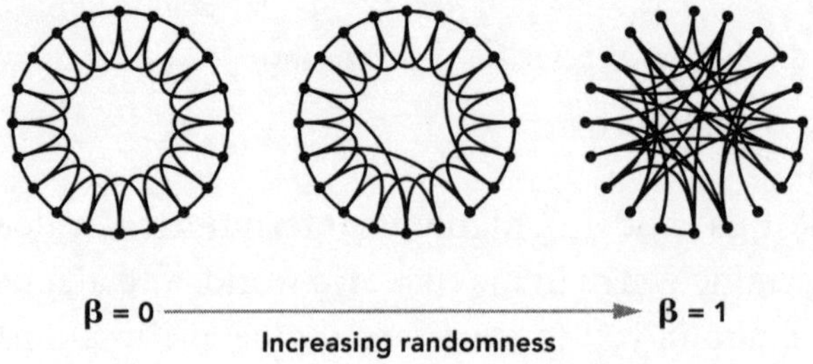

FIGURE 2.5 The Beta Model

The beta model (Figure 2.5) works like this: Imagine you're in a football stadium, standing with a ring of spectators around the circumference. You can communicate pretty easily with those standing close to you, but those across the stadium might as well be out in the parking lot, or even in another city. Although they're connected to you through the other people in the ring, the connection is so loose that they might as well not be. Now hand out a few mobile phones randomly. Suddenly, the social distance of the ring collapses. You can call someone on the other side of the stadium and that person can get the message to anyone near him or her. The social distance collapses, and all it takes is a little random mixing.

This is exactly what Watts discovered mathematically. The more he looked, the more it became clear that it takes very few random links in the network to shorten path lengths considerably. In fact, adding only five random links, he found, would cut social distance in half, regardless of the size of the network. Not only was it possible for tight clusters to combine with short social distance; *networks actually have a strong tendency to become tight clusters combined with short social distance.* In effect, Watts's mathematical model predicted that small-world networks are not a special case, but a natural state.

These random links played exactly the same role that Granovetter's "weak ties" did in his job-hunting studies. In one fell swoop, Watts had found an explanation that agreed both with Erdős, Rényi, and Rapaport's mathematical investigations and with the real-world studies of Milgram and Granovetter. Networks really are "small worlds," clustered into tight communities, but also connected through links over long distances. Small groups, loosely connected, have a strange power to synchronize.

When Watts and Strogatz applied their model to actual data—the network of movie actors in the Internet Movie Database (IMDB), the neural network of the worm *C. Elegans*, and the power grid of the western United States—their theory fit precisely with the behavior of real-world networks. The paper Watts wrote with Strogatz, Collective Dynamics of 'Small-World' Networks, would prove to be a landmark in the study of how things connect and remains one of the most highly cited papers in the field today, 20 years later.[22] High clustering going hand-in-hand with massive reach, it seemed to be a universal law. Loosely connected small groups can drive massive synchronized behavior, as long as some element of randomness is introduced in the system (and in the real world, randomness almost always comes into play).

THE MAKING OF A CASCADE

The unlikely success of his network studies led Watts to begin studying another network-related phenomenon known as cascades. A particularly vivid example of a cascade occurred during the summer of 1996.[23]

On August 10 of that year, an exceedingly hot day, air conditioners across the West Coast were going at full blast when a transmission line near Portland, Oregon, failed. This was not an unusual occurrence, and redundancies were built into the system to cover for just such a failure. The load of electricity was supposed to be rerouted by a relay to another substation. However, with the entire system operating at its limit, the surge caused another line to fail. The excess power from that backup line was rerouted to yet another overly taxed component of the system, causing yet another failure. Soon, power surged throughout the system, causing cascading failures wherever it went. Within 70 seconds, the entire power grid between California and Oregon was out. Then the surge moved east, creating outages in six other states.

The power company's report on the blackout listed many possible causes: maintenance problems, failure to address warning signs, and bad luck. Yet a general comment slipped in at the end of the report caught Watts's attention—the power company admitted that it simply didn't fully understand the interdependencies of the system.

Although it may not be immediately obvious, the disruptions we've discussed up to this point are very much like the West Coast blackout of 1996. They are also cascades. A disturbance in one part of the system eventually ripples through every other part of the system, finding vulnerable clusters as it travels. Eventually, the entire order is disrupted, much like the cascading failures in the electrical grid.

The electrical grid was also a network, and Watts, fresh off identifying the structure of small-world networks, moved quickly to study it. What he found was that while cascades were known to occur in a variety of environments, most of the examination focused on the nodes, not the networks. When a flu epidemic spreads through a school, or financial contagion spreads from a crisis in one country to entire continents, we tend to look for a cause in the initial failure rather than in the system as a whole. Social fads work in a similar fashion. Whether the craze is for Harry Potter or the iPhone, we tend to think there's something magical about the idea itself and often fail to notice the network the idea travels through.

Yet in our rush to ascribe significance to a particular node, we often miss the dynamics of the network. Certainly, there was nothing particularly special about the transmission line that started the blackout of 1996. So why do we tend to assume that there's something special about the idea of Harry Potter or the iPhone? Sure, they are powerful ideas, but so are many others that die on the vine. What's the difference between those and many fairly ordinary ideas, like LOLCats and other Internet memes, which somehow get uplifted by extraordinary cascades?

Just as important, Watts argued, is the structure of the network, which can influence a cascade's probability.[24] If you think about it, that's undeniably true. Would the financial crises of 1997 and 1998 have happened if the emerging markets of Asia and Eastern Europe were stable to start with? Was the amazing success of Harry Potter due only to the talents of J.K. Rowling, completely removed from context of time and place? Would the iPhone have been as successful if it had not been created by Apple, with its dense network of brand loyalists?

That's a crucial point, because the structure of networks is something that we can do quite a bit about and that can have a dramatic effect on whether a movement cascades or not. We can choose to depend on a few all-stars, or we can disperse responsibility around the organization. We can insulate ourselves, like Milošević in Serbia, Yanukovych in Ukraine, and the various dictatorships in the Arab Spring, or we can choose to build open, transparent management structures, like

General Stanley McChrystal did in Iraq. We can lock up our organizations in airtight, siloed fortresses, or we can encourage communication across the enterprise.

We tend to see success and failure through the prism of strategy and tactics, and that is, to a certain extent, true. But we also act according to how we see the world. If we see the world as a chessboard, with various powers vying for dominance, we will act one way. However, if we see the world as a series of networks and ecosystems, we are likely to act differently. What we see determines how we will act.

SEEING THINGS FROM A NETWORK VIEW

In the Introduction to this book, we looked at three pairs of examples: Occupy and Otpor, Blockbuster and McChrystal's forces in Iraq, and Route 128 outside Boston and Silicon Valley. Look at these cases one by one, and you will see differences in strategy and tactics. While Antioco changed his business strategy, McChrystal transformed his culture. The Route 128 companies sought proprietary competitive advantage, while Silicon Valley companies created an open industrial ecosystem. Occupy chose angry rhetoric, while Otpor chose street pranks.

Yet when taken collectively, a different picture emerges. Antioco, the Route 128 firms, and Occupy saw hierarchies and framed the challenges they faced in terms of traditional resources, such as strategic capacity, competitive pressures, and market dynamics. McChrystal, the Silicon Valley firms, and Otpor, on the other hand, saw networks to integrate, and that made all the difference. They looked to build connections to other nodes in the system and recognized that true power resided in those linkages.

Otpor set out to identify pillars supporting the existing power structure—not to knock them out, but to draw them in. So for them, every arrest was a chance to win converts at the police station, and those converts, in the end, were what proved to be decisive. Occupy, on the other hand, eschewed all connections to the existing order and quickly devolved. McChrystal saw that, "to defeat a network, you must become a network" and transformed his organization from one that relied solely on a top-down command structure to one that worked to build horizontal connections that empowered a "team of teams." Antioco and his executive team at Blockbuster merely saw a strategy to be executed and neglected internal networks. Silicon Valley saw an ecosystem that needed to be constantly nourished and renewed, while the Route 128 firms believed in vertical integration.

In *The End of Power*, Moisés Naím pointed out that "power is easier to get but harder to use or keep." That is undeniably true, but I also think it misses the point somewhat. The greater truth is that in a world connected by digital technology, power no longer lies at the top of hierarchies, but at the center of networks. We move to the center by making new connections and drawing others in.

Networks have important advantages over hierarchies. Hierarchies are expensive and difficult to maintain. Leadership must provide standards, governance, oversight, and resources. The Tea Party, to take just one example, was able to take the country by storm, seemingly overnight, because it didn't have to provide any of those things. It only needed to empower the groups that formed of their own accord, let them connect with each other, share ideas and practices, and, most of all, help them to understand that they were not alone, but there were many others who shared their ethos.

This kind of distributed authority can be amazingly effective. Consider the Orpheus Chamber Orchestra, one of the most accomplished ensembles in the world. It operates without a conductor. By giving everybody a voice in which arrangements will be performed, how they will be interpreted, and what role each instrument will play in a particular piece of music, it has unleashed the creative energy of its members and won multiple Grammy awards in the process.[25] In a similar vein, Morningstar, a $700 million dollar food processing business, operates without any management hierarchy at all.[26]

Networks, unlike hierarchies, push authority down to the lowest level of an organization. They recognize that people on the ground have the most current information and are most able to act on it quickly and effectively. However, there is a catch. Just as well-functioning networks can cascade toward a common purpose, poorly governed ones can spin wildly out of control. One or two rock throwers can quickly transform a peaceful demonstration into a horrifying riot. Factions can form in an organization and go off in competing directions. Much like Tolstoy wrote about families, all well-functioning networks are alike, but each can go wrong in a multitude of ways.

Every movement for change has a trigger. In Serbia and in Ukraine's Orange Revolution, an election triggered the mass protests that brought down the respective regimes. Later, during Ukraine's Euromaidan protests, it was the pullout from an EU agreement that set things off. With Occupy, it was the financial crisis, and in Silicon Valley it was the shift from microcomputers to PCs that set the stage for Bay Area dominance and sealed the fate of Route 128. More recently, videos of police violence have led to massive protests and the Black Lives Matter movement, while the mass shooting at Marjory Stoneman Douglas High School in Parkland, Florida, ignited the March for Our Lives movement.

Yet notice that not all of these movements have been successful. A cascade makes change possible, but it doesn't make it inevitable. As impressive as the mass protests that Occupy was able to mobilize were, they never amounted to much. They made a point, but they never made a difference.

And that's what's crucial to understand about cascades. They are a means to an end, not an end in themselves. Mobilizing thousands of people to walk the streets or sleep in parks or post messages on social media do not in themselves make change happen. In fact, such actions can—and often do—backfire if they motivate those who oppose change to mobilize themselves. Every revolution sets the stage for a counterrevolution. Cascades are only useful if they result in influence, and to do that, they must travel far beyond where they start.

That is what we turn to in the next chapter, in which we will see how small groups, loosely connected, but united by a common purpose, lead to transformational change and how harnessing these forces often determines whether a movement succeeds or fails.

CHAPTER 3

How Cascades Create Transformational Change

What all information cascades have in common, however, is that once one commences, it becomes largely self-perpetuating; that is, it picks up new adherents largely on the strength of having attracted previous ones. Hence, an initial shock can propagate throughout a very large system, even when the shock itself is small.[1]

—DUNCAN WATTS

My best friend growing up was a boy named Robbie, and he had a special gift. He was the kind of guy everyone loved to be around. Although he was not a great student, teachers had a soft spot for him. He was a good athlete, but not a star. Coaches loved him anyway. He was not what you'd call suave or debonair. Nevertheless, girls liked him. Robbie *had something.* He was funny, had a zest for life, and loved being around other people. He had a certain way of saying and doing things. He would tell a joke in the locker room, and the next thing you knew, everybody was repeating it.

I think everyone knew someone in high school like Robbie. So, when Malcolm Gladwell published *The Tipping Point*, which offered an explanation why people like Robbie can be so infectious, it became an instant bestseller, in part because he claimed people like Robbie can lead to much bigger things. Many great movements have charismatic leaders. We see Mahatma Gandhi, Martin Luther King Jr., and other legendary figures leading the charge, inspiring large masses of people to act in the service of a cause. In business, we see larger-than-life figures like Steve Jobs and Elon Musk at the head of their own revolutions.

So the idea that the personal qualities of rare individuals determine whether a change effort succeeds or not makes intuitive sense, although as we will see, things don't really work that way. It is, in many ways, an urban myth, and if we try to create change based on that assumption we are unlikely to succeed. So it's important to understand why it doesn't hold water. It is not "influential" people who create change, but as Duncan Watts put it to me "easily influenced people influencing other easily influenced people"[2] that creates a cascade.

Gladwell's explanation for how personal qualities drive change is based on what he calls the "Law of the Few."[3] "The success of any kind of social epidemic is heavily dependent on the involvement of people with a particular and rare set of social gifts," he writes and then goes on to classify these gifts according to three classes of highly influential people: Connectors, Mavens, and Salesmen. Connectors know a lot of people, but they are more than just social butterflies. They actively seek out folks to introduce and, by doing so, attract even more people to them. The Mavens influence others through their deep knowledge and expertise. They are subject matter experts that others actively seek out for advice. Salesmen seem to have supernatural powers of persuasion.

We've all met people like this and we remember them. Connectors, Mavens, and Salesmen have played important roles in our lives because they have, as Gladwell notes, skills that are rare and valuable. So the idea that people like these play an outsized role in creating change just feels intuitively right. It is, in many ways, a more modern and trendy version of the "Great Man" theory of history. If true, the question of how to create transformational change would be relatively easy. You simply have to find a transformational changemaker (an "influential" in popular modern parlance), and this person could then convince everyone else to join in.

Unfortunately, the Law of the Few, while seemingly plausible, is dangerously misleading. As we will soon see, it is not "special people" who create change, although some with great talent can help to inspire it, but small groups, loosely connected, and united by a common purpose. Each of those three elements is crucial, because small groups engender strong bonds, loose connections provide greater numbers, and a common purpose gives direction. Every change effort, if it is to succeed and provide lasting results, needs each of those elements because it requires *long chains of sustained influence* to make a real difference.

However, in order to understand how small groups, loosely connected, but united by a common purpose, give rise to cascades and lead to transformational change, we first must understand why the Law of the Few and the idea of influentials isn't a viable explanation for what makes a movement succeed. To do that, we first need to understand where Gladwell's idea came from.

OPINION LEADERS AND THE TWO STEP FLOW COMMUNICATION MODEL

Long before Gladwell published *The Tipping Point*, Paul Lazarsfeld and Elihu Katz, two eminent sociologists, developed what they called the Two Step Flow Communication Model. It was based on Lazarsfeld's earlier research into the 1944 presidential campaign,[4] which had inspired subsequent studies throughout the 1940s and 1950s.[5]

The basic argument was that mass media doesn't actually affect the masses, but works through "opinion leaders" who amplify messages. The existence of these special people was predicated on three findings from their research of presidential politics. First, they found that people who had changed their minds or selected their candidate late in the campaign were likely to cite the personal influence of those they knew as a factor in their choice. Second, they found that the "opinion leaders" who influenced the choice of others tended to be of the same social class as the people whom they influenced. So, and this is a crucial point, the opinion leaders weren't influential by virtue of celebrity or position, but through a personal relationship. Third, the opinion leaders were exposed to mass media more than others.

Katz and Lazarsfeld concluded that the real reason mass media was effective in forming opinions wasn't simply because it reached a lot of people, but because of its ability to influence the influencers. Their work eventually became a core principle for generations of marketers and political consultants: reach those whose opinions can affect the opinions of others and you can sell just about anything. Inspiring word of mouth became a fixture of every political and promotional campaign.

Subsequent studies revealed three characteristics of opinion leaders: the personification of values (who one is); competence (what one knows); and strategic social location (whom one knows). We'll look at each in turn:

1. **Personification of values (who one is).** The studies found, not surprisingly, that influence isn't a universal quality. While a middle-aged mother might wield influence in such areas as what products to buy at the market (remember, these studies were done in the 1950s), her daughter may be more persuasive in areas such as fashion and what to watch at the movies.
2. **Competence (what one knows).** It was also found that people who were seen to be more competent had more

influence, but this was highly situational. For example, doctors who were seen to be more "scientific" were often able to form the opinions of their peers, while young people who go to the movies often and can rattle off the works of acclaimed directors are seen to be knowledgeable and influential in that realm.

3. **Strategic social location (whom one knows).** Social connections play a role in two ways. First, people tend to trust others they feel are part of their group, a principle that seems to be fully grasped by politicians whose accent changes slightly depending on which part of the country they happen to be in at any given time. This phenomenon is often referred to as *homophily.* Second, those who travel outside the group are seen as being privy to information others don't have and can therefore leverage the knowledge they gain to persuade others within their group. So a person who is seen as part of a tight-knit group, but also has links to the outside world, can be particularly influential.

All of this seems perfectly plausible and in accordance with our daily lives. We all have people we go to for information in particular spheres of our lives: The niece who is a veritable encyclopedia of the best mobile apps to use, the uncle who is glued to CNN and knows all there is to know about politics, the friend from college who knows just where to take a particularly promising date. So it's easy to believe that those same people can lead to large-scale change. However, that's not how the world really works.

DEBUNKING THE INFLUENTIALS MYTH

In a very large sense, Malcolm Gladwell's Law of the Few can be seen as an update of Katz and Lazarsfeld's decades of research. We can easily see how Connectors, Mavens, and Salesmen have "rare qualities" that make them adept at influencing others. However, in ascribing these personal qualities to large-scale social phenomena, Gladwell misunderstood the data.

The problem with his idea is that to create a significant impact, you need a lot of people to buy into an idea. So, while a Connector, a Maven, or a Salesman may be able to influence those around them, those people would have to influence others, and those people, in turn, would have to influence others *still.* To create something like the Orange Revolution, it takes literally millions of people to join in. So, if the Law of the Few were true, we would expect people with "rare social gifts" not only to be able to persuade those around them, but to create long chains of influence more reliably than a normal person would. That's a very testable hypothesis, and researchers who have studied it have found it wanting.

One e-mail study that incorporated 60,000 respondents to replicate Milgram's small-world research found that, while the principle of six degrees of separation held true, messages didn't need to go through "hubs" (highly connected people) to reach their recipients.[6] Another study of 1.6 million Twitter users found that, while highly connected users were slightly more likely to initiate large viral cascades, the difference between them and normal users was so small that it's probably not economically feasible to waste resources seeking them out.[7]

So the empirical evidence debunks Gladwell's Law of the Few. Not only are people with "rare social gifts" not sufficient to initiate a social epidemic, they aren't even necessary. Just because someone has a lot of connections to other people, specialized knowledge, or ample powers of persuasion doesn't mean that he or she is more likely to initiate messages that get passed on by long chains of people.

Beyond the scientific evidence, there is a more compelling reason to discount Gladwell's Law of the Few. Does it stand to reason that Slobodan Milošević in Serbia or Viktor Yanukovych in Ukraine lacked influence or access to influential people? That certainly doesn't seem right.

On the other side of the ledger, if those who played a part in the Orange Revolution and the Arab Spring had magical powers of influence, why did these powers fail them in the aftermath? The protestors that overthrew Mubarak in Cairo were overrun by the Muslim Brotherhood in the elections that followed the uprising. What happened to their "rare set of social gifts" then? The members of the Pora student movement, which played such a central role in the Orange Revolution, also played little, if any, further part in public affairs in Ukraine. For that matter, the leaders of the Boston tech firms were highly influential within the tech industry until they were steamrolled by the mostly anonymous (at the time), but highly interdependent, Silicon Valley entrepreneurs. Clearly, if we're going to understand how ideas spread and create change, we're going to need a different model based on the best available empirical evidence.

To understand why people who are influential personally often fail to create widespread change, let's go back to my friend Robbie. Sure, he could do or say something goofy in the locker room, and the next thing you knew it seemed like everybody was repeating it, but we were all deeply connected in a school environment. The kids in the next town over were oblivious to Robbie's charms and therefore completely unaffected by the memes floating around our school.

What belies the theory of "influentials" or "opinion leaders" or whatever you want to call them is that change is a matter of networks and not nodes. While it is easier and more cognitively pleasing to single out individuals, the truth is that it is the *connections between people* that are decisive. True power does not lie at the top of hierarchies, but emanates from the center of networks. Moreover, as digital technology enables connections to form faster and more pervasively, networks are becoming even more salient and essential to create transformational change.

So while we always need to be careful when considering the explanatory power of any theory,[8] I do believe that there is a body of research that much better fits the data than Gladwell's Law of the Few which can help us understand how cascades form, how they can result in transformational change, and how we can harness many of these same forces, albeit imperfectly, to bring change about.

THE INFLUENCE OF LOCAL MAJORITIES

When you go to a new country, or even just enter a new business environment, one of the first things you'll notice is that people do things much differently than you're used to. Sometimes these differences are startling and you find yourself objecting vigorously, but when challenged you can't really say why you have a problem with the seemingly strange custom. It just feels wrong to you. After a while, though, what once seemed alien and exotic starts to feel normal. You begin to conform to your local environment.

Solomon Asch noticed this phenomenon when he was a small boy at a Passover Seder. When he asked his uncle why an extra glass was being left on the table, he was told that it was for the prophet Elijah. When the time came and the door was opened for the legendary prophet, the young boy actually thought he saw the level of wine in the glass drop ever so slightly.[9]

Later, when he became a prominent social psychologist, Asch wanted to study the effect of suggestion and expectation. So he designed an ingenious experiment. A group of seven to nine subjects were brought into a room and told that they would be evaluating the length of lines. They were then shown pairs of cards like the ones in Figure 3.1.

The subjects were asked to choose which line on the right matched the line on the left. The answer was made to be deliberately obvious, but as the administrator went around the room, every person answered that "A" was clearly the same length as the sample line. The last person in the group (in fact, the only

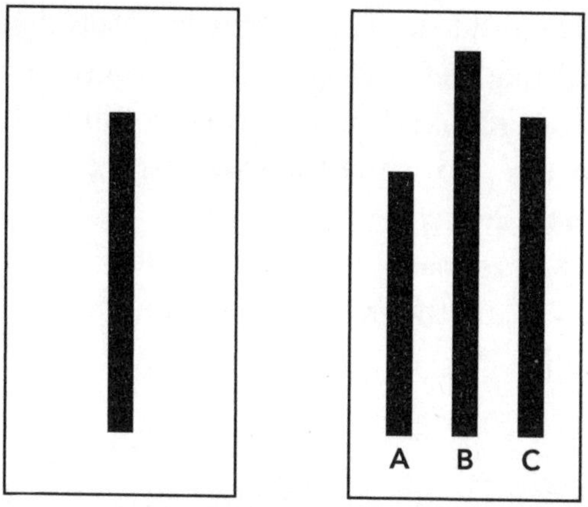

FIGURE 3.1 Cards from Asch's Experiment

real subject, the rest were collaborating with the researchers) paused nervously and then slowly stuttered out that he too agreed that "A" was the correct answer.

The experiment was run 123 times, with confederates purposely giving wrong answers to 12 out of 18 trials. Subjects gave incorrect answers 36.8 percent of the time compared to only 1 percent of the time under ordinary circumstances.[10] The experiment was replicated many times by Asch as well as others, and while the precise conditions and results would change slightly, the conclusion was always the same—we have a natural tendency to conform to a local majority.

In a sense, this shouldn't be surprising. The idea that people have a tendency toward conformity is nothing new. But that people would give obviously wrong answers to simple and unambiguous questions was indeed shocking.

Asch's experiment should give us some pause in how we think about influence. While much discussion has focused on influential individuals, groups exert considerable sway that should not be ignored. In fact, in their study of opinion leaders, Katz and Lazarsfeld found a large degree of "political homogeneity" among groups of family and friends, but attributed it to an individual's influence rather than a group dynamic. They also reported that many people who changed their opinions during the research were actually just coming back into line with their peers.[11] So while the studies gave rise to the concept of "opinion leaders" and, indirectly, to Gladwell's Law of the Few, it appears that a group dynamic would fit the data at least as well. While the evidence was sound, the conclusions were not.

THE THRESHOLD MODEL OF COLLECTIVE BEHAVIOR

One important aspect of Asch's conformity studies was that the results were far from uniform. A quarter of the subjects never conformed, some always did, and others were somewhere in the middle. We all have different thresholds for conformity based on our own personal characteristics, confidence in our knowledge of the subject at hand, our opinions about other people in the group, and so on.

We are always influenced by people around us, but not in a uniform manner. It varies. Maybe we are slaves to fashion in the clothes we wear, but more independent in the books we choose to read. If everyone we know reads a certain novel, we might succumb, but it would have to be an overwhelming majority. Most of the time, we are keeping an eye on both our inner compass and our peer group, considering both our own preferences and those around us.

Mark Granovetter, whom we met in the last chapter in connection with his theory of "the strength of weak ties," proposed a model for understanding group dynamics as a series of thresholds of resistance. As a thought experiment, he asks us to imagine a diverse group of people milling around in a square. Some are natural deviants, always ready to start trouble, most are susceptible to provocation in varying degrees, and the remainder is made up of unusually solid citizens, almost never engaging in antisocial behavior.[12]

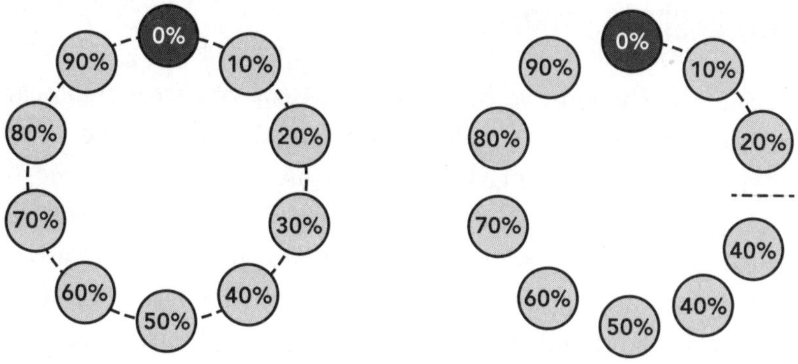

FIGURE 3.2 Two Possibilities of Granovetter's Threshold Model

A graphic representation of two possibilities of Granovetter's scheme can be found in Figure 3.2. In the example on the left, a troublemaker with a zero threshold decides he wants to throw a rock and break a window. His friend with a slightly higher threshold sees him, and that's enough for him to throw a rock too. As more and more people join in, the threshold of others in the group is met, and before you know it, everybody is engaging in a full-scale riot.

The example on the right is slightly different. After the first two troublemakers start, there is no one around with a low enough threshold to join in. Rather than the contagion spreading, it fizzles out, the three miscreants are isolated, and little note is made about the incident. In the first case, news reports the next day would be likely to attribute the full-scale riot to a sociological phenomenon, such as race, class, political discord, or some other external factor. However, the real cause had more to do with a slight difference in the distribution of resistance thresholds.

Granovetter pointed out that the model can be generalized to a variety of social situations, such as whether to adopt a new technology, leave a party, go to college, join a strike, and so on. We naturally take social cues from those around us, whether they have "rare qualities" or not. Majorities don't just rule, *they also influence.*

HOW CASCADES FORM

In the last chapter, we discussed the issue of cascades. Local problems tend not to stay local, but spread through a network of connections and interdependences. Just as it would be nonsensical to describe the first power line that failed in the 1996 blackout as having "rare qualities," it is unreasonable to attribute informational cascades, such as business fads, financial contagions, and political ideas, solely to individuals. The structure of the connections within the network matters—a lot.

We can, in fact, take Granovetter's threshold model further by combining it with his principle of the "strength of weak ties" to understand how the threshold model can lead to viral cascades. Take a look at Figure 3.3 on the next page. Now, instead of one group of people, we have three. The one at the top, marked "A," is identical to the group in the previous diagram that resulted in a riot. Now, however, we add two new groups, "B" and "C," that are weakly connected to the first group. As the contagion infects the entire first group, it quickly spreads to highly susceptible members of the other two groups, and before you know it, a large cascade ensues. Physicists have a name for this type of phenomenon—*percolation*—and a configuration like the one in Figure 3.3 is called a *percolating cluster.*

Notice that no individual in this model has any more influence than anybody else. Small groups, loosely connected, but united by a common purpose give rise to a cascade regardless of the personal qualities of the individuals involved. Once again, it is not the nodes, but the network that drives transformational change. That may not be as simple and intuitively pleasing as Gladwell's "Law of the Few," but it is the explanation that empirical research supports.[13]

The threshold model of cascades also provides a helpful explanation of the events I witnessed during the Orange Revolution. The tent city phenomenon got started at one university in the form of student meetings, soon spread to others in Kyiv, and eventually spread across the country through participants'

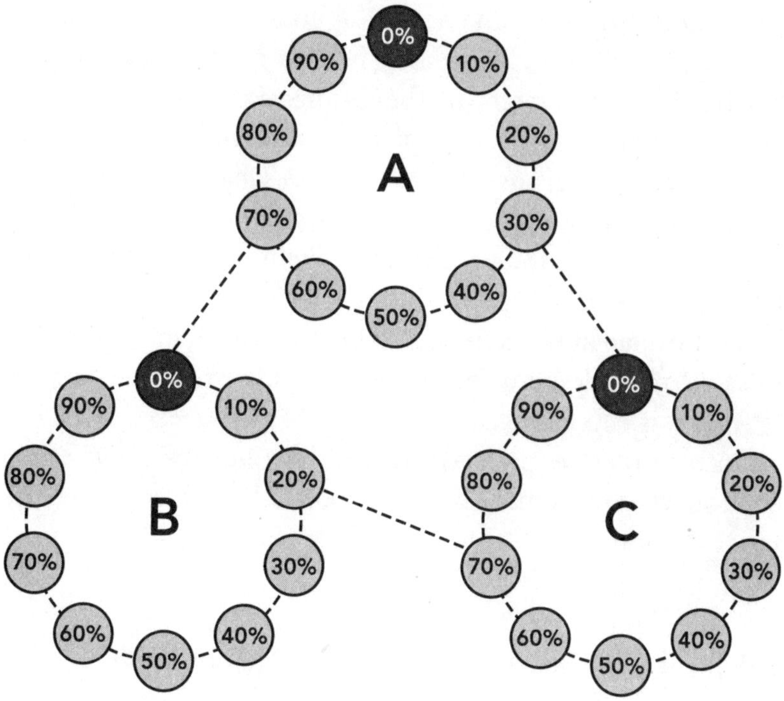

FIGURE 3.3 A Percolation Model with Weak Ties

personal connections such as their parents, aunts, uncles, and neighbors. As the idea spread, others with higher thresholds—like my fiancée, our friends, and me—began to join in. We weren't convinced to act by people with special qualities, but by those close to us. They were friends, coworkers, neighbors, and family members. In Otpor's Serbian revolution, a crucial component of the movement was the mothers who saw their children arrested for taking part in peaceful protest. Again, it is not special qualities of individuals that spread an idea, but vulnerable clusters influencing other (often slightly less) vulnerable clusters that drives a cascade.

Another interesting aspect of the threshold model of cascades is that there is no reason that thresholds need to be static, intrinsic qualities of individuals. Instead, thresholds can change over time and according to environmental factors as well as to differences in how the idea is presented.[14] In the heightened environment of the Orange Revolution, the lowering of thresholds became palpable and contributed to the abundance of viral memes discussed in Chapter 1—the horn protest outside of the Central Election Commission, the no-drinking rule, and the *Razom Nas Bahato* chant being three of the most salient examples. With revolution in the air and millions of people in the streets, it didn't take much for something to catch on. Everybody felt connected and wanted to be a part of what was happening.

So now that we understand in theory how cascades effect change, let's take a more practical look at how they play out in the real world.

THE DIFFUSION OF INNOVATIONS: A NETWORK VIEW

Let's put ourselves in John Antioco's place in 2000. He had been a phenomenally successful retail executive, pulling off turnarounds of major brands like Circle K and Taco Bell, and he had thrived in his role of CEO at Blockbuster, leading it to market dominance and serious profitability. When the Netflix team flew to Dallas to propose a partnership to his team, their company was little more than a start-up renting movies through the mail. The deal that Netflix offered, to basically license Blockbuster's brand name for the web, was not attractive. In fact, when Toys "R" Us entered a similar deal with Amazon, it proved to be a disastrous mistake. At the time, Netflix had little to offer him and his company.

Seemingly more questionable was his dismissal of Netflix as a niche product. After all, every product begins with a small following—the question is whether it has the potential to grow beyond that. Yet if Antioco had reacted to every potential disruption, he would have had to consider not only Netflix, but every niche competitor, as a serious threat. That too would have been problematic. After all, if Antioco rang alarm bells every time anybody came up with a new way to rent videos, he wouldn't have been able to run his company in the orderly, disciplined way that had made him successful in the first place.

Clearly, what Antioco and Blockbuster needed was a basis for evaluating niche competitors that would allow them to assess and respond to disruptive threats without overreacting and changing strategy every time a marginal competitor appeared. Ironically, the solution to this problem can be found in a very unlikely place: Iowa seed corn.

Hybrid corn in the middle of the twentieth century had some important similarities to Netflix's business model in 2000. Like Netflix's no-late-fee policy, there were obvious benefits to hybrid corn seed, namely 20 percent higher crop yields and resistance to drought. In both cases, there were also some important obstacles to adoption. In Netflix's case, there was the inconvenience involved in ordering videos through the mail versus the ease of just popping by a nearby Blockbuster location after work. In the case of hybrid corn, the higher up-front cost was more immediately apparent than the benefits at harvest time.[15]

In 1962, a young sociologist named Everett Rogers combined studies of innovations like hybrid corn in a book called *The Diffusion of Innovations*, which has been the model for thinking about how ideas spread ever since.[16] In each case he studied he found the same pattern. It looked like Figure 3.4.

What Rogers found was that an innovation is first adopted by a small core group of innovators and then spreads slowly to a slightly larger market of early adopters before it hits the majority of people in the middle and begins a period of explosive growth. When the Blockbuster executives met with Hastings, Netflix was most probably still in the "Innovators" or "Early Adopters" stage and therefore easy to dismiss as "niche."

Rogers was aware of, and greatly influenced by, Katz and Lazarsfeld's research on opinion leaders. So, not surprisingly, he attributed special qualities to the innovators and early adopters.

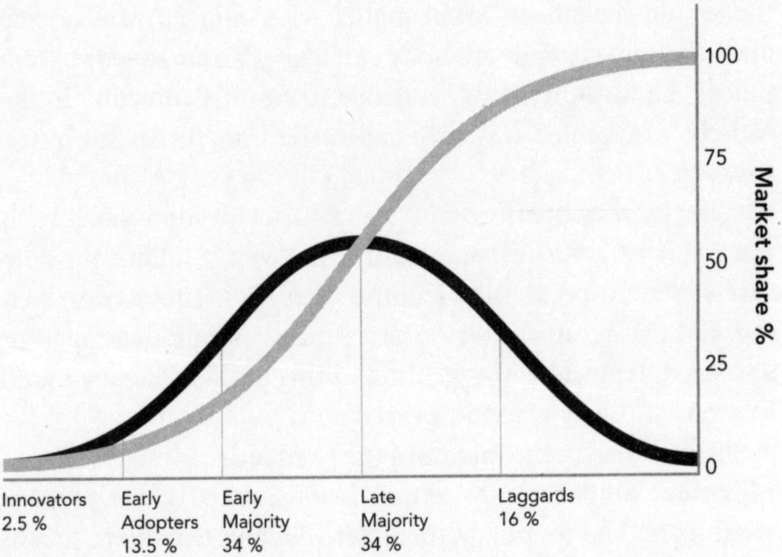

FIGURE 3.4 The Diffusion of Innovations

However, it should be clear by now that's not necessarily true. Rogers himself noted that his father "loved electro-mechanical farm innovations; but was resistant to biological-chemical innovations such as the new hybrid corn."[17] In much the same way, I might jump on the chance to try a cheesesteak place in my hometown of Philadelphia, but have kept the same hairstyle for 30 years. Our resistance thresholds to new ideas are highly situational. Early adoptership is a matter of context, not destiny. Once again, it is the connections between vulnerable clusters that drive a cascade, much as we saw in the example of transmission lines failing in the last chapter.

In his highly influential book *Crossing the Chasm*, Geoffrey Moore notes that most innovations never make the jump from early adopter to early majority and end up fizzling out.[18] However, the threshold model of cascades gives us some clues that can help predict which ideas have the potential to cross the chasm and which do not: how the early adopters and early majority are connected.

If Antioco had analyzed Netflix in 2000, he would have most likely seen that the niche it occupied had specific characteristics, most probably film enthusiasts in California, where Netflix was located. These people were happy to trade the convenience of a nearby Blockbuster location for the greater selection and economic benefits of Netflix's mail order model. The logical question would then be, where is it spreading? If new Netflix customers looked much like the old ones, then it probably wasn't much to worry about. However, once an idea starts infecting new groups with higher thresholds of resistance, it's begun to cross over from early adopters to early majority consumers and a change is brewing.

In fact, it appears that is essentially what Antioco and his team did, which is why he was able to recognize the potential of the online video rental business and develop and implement a viable strategy. Remember, it was internal networks that led to Blockbuster's demise. First shareholders, skeptical about the digital strategy and the unrest it caused with the franchisees, diminished the stock price. The undervalued stock, in turn, attracted corporate raider Carl Icahn to take a major position and take control of the company. That, in turn, led to the compensation dispute, Antioco's departure, the reinstatement of late fees, and the retrenchment into retail stores. If Antioco had shown the same acumen in aligning internal stakeholders as he did in marketing to customers, it is likely that Blockbuster would still be thriving today.

The same principles applied in the Orange Revolution, which started out in low threshold areas like universities but gained steam when the movement spread to higher threshold groups such as young professionals (like my fiancée). By the time the election was falsified, even high threshold groups, such as the babushkas who brought food to the tent city and helped enforce the no-drinking rule, were out in great numbers as well. As we will see later on in this book, changemakers of all stripes, whether they are corporate executives, entrepreneurs, public servants, or community activists, succeed when they actively court those who have not yet joined their movement and fail when they insist on strict obedience to a rigid ideology.

As Duncan Watts noted in a scientific paper on the dynamics of cascades, "The success or failure of an innovation may depend less on the number and characteristics of the innovators themselves than on the structure of the community of early adopters. Clearly, the more early adopters exist in the network, the more likely it is that an innovation will spread. But, the extent of its growth, and hence the susceptibility of the network as a whole, depends not only on the number of early adopters, but on how connected they are to one another and to the much larger community consisting of the early and late majority, who do not tend to respond to the innovators directly, but who can be influenced directly if exposed to multiple early adopters."[19]

I would also add that these connections do not form automatically. You have to be proactive about building them. You can't seek to overpower by ranting and raving. You have to work to attract others to your cause, particularly those with higher thresholds of resistance.

The threshold model offers a possible explanation for why Occupy failed. While it did indeed spark a cascade, it didn't "cross the chasm" and never spread beyond early adopters. In fact, many in the mainstream, even those who were concerned about income inequality and sympathized with the activists' "We are the 99%" slogan, were appalled by the unkempt, often vulgar protestors. So it's not surprising that they failed to connect with higher threshold groups. In Ukraine, the Maidan was a place where people wanted to be. Families would take their kids to see how change was finally coming to their nation. Nobody was going on family outings to Zuccotti Park.

In fact, at times, the Occupy protestors seemed to actively spurn the notion of reaching outside their milieu. When Congressman John Lewis, a hero of the civil rights movement, asked to speak at a rally in Atlanta, he was rebuffed.[20] Many attributed the snub to racism among the privileged white protestors. The activist who led the charge to block him from speaking would later explain in an interview that his objection was not so much against the Congressman himself, but against any "member of the two-party system."[21] A post on the liberal site Daily Kos explained that the problem was that John Lewis simply didn't understand the complex rules of an Occupy event.[22] Whatever explanation you want to accept, the result was that an opportunity to build a connection and spread the movement was lost.

Make no mistake. You create change by bringing people in, not pushing them away. You don't get points for purity or rigid adherence. To spread an idea, you have to connect. Unlike the Occupy protestors, the Otpor activists didn't seem to be angry. Instead they strived to be *funny*, because humor was inviting. In Iraq, General McChrystal was willing to sacrifice some of the efficiency of his commando teams in order to invite greater collaboration among key stakeholders. When employees left tech firms in Silicon Valley, they weren't considered to be pariahs like they would be in Boston, but allies and assets, and they were encouraged to stay connected. Wherever you see a change effort succeed, you'll find connection at its core.

Yet it is not connection alone that creates a cascade, it is connection to *higher threshold groups*. That's a challenge, because it means that you cannot only seek out the like-minded, you must also bring in the unconvinced, the skeptical, and the oblivious. If the desire for change remains with the zealots, it won't go anywhere. It's only when everybody else joins in that a transformational change can take place, whether that change is in a community, an organization, an industry, or throughout society as a whole.

THE EVOLVING ROLE OF LEADERS

As I noted in the Introduction, the world used to be ruled by institutions that were set up as hierarchies. Those at the top planned and directed action, which was carried out according to formal lines of authority that ran vertically through an organization. Today, however, the world is increasingly organized into networks, which are informal lines that often run horizontally, and, as we will see in greater depth in Chapter 6, it is a leader's job to shape them.

It is along these horizontal lines that cascades often take place, so it shouldn't be surprising that hierarchically oriented leaders often miss them. John Antioco at Blockbuster saw the threat that Netflix posed as merely one of a competing business model. It's not that he didn't recognize the importance of the concerns of investors and franchisees; he did and made efforts to quell these concerns. Still, these were secondary to the execution of his strategy through vertical lines. Contrast that with General McChrystal, whose primary focus was to transform his organization into "a network that could defeat a network."

In much the same way, the Route 128 firms saw the marketplace as a quest for dominance among competing firms. That's why they strongly discouraged employees jumping from company to company or mixing socially with colleagues from other companies. It's also why they pushed local governments for tax cuts and other giveaways, because in a stable marketplace, a low cost structure can be a considerable competitive advantage. The Silicon Valley entrepreneurs, on the other hand, recognized that technology was cascading rapidly, and they focused on building an ecosystem that would adapt to changes that hierarchies usually miss until it's too late.

Even Occupy, in its own way, saw things in terms of hierarchies and missed the value of cascades. In effect, they considered the challenge to be a battle between themselves on one side and the banks and politicians on the other. What they failed to recognize was the importance of everybody else, so they turned away many potential supporters. Otpor, on the other hand, saw the struggle ahead as one of mobilizing their fellow citizens. They sought, through humor, pranks, and meticulous planning, to crash through thresholds of resistance and bring everyone else in. Everything—even arrests—was an opportunity to recruit or, at the very least, to soften objection.

Make no mistake. Cascades are forces of nature. Small groups, loosely connected, but united by a common purpose is a valid principle whether the network is citizens in a revolution, employees in an organization, consumers in a marketplace, or snowy tree crickets in a forest. We cannot control cascades or conjure them into existence through sheer force of will. They happen either when new connections form that we are scarcely aware of or some external event that is outside of our control lowers thresholds and makes the system more susceptible to a trigger.

That's why cascades, as important as they are, are only the first aspect of transformational change. As we have seen, cascades can be immensely powerful, but once they manifest themselves into concrete action, they can also inspire opposition. As Moisés Naím has put it, "power is now easier to get and harder to use or keep." Every revolution has the potential to inspire a counterrevolution.

That's why, as crucial as it is to understand how cascades function, the second aspect of transformational change—organization, planning, and discipline—is just as important, because it's what allows us to put cascades to productive use. We now turn to that very subject in Part Two of this book: how you organize for action, because it is only through action that we can effect real change.

PART TWO

HOW CHANGE MOVEMENTS SUCCEED—AND FAIL

CHAPTER 4

Identifying a Keystone Change

You must be the change you wish to see in the world.

—MAHATMA GANDHI

At midnight on December 31, 1929, the Indian National Congress adopted a resolution for *Purna Swaraj*, full independence from Great Britain and the intention of self-rule. A few weeks later, the body issued a formal declaration to that effect.[1] Reminiscent of the American Declaration of Independence, it spoke of "the inalienable right of the Indian people, as of any other people, to have freedom and to enjoy the fruits of their toil and have the necessities of life." Yet unlike the American version, it pledged a commitment to nonviolence, even under provocation. The declaration also promised a massive campaign of civil disobedience to come. The task of organizing this effort fell to Mohandas Gandhi, already renowned as both a political and a spiritual leader.

Gandhi withdrew to his ashram to contemplate the task ahead. It was an enormous responsibility as well as a task full of complexity and nuance. The campaign would have to unite a diverse population of Hindu, Muslim, Sikh, and outcaste Indians, who were often at odds with each other, into a single national effort. At the same time, it would have to somehow avoid getting people so riled that it would devolve into violent outbursts, violate Gandhi's cherished principles, and cede the moral ground. When his friend, the internationally famous poet Rabindranath Tagore, visited him in January, Gandhi told him, "I am furiously thinking day and night and I do not see any light coming out of the surrounding darkness."[2]

This is not uncommon for transformational change efforts. Every movement starts with a sense of grievance. Yet to succeed, you must go beyond grievance to identify an affirmative vision for what you would like to be different and then identify a single, fundamental change that will bring that vision about. That's no small task. The women's movement in the nineteenth century, to take just one example, struggled for decades to identify a single, fundamental change that would uplift women everywhere. At the time, women were treated almost like property—they couldn't own land, get a substantial education, or seek legal protection from an abusive husband. So it wasn't at all obvious that voting rights would become the focus of the movement. Yet that's what led to greater equality.

Talia Milgrom-Elcott, who leads 100Kin10, a movement to train 100,000 STEM teachers in 10 years, calls this a "keystone change," based on the ecological concept that an entire ecosystem is highly dependent on the existence of one or two species. Identifying that keystone change is the first major challenge of any change movement, and until you meet that challenge, your efforts will likely be in vain.

So Gandhi continued to meditate on the problem. January turned into February. February turned into March. And still nothing. Finally, he emerged from his ashram. Then, in a letter to the British Viceroy offering one last invitation to negotiate before the campaign began, Gandhi announced his plan:

He would march for salt.

It seemed like some sort of joke. *The Statesman*, a prominent English language newspaper, noted at the time, "It is difficult not to laugh, and we imagine that will be the mood of most thinking Indians."[3] The British Viceroy, for his part, wrote, "At present the prospect of a salt campaign does not keep me awake at night."[4] Nobody seemed to take Gandhi's plan seriously.

But it was no joke. In fact, identifying salt as a keystone change was to be remembered as Gandhi's greatest stroke of genius and the culmination of two decades of seeking to bring truth to power.

Mohandas Gandhi was born to a middle-class family in Gujarat, on the coast of India, about halfway between Mumbai and Karachi. His father, prime minister to a local autocrat, died when he was 16, putting pressure on the family finances. Still, a family friend suggested that he go to England to get a law degree and assume his father's former stature. While there was significant resistance in the family to his going abroad, Gandhi refused to be dissuaded.[5] Gathering money from relatives, he traveled to London to study and, a few years later, won admittance to the bar.

When he returned to India, however, he proved to be poorly suited to the legal profession. Due to his inherently shy nature, he had trouble speaking in public and was unable to cross-examine witnesses. He soon found himself reduced to filling out petitions to the court. It was hardly the makings of a fruitful practice. So when he was offered the opportunity to work on a case in South Africa for a prosperous Indian merchant, Gandhi took it eagerly.[6]

It was in South Africa that the young Gandhi had his first experience with true color prejudice. Having paid for a first-class train ticket, he was asked to move to a third-class compartment. When he refused, he was kicked off the train. On a later train during the same trip, he was forced to ride outside the compartment in the cold. Although a well-educated lawyer, he was nonetheless considered a "coolie," who was unfit to reside with Europeans or even to share a footpath with them.[7] "I saw that South Africa was no country for a self-respecting Indian," he would later write, "and my mind became more and more occupied with the question of how this state of things might be improved."[8]

After his case was finished, Gandhi chose to stay and help with the struggle to gain rights for Indians in South Africa. With newfound confidence, he became more assertive, built a prosperous law practice, and eventually brought his wife and young child to join him. He would spend 21 years in South Africa, fighting for the rights of his fellow Indians.

It was there he would develop his own brand of civil disobedience, which he called *Satyagraha* or "truth force." The aim, as he put it, was "the vindication of truth not by affliction of suffering on the opponent, but on one's self." In his view, the opponent must be "weaned from error by patience and sympathy."[9] He took pains to distinguish it from passive resistance, which he felt was a "weapon of the weak." His vision was something more forceful, to expose the faults of a repressive regime.

One of the first principles of Satyagraha was *ahimsa*, or nonviolence, which was rooted in the quest for truth. If no one could claim to have absolute knowledge of the truth, then it followed that using violence (or any other means of coercion for that matter) to compel people to accede to one's will would be to undermine, rather than support, truth. For much the same reason, means were given equal significance as ends, because any victory brought about by unjust means would be a pyrrhic one. After all, how could you build a just society on an unjust foundation? And if a just society wasn't the objective, then what was the point?[10] "But all my life through," Gandhi would write in his autobiography, "the very insistence on truth has taught me the beauty of compromise."[11]

To the modern ear, Gandhi's views seem idealistic at best, if not completely naive, yet there was much more to his philosophy than met the eye. In fact, he thought about things in very strategic terms. His aim was to undermine his opponents' legitimacy, and in doing so, their freedom of action. He sought to back them into a corner in which both action and inaction would yield essentially the same result—an upending of the existing order. As Gandhi himself put it, "Men say that I am a saint losing myself in politics. The fact is I am a politician trying my hardest to be a saint."[12]

It was during his South African years that Gandhi ceased to be an ambitious young lawyer and took on the legendary persona we know today. He eschewed Western dress, memorized the *Bhagavad Gita*, took a vow of celibacy, and began fasting and living a life of austerity. He also worked to control his violent temper. In sum, he sought to sublimate his ego to his cause, so that he could uplift his fellow Indians in South Africa.[13]

The plight of Indians in South Africa was profoundly unjust. They were originally brought to the country to work on British plantations, as indentured laborers, for a term of five years. Many, finding conditions somewhat better than they had in India, stayed on as free men. Some of these prospered as merchants who brought other Indians to work as tradesmen and professionals, much as Gandhi himself had. By the end of the nineteenth century, they greatly outnumbered Europeans.[14]

In order for the Europeans to maintain control, a series of increasingly repressive laws were adopted that were designed to make life unbearable for Indians. In addition to the restrictions on what train car they could ride in and where they could walk, a number of bills were passed to restrict immigration and require them to carry registration cards. A three-pound tax (a prohibitive sum) was levied on all previously indentured servants who remained in the country, and travel restrictions were put in place that greatly hampered the ability of Indians to earn a living. To add insult to injury, a court ruling decreed that only Christian marriages would be considered legitimate.

Gandhi led a series of Satyagraha campaigns that defied these laws, including mass border crossings, strikes, and burning of registration cards. The struggle went on for years, and thousands went to jail. Gandhi himself was imprisoned three separate times. Yet the position of the South African government became increasingly untenable and, in 1914, Gandhi signed an agreement with the Boer General Jan Christiaan Smuts to retract the repressive tax along with many of the discriminatory regulations. Satyagraha had its first major victory.[15]

When Gandhi returned to India in 1915, he was already a confirmed nationalist. His book, *Hind Swaraj* or "*Indian Home Rule*," published in 1909, laid out his principles. First, he advocated for Satyagraha while condemning terror as an illegitimate, and ultimately ineffective, tactic. Second, he stressed the need for self-reliance. It was, in his view, the mutual reliance with the British that kept Indians enslaved. Third, he insisted that the goal was not mere independence, but to return to a more authentically Indian existence. If they replaced British rulers with Indians who would rule the same way, then what was the point of the struggle?[16]

The India that Gandhi found upon his return was far removed from his ideal. The most significant nationalist institution was the Indian National Congress. Established in 1885, it was, for the most part, a talking shop, which gathered delegates from all over the country every December to make speeches and pass resolutions. These would then be sent on to the British overlords to be considered.

On the other end of the spectrum, there were splintered terrorist groups who thought they could get the Raj to leave by force. In between were the majority of the Indian population, mostly poor peasants and "untouchables." They didn't really care if they were ruled by British elites or Indian elites. Either way, their lives would be filled with poverty, privation, and struggle. To make matters more complex, there were significant tensions between Hindus and Muslims, caste Hindus and untouchables, and regional rivalries as well as concerns among minority Sikh and Christian populations.

It should be noted that this is not at all an uncommon situation. Most change movements start out in a small, distinct group that has little in common with many potential constituents and supporters. To take just one example, the Occupy movement was largely made up of college-educated elites rather than the disaffected working class most impacted by the financial crisis.[17] That's why it's so important to reach out and build links to weave a network.

Gandhi, however, was determined to internalize the struggles of those he wished to liberate. For a year after his return, he traveled around the country. Unlike his earlier insistence on first-class train compartments in South Africa that led to his initial activism, he now gladly traveled third class. As had become his custom, he wore little more than a loincloth made out of fabric he spun himself. Already renowned as a "Mahatma" or "saintly man" after his exploits in South Africa, he agitated for women's rights, acceptance of "untouchable" outcastes, and for "khadi," the home spinning of cloth that would reduce reliance on foreign imports. "We may petition the Government, we may agitate . . . for our rights, but for a real awakening of the people, the more important thing is activities directed inwards," he wrote.[18]

His actions were, in no small measure, a challenge to the elite nationalist movement. "How could leaders in Bond Street suits or Bombay coats and trousers reach the peasants' hearts: how could English-speaking orators touch their minds?" he asked in a speech surrounded by Indian politicians in European dress.[19]

He also put Satyagraha to work in the struggle for peasants' rights. The first notable example was in the Champaran district in the region of Bihar, which lay in the foothills of the Himalayas, on the other side of the subcontinent from Gandhi's native Gujarat. He was implored to go to the region by a farmer named Raj Kumar Shukla, who approached the Mahatma at the 1916 Indian National Congress and then followed him to his ashram. Impressed by Shukla's tenacity, Gandhi agreed to go to Champaran and see what was going on for himself. He had planned to visit for a few days, but ended up spending almost a year.[20]

The situation in Champaran was indeed troubling. The landlords had required the peasants to use 15 percent of their land for the cultivation of indigo, which was then sold on the global market, as rent. Yet industrialists in Germany had developed a process for producing synthetic indigo, causing prices to collapse. So instead of allowing rent to be paid in indigo, the landlords now required cash. They also took advantage of an old agreement that stipulated that rents could be raised if indigo was not grown. So the peasants, already impoverished, were getting squeezed twice over.

The first thing that Gandhi did upon his arrival was to make appointments to see the secretary of the Planters Association and the commissioner of the Divisional Government. The secretary told him that he was an outsider—the designation of "outside agitator" has long been a common refrain of those who seek to resist change—and had no business meddling in the affairs of the landlords and their tenants. Gandhi told him that he did not consider himself an outsider and that he had every right to advocate for the peasants if they asked him to. The commissioner tried to bully him and advised him to leave the region.[21]

Soon after, as Gandhi proceeded with his investigations, he was overtaken by a messenger from the local police superintendent who asked him to return to town. When he arrived, he was given an official notice to leave the district. He signed the order to confirm he had received it, but also announced his intention to disobey. Upon doing so, he was given a summons to appear in court the next day.

When the Mahatma arrived at the courthouse, enormous crowds had gathered to support him. The officials asked him to help pacify the crowds to prevent a riot, which he did willingly. Inside the court, Gandhi explained that he understood the order, but could not obey it because he felt it violated his conscience. Unsure of what to do, the magistrate ordered a two-hour recess and announced that Gandhi would be released on bail. He refused to pay it and was released anyway.

When the court reconvened, the magistrate announced that he would wait for orders from his superiors. The Bihar government, aware of Gandhi's exploits in South Africa and how the Afrikaners' rough treatment of him only increased his power, was cautious about making the same mistake. It ordered him to be released and for local officials to cooperate with his investigation. "According to law," Gandhi would later write, "I was to be on trial, but truly speaking Government was to be on trial. The Commissioner only succeeded in trapping Government in the net which he had spread for me."[22]

So Gandhi continued to investigate, working with local lawyers and businessmen to take the statements of the peasants (a practice similar to that employed by Thurgood Marshall decades later in the struggle for civil rights in America).[23] He also worked to improve the lives of the peasants by setting up schools, improving sanitary conditions, and bringing in medical care. Eventually, a committee to arbitrate the dispute was convened and Gandhi was invited to sit on it. The landlords agreed to rescind the rent increases and refund 25 percent of the increases already collected.[24]

Satyagraha had triumphed, but Gandhi had achieved even more than that. He had shown himself to be a very different kind of nationalist. Unlike the urbane Congress delegates, who were often blinded by high-minded rhetoric, he proved to be a true and effective advocate of the Indian people. It would serve him well in the years to come, but as he would soon learn, there were unforeseen challenges ahead that had less to do with the British and more to do with the movement Gandhi was building itself.

The next phase in Gandhi's journey came in 1919, with the institution of the Rowlatt Acts. During World War I, the Defense of India Act was passed in order to control terrorism. Now, these new laws, including administrative detentions and trials by judges instead of juries for acts determined to be seditious, were to be extended. Gandhi, as well as many other Indians, was appalled. He set up a new organization, called Satyagraha Sabha, to resist them.

His plan began with two major actions. The first was the sale of banned literature. The second, which came to him as an inspiration in the early hours of the morning, was a nationwide *hartal*—a day of fasting and prayer in which Indians would stop work and cease to do business. It was an enormous success. In Bombay, 80 percent of shops were closed.[25] Once again, Gandhi had proven himself to be not only a spiritual leader, but a master strategist.

Yet after that, things spun out of control. The hartal, while successful, sparked further protests, many of which turned violent. Riots broke out, buildings were burned, and there were a number of violent confrontations with police. In the Punjab city of Amritsar, General Reginald Dyer banned all public gatherings. When his order was ignored, he allowed the protestors to assemble in a large square with just a few exits and then drove up with his men in two armored cars. Without warning, he gave the order to fire, killing hundreds and severely injuring even more.[26] As Dyer himself would say in the inquiry that followed, "It was no longer a question of merely dispersing the crowd, but one of producing sufficient moral effect not only on those who were present, but more especially throughout the Punjab. There could be no question of undue severity."[27]

Afterward, India plunged further into violence, and Gandhi would fast for three days in penitence. It was, as he would later call it, a "Himalayan miscalculation." "I had called on the people to launch upon civil disobedience before they had thus qualified themselves for it, and this mistake seemed to me of Himalayan magnitude," he wrote in his autobiography. "I realized that before a people could be fit for offering civil disobedience, they should thoroughly understand its deeper implications. That being so, before restarting civil disobedience on a mass scale, it would be necessary to create a band of well-tried, pure-hearted volunteers who thoroughly understood the strict conditions of Satyagraha."[28]

These early disappointments were surely on the Mahatma's mind when he retreated to his ashram a decade later to contemplate a new campaign of civil disobedience in support of *Purna Swaraj*. He spent most of the previous 10 years preparing the Indian people for the rigors of Satyagraha. He promoted the spinning of cloth and the reduction of reliance on foreign goods, worked to bridge the divides between Hindus and Muslims, and campaigned against the discrimination of the untouchable outcastes. Yet still, he saw that there was great potential for violence in any political action, and that's what he meant when he told his friend that he was struggling to see "any light coming out of the surrounding darkness."

The precipitating event was the Simon Commission, which was convened in November 1927. Ostensibly, its purpose was to propose further reforms in the governance of the Indian people. Yet the Commission did not include a single Indian among its members and was widely considered a farce. Gandhi himself called it an "organized insult to a whole people."[29]

The Indian National Congress responded in December 1928 by adopting the Nehru Report, named for Motilal Nehru, father of Jawaharlal, the future prime minister of India. The report proposed a draft constitution that would include autonomous dominion status for the country and self-government by a legislature elected by Indians. The British were given a year to consider the proposal. When the Congress met the next December there had been no progress. That's when the declaration of *Purna Swaraj*, or complete self-rule, was issued. It now fell to Gandhi to formulate the next steps.

His previous efforts at Satyagraha had proven successful in limited settings, when the Mahatma himself was there to impose some discipline and head off the potential for violence.

In the interim between the mass campaigns that ended in violence, which followed the Rowlatt Acts, and the meeting of the Simon Commission, Gandhi had done much to prepare his followers for the rigors ahead. His tireless work on behalf of India's downtrodden, his promotion of self-reliance, and his well-earned reputation for wisdom and common sense among the country's elite made him uniquely qualified to lead the campaign ahead. Still, he harbored no illusions, and his "Himalayan miscalculation" still weighed heavily on him.

Although few saw it at the time, the salt law was an inspired choice for a target. It was almost ridiculously repressive, outlawing the production of a natural resource by the people who inhabited the country. In fact, Ramsay MacDonald, a prominent British politician who would be named Prime Minister in June 1929, had himself previously denounced the salt law as unjust. It was also a grievance that everybody in the country shared, regardless of religion or caste, but particularly impacted the poor. Perhaps most importantly, participation was easily accessible to anyone. All that was needed was to take some water from the sea and boil it. Salt, in a sense, already had a connected network of grievance. This network only needed to be activated, and a cascade would ensue. At the same time, the revenue gained from the tax was not significant enough to provoke a vigorous initial response from the British Raj. As the Viceroy himself had written, it didn't seem like anything to lose sleep over.

Gandhi had found his keystone change.

He began the march from his own ashram on March 12 with a small, tight-knit group of 80 of his most disciplined and devoted followers, well versed in the principles of Satyagraha, so there would be no possibility of violent outbursts. They would march over 200 miles in 24 days to the coastal village of Dandi, where they would defy the oppressive British law by making their own salt.

The Salt March was an enormous success from the start. Gandhi and his band walked in the morning and the afternoon, avoiding the most oppressive midday heat. At each village he would speak, exhorting the people to spin their own cloth, avoid alcohol and opium, and live clean lives. Tens of thousands came out to see him. Hundreds of village officials gave up their government jobs after the Mahatma encouraged them to do so.[30] All across India, newspapers featured Gandhi and his followers on the front page, chronicling each leg of the march and his message of civil disobedience. By the end of 1930, *Time* magazine would proclaim Gandhi its "Man of the Year."

On April 5, the marchers reached Dandi and spent the night praying. The next morning, the Mahatma picked up a lump of salt from the shores of the ocean, and his followers immediately began filling pots with seawater to be boiled. It was, as Jawaharlal Nehru would write, "as though a spring had been released."[31] In a single stroke, he had not only shown defiance of British rule, but also displayed the power of civil disobedience. Within weeks a cascade ensued and people all over India were brazenly manufacturing their own salt. To create further pressure, Gandhi encouraged his fellow Indians to boycott foreign cloth and liquor. Then, on April 24, he announced that he would lead a march on the Dharasana Salt Works, raising the level of provocation even further.

The British Viceroy, for his part, was caught in a dilemma. If he allowed Gandhi to continue unhindered, he risked making British rule a farce. However, if he had Gandhi arrested, he risked fanning the flames even further. The Viceroy chose the latter, and on May 4, a month after the Mahatma reached his hand into the sea at Dandi, he was brought into custody. There was an immediate outcry, with mass demonstrations and hartals, and the cascade accelerated. Roughly half of the country's textile mills shut down. 128 villages in the Bardoli district, where Gandhi had previously led successful Satyagraha campaigns, refused to pay land taxes, and dozens of other villages followed suit. The entire country, it seemed, was in open revolt.[32]

The action at Dharasana went forward as well. Abbas Tyabji, a seventy-six-year-old retired judge, announced that he and 300 of the Mahatma's followers would continue with the march with him and Gandhi's wife at the lead. They were both arrested. Next Sarojini Naidu, an internationally known poet and former president of the Indian National Congress, stepped into the breach. She told the demonstrators, "You must not use any violence under any circumstances. You will be beaten but you must not resist: you must not even raise a hand to ward off the blows."[33]

As the marchers approached the salt works, they were ordered to stop, but refused to obey. As each column approached, they were clubbed down by police, only to be replaced by another, who were bludgeoned in a similar manner. The confrontations went on day after day, and throughout, the nonviolent discipline of the protestors held even while they were being savagely beaten. It was an appalling sight, and foreign correspondents were there to record it.[34]

Public opinion, even in Great Britain, shifted sharply against the Raj. Those charged with defending British rule in India were also demoralized. John Court Curry, a British police officer in Bombay, remarked that he disliked dispersing the nonviolent demonstrators so much that being called to duty made him physically ill.[35]

The struggle was punishing for both sides. Thousands of protestors had been imprisoned, and many had been severely beaten. For its part, the British Raj suffered a significant decline in tax revenues and increasing costs associated with enforcing the contested laws. Finally, Gandhi was released from jail and entered negotiations with the Viceroy. A settlement was made on terms generous to the British. All prisoners would be released, those who quit their government jobs would get them back, but the salt laws would stay in place, except for provisions for small-scale manufacture.[36]

Yet the terms of the agreement were never the point. Constitutional reforms were always secondary for Gandhi. His primary objective was to create a state of Satyagraha, a force for truth and dignity among his countrymen, and in that, he succeeded brilliantly. The fact that the British were forced to come to the table and negotiate with Indians as equals broke the spell of dominance. British rule had lost much of its legitimacy and therefore its power. For Indians, going to jail was no longer a cause for shame, but a badge of honor. As one of Gandhi's followers remarked, before the British sat down with Gandhi, they "were all sahibs and we were obeying. No more after that."[37]

From that point on, it was only a matter of time. Once salt had been identified as a keystone change, the movement would only gather steam in the years to come. India became an independent country in 1948.

SHARED PURPOSE AND SHARED CONSCIOUSNESS

When General Stanley McChrystal took command of the Special Forces Task Force in Iraq, he encountered a situation not very different from what Gandhi found upon his return to India. Where Gandhi found his country splintered into factions of Hindu, Muslim, Sikh, Christian, high caste, peasant, and untouchable, McChrystal's forces were split into their own tribes, which included Navy SEALs, Army Special Forces, Night Stalker helicopter pilots, and others, each with its own ethos, codes, and traditions. Additionally, there were a number of stakeholders outside his command, which included operatives within intelligence and law enforcement agencies as well as diplomatic corps stationed at embassies and other posts that were also essential to his mission.

In his book *Team of Teams*, McChrystal likened the situation to that of the famous game theory thought experiment, the Prisoner's Dilemma.[38] In the classic example, two criminals are arrested and taken to separate interrogation rooms, where each is offered the same deal. If one informs on his partner and his partner stays silent, he goes free and his partner gets a five-year sentence. If they both confess, they will each get a three-year sentence, and if neither confesses they will each serve a one-year sentence on a lesser charge. The payoff matrix looks like Figure 4.1.

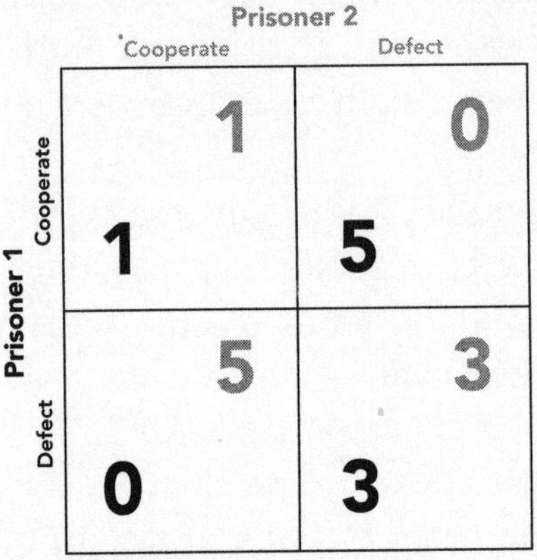

FIGURE 4.1 Prisoner Payoff Matrix

The basic gist of the game is that they are collectively better off if they cooperate with each other, but each will cut two years off his sentence individually by defecting no matter what his partner does. So if both follow the same logic, they will collectively serve a total of six years, the very worst possible outcome. What makes the Prisoner's Dilemma so devilishly hard to overcome is that the worst outcome is also the most stable, because it arises when each player acts according to his own self-interest. The only way to win is to build a bond of trust that supersedes the economics of utility. That's the function a keystone change fulfills. It brings together competing interests without inciting opposition.

Under McChrystal's command, similar forces were at play. Certain resources, such as air support and intelligence resources, were limited. Everybody knew that it was best for those assets to be deployed where they were needed most, but it was natural for each unit to want to maximize its own capability. So if, say, a team of Army Rangers had been assigned air support but found themselves encountering little resistance, they might want to hold on to it just in case, even though a Navy SEAL unit might desperately need the same resources to accomplish its mission.

The situation was even worse when it came to interagency cooperation. Commandos were responsible for killing and capturing terrorists, for which they depended on the work of intelligence analysts. The intelligence analysts, for their part, depended on the commandos capturing enemy assets. Clearly, their functions were interdependent, but their responsibilities were distinct. The Special Forces operators were responsible for killing and capturing bad guys, and the intelligence analysts were responsible for interpreting the information given to them. Each had their own specific mission, but neither was responsible for seeing the whole system.

McChrystal's key insight was that he needed to forge a sense of shared mission and shared consciousness among his troops and partner agencies, much like Gandhi created a shared mission and a shared consciousness with his targeting of the Salt Act, which united the elite nationalists, the downtrodden peasants, and also Muslims, Sikhs, and others. And, much like Gandhi, McChrystal framed the challenge not as a simple matter of defeating an enemy, but as an internal struggle to change the military culture. Rather than task his forces with killing more terrorists or taking more ground, he called upon them to embrace a simple equation:

Credibility = Proven Competence + Integrity + Relationships[39]

Competence and integrity were nothing new among the troops under McChrystal's command, but relationships added a dimension. It put the objectives of other teams on par with one's own. A commando team's responsibilities no longer ended with capturing intelligence assets, but also building relationships with the teams those assets would go to. He also, as we will see in Chapter 6, put specific procedures in place to foster networks that would help reinforce this directive.

For McChrystal, building key linkages between diverse and disparate units both under and outside his command was the keystone change.

USING A KEYSTONE CHANGE TO DRIVE TRANSFORMATION FORWARD

When Lou Gerstner was chosen to lead IBM in 1993, what most people saw was an old dinosaur that had lost its way. Overtaken by nimbler upstarts like Microsoft in software, Compaq in hardware, and Intel in microprocessors, many observers believed that IBM needed to be broken up into smaller, more focused units to compete on a more even playing field in the new economy. A huge, sprawling enterprise like IBM, competing in so many technologies at the same time, seemed like it was from another time, and like the dinosaurs, it was dying.

Gerstner saw the situation differently. As a longtime IBM customer, he saw the value of what IBM could potentially deliver: integrated solutions. From his point of view, enterprise customers were struggling to adapt to new technologies and needed a partner that had the breadth of expertise to solve their problems. IBM was uniquely qualified to play that role, but was failing to capitalize on the opportunity because it lacked shared purpose and shared consciousness.

"Units competed with each other, hid things from each other, and wanted to control access to their territory from other IBMers. . . . Instead of facilitating coordination, they manned the barricades and protected the borders." Gerstner would later write in his memoir, *Who Says Elephants Can't Dance*. "Huge staffs spent countless hours debating and managing transfer pricing terms between IBM units instead of facilitating a seamless transfer of products to customers. Staff units were duplicated at every level of the organization, because no managers trusted cross-unit colleagues to carry out the work. Meetings to decide issues that cut across units were attended by throngs of people because everyone needed to be present to protect his or her turf."[40]

"A lot of people thought IBM should be broken up," Irving Wladawsky-Berger, one of Gerstner's key lieutenants during that time, told me. "Others thought we should embrace new computing architectures for mainframes. Still others thought that the new operating system we were developing, OS/2, could return IBM to its former glory days. There were many people with different ideas, but no consensus of how to move forward."

"Lou refocused us all on customers and listening to what they wanted, and he did it by example," he continued. "We started listening to customers more because he listened to customers. Once we did that, we realized that customers didn't want IBM to fail or to be broken up. They needed our mainframes, software, and services to run their mission critical business processes, as well as to help manage their growing IT infrastructures, so the prospect of losing IBM as a supplier terrified them. Once we understood that, it led us to design our mainframes to be more competitively priced, to build a services business, and to embrace the Internet, all the things that led us to be in greater harmony with the market and brought about our rebirth."[41]

What Gerstner understood was that what IBM needed wasn't a strategy. In fact, at his very first press conference, he said, "The last thing IBM needs right now is a vision,"[42] which immediately became one of the most quotable statements in American corporate history. What IBM needed was alignment behind a strategy. So Gerstner set out to create a movement within his own organization. He changed the focus from forcing IBM's proprietary stack of technologies down customers' throats to a new model aimed at helping customers with their "stack of business processes."[43] In doing so, he led one of the most dramatic turnarounds in corporate history.

For Lou Gerstner and IBM, switching the company's focus from its own proprietary stack of technology products to its customers' "stack of business processes" was the keystone change.

In a similar fashion, when Paul O'Neill took the helm of Alcoa in 1987, the once-great company was struggling. In his first public comments, he didn't talk about strategy or profits or increasing shareholder value or anything that an incoming CEO would typically say to quell investors' fears. Instead, he talked about safety. It wasn't that Alcoa had a bad safety record. In fact, it was better than average. Nevertheless, O'Neill proudly declared, "I intend to make Alcoa the safest company in America. I intend to go for zero injuries."

Much like the Indian elites when Gandhi announced he would march for salt, the reporters and analysts were puzzled. They began asking the typical questions about performance. O'Neill would have none of it. "I'm not certain you heard me," he said. "If you want to understand how Alcoa is doing, you need to look at our workplace safety figures. . . . Safety will be an important indicator that we're making progress in changing habits across the entire institution. That's how we should be judged.[44]

For Paul O'Neill and Alcoa, safety was the keystone change, and like Gerstner, he led his company to a historic turnaround.

What O'Neill understood, much like Gandhi and Gerstner, was that to create a movement for transformational change, you need to create shared purpose and shared consciousness on a fundamental level. Concepts like "independence," "freedom," and "shareholder value" might check the boxes of elite opinion, but they mean little to the masses that are needed to actually make change happen. That's why shared purpose means little if it's not combined with shared consciousness and vice versa. In the 2016 US presidential election, Hillary Clinton proposed policies that shared purpose with the working class, but her opponent Donald Trump displayed shared consciousness and won many over to his side.

To create a powerful movement for change, you need to show both shared purpose *and* shared consciousness among a wide swath of constituents. All too often, this is cast as a mere issue of messaging. Leaders try to devise a strategy that gives a little of something to everyone, attempting to piece together a coalition that will add up to 51 percent majority support. Politicians vow to help the poor, support businesses, and give a little something to the middle class. CEOs promise to champion the interests of workers and profits. In the end, it all comes off looking like exactly what it is, pandering to constituencies to get them to back your program.

To create real change, change that sticks and won't be soon reversed, you need to identify a fundamental issue that encapsulates the value of the mission—a keystone change that is concrete and tangible, unites the efforts of multiple stakeholders, and paves the way for greater change. Revolutions don't begin with a slogan—they begin with a cause.

MAKING CHANGE FOUNDATIONAL

At the height of the Occupy protests in 2011, Srdja Popović of CANVAS was called in to talk to its leaders. He asked them what change they wanted to see, and they spoke about their grievances. They told him, in excruciating detail, about the greed of the banks and the travesty of oppressive student loans. They had no shortage of complaints that they demanded to be addressed. But when Popović asked them about what change they actually wanted to see happen, they couldn't say. "Imagine you are like Harry Potter with a magic wand and you can change anything," he told the activists. "What would that change look like?" They didn't have the first idea.[45]

It is never enough to merely state grievances to challenge the status quo. To create meaningful change, you must put forward an affirmative vision for what you want the future to look like. Again, this is not about messaging. It's not enough to merely express your grievances more artfully. You have to define an alternative that is actually better, not just for those who agree with you, but for the vast majority of those who will be affected by the change you seek.

That may seem like a very simple thing, but it isn't. Remember, Gandhi struggled for weeks to identify a cause that would encapsulate the change he wanted to see. In his book on the history of the LGBT movement, *Awakening*, Nathaniel Frank explains how the activists struggled for decades before they came to understand that same-sex marriage was the issue that would give them their strongest case for equality. After all, while it can be hard to internalize another's sexual preference, everybody can recognize the importance of being in a committed relationship and raising a family. Denying it to fellow citizens just seems fundamentally unjust.

In much the same way, during the nineteenth century there were many issues facing women. In most cases, they couldn't own property, receive a real education, or take legal action against abusive husbands. They were, in many respects, treated like property. So it wasn't at all obvious that voting rights would become their keystone change, but today we know their struggle as the women's suffrage movement.[46] However, voting rights were not the ultimate vision, equality was, and while the struggle for full gender equality continues, the right to vote paved the way for significant advancement over the last century.

In some cases, keystone changes have a technical dimension. Don Berwick, Founder of the Institute for Healthcare Improvement (IHI), was a doctor who was introduced to W. Edwards Deming's quality methods for manufacturing. He soon became convinced that similar methods could be the keystone change that would transform the healthcare system and cut down on medical errors, which result in tens of thousands of needless deaths each year. Yet it would take years of research to identify exactly which practices could have the greatest impact before the effort could be scaled up enough to launch the "Campaign to Save 100,000 Lives." We will discuss that campaign further in Chapters 6 and 8.[47]

In other cases, keystone changes are nested, as in the case of Wyeth Pharmaceuticals' quest to cut costs by 25 percent. Lean manufacturing methods were identified as the keystone change that could transform the company and achieve its objectives, but to implement those methods meant transforming the behaviors of 20,000 employees across 16 large facilities, most of whom were skeptical of the change. So they started with one process, factory changeovers, and reduced the time it took to switch from producing one product to another in half. "That changed assumptions of what was possible," an advisor that worked on the project told me. "It allowed us to implement metrics, improve collaboration, and train the supervisor to reimagine her perceived role from being a taskmaster that pushed people to work harder to a coach that enables improved performance."[48]

Lean manufacturing was the keystone change for Wyeth, but factory changeovers were the keystone change that made the lean manufacturing transformation possible. The company exceeded its goals and saved $250 million from its operating budget.[49]

In a similar vein, the rise of cloud architectures created a dilemma for big data giant Experian. For decades, it had built up a reliable data architecture to service large banks with credit data and built other data businesses on a similar infrastructure. Yet when Barry Libenson began his tenure as chief information officer, he saw that customers were demanding more access and flexibility that could only be achieved if the company moved from its traditional systems to the cloud. However, that was easier said than done.

"There was a lot of concern that we were going to disrupt our own business and that we would lose control of our data," he told me. "For years, Experian's business model was based on a traditional architecture. There were also security concerns. So there were obviously lots of important questions that we needed to be sure to address."

Libenson set out to identify a keystone change. He started by developing APIs for internal use rather than going straight to customer-facing features. The effect of the initiative was subtle, but important because it got people working together and showed what was possible. Building the APIs required collaboration across the IT organization. Application developers found that they could access data more easily, business unit leaders were able to get new products out the door more quickly, and customers started to notice better service. It was a relatively small step, but got the ball rolling. "Once we developed some internal APIs, people could see that there was vast potential and we gained some momentum," Libenson remembers.

Much like with voting rights for women, the internal APIs and, in fact, the move to the cloud weren't the end of the journey, but rather a concrete and tangible accomplishment that paved the way for future change. "I think the most impactful technology that's emerging right now is machine learning," Libenson told me. "For example, we've started using machine learning to help manage our infrastructure, predict problems, and suggest possible solutions. We have also begun using similar technologies for fraud detection, security, and to improve decision results. Having gone through this transformational process over the past three years and seeing concrete business results, we are much better positioned to adopt those technologies. We've made the changes in culture, our organizational structure, and skills to be able to adopt new technologies quickly, completely, and with better collaboration with our customers."[50]

Notice that none of these keystone changes are obvious. In every case, it took a great deal of deliberation—and often no small amount of trial and error—before they could be identified. What makes a keystone change so difficult to identify is that, while grievances are what drive the passion of some, a keystone change needs to resonate with those outside the early adopter group if it is going to spread. Movements, as the name implies, need to be kinetic. They start somewhere and need to end up somewhere else. So it's never enough to just speak to the hopes and aspirations of the loyal and faithful. You need to speak to common values shared by those outside your movement for change to occur. Driving change is always about attracting, never overpowering.

That's why Martin Luther King Jr., who studied Gandhi closely, when he spoke to a mass meeting of protestors at the beginning of the Montgomery Bus Boycott, framed the struggle not in terms of a distinctly black experience, but that of America and Christianity. "If we are wrong," he said, "the Supreme Court of this nation is wrong. If we are wrong, the Constitution of the United States is wrong. If we are wrong, God almighty is wrong. If we are wrong, Jesus of Nazareth was merely a utopian dreamer that never came down to earth."[51]

It was that appeal to common values that helped the movement for civil rights spread far beyond the black Americans who experienced discrimination personally. White liberals, mostly in the North, but also in the South, took up the cause as well. Eventually, the movement reached the politicians in Washington who had the power to effect change. As the civil rights leader John Lewis would remember in his autobiography, *Walking with the Wind*, at one point Robert Kennedy, Attorney General of the United States and brother to the president, would say to him, "John, the people, the young people of the SNCC, have educated me. You have changed me. Now I understand."[52]

That's what really makes change happen. Not a strident call to the faithful, but the forging of a common cause among diverse constituencies. As we have seen, for any cascade to form, linkages need to be built to higher threshold groups, and that can only be done by reaching out and learning about the needs, desires, and fears of others. That was as true with Gandhi as it was with Gerstner, McChrystal, O'Neill, the Institute for Healthcare Improvement, Wyeth Pharmaceuticals, and Experian. In each case, it was the forging of shared purpose and shared consciousness through identifying keystone issues that made change possible.

Just as building a clear sense of purpose is essential for a movement to succeed, the lack of a clear purpose can hobble one almost before it starts. While Occupy's slogan of "We are the 99 percent" caught the imagination of millions, the activists were never really clear about what they actually wanted to be done. As columnist Joe Nocera noted in the *New York Times*, "they had plenty of grievances, aimed mainly at the 'oppressive power of corporations,' but never got beyond their own slogans."[53] Before long, everyone lost interest.

Creating a clear sense of purpose and identifying a keystone issue that can achieve that purpose is absolutely essential to create transformative change. However, it is merely a first step. Once you figure out what the end game should look like, you need to develop a plan to get there.

That is what we turn to next.

CHAPTER 5

Making a Plan

When evil men plot, good men must plan. When evil men burn and bomb, good men must build and bind.

—MARTIN LUTHER KING JR.

The March on Washington in 1963 remains a defining moment in American history. It was the brainchild of A. Philip Randolph who, at age 74, was considered to be an elder statesman of the civil rights movement. Randolph had been elected the president of the Brotherhood of Sleeping Car Porters in 1925 and quickly built a reputation as one of the most effective labor organizers in the country. In 1941, as America was gearing up for war, he had threatened a mass march on Washington, but President Roosevelt invited him to the White House and offered to issue an executive order forbidding discrimination in the defense industry if Randolph called it off. He did, and tens of thousands of black workers got good paying jobs.[1]

By 1963 civil disobedience had won significant victories throughout the American South and exposed the ugliness of segregation in places like Birmingham and Montgomery. President Kennedy had announced that he planned to send a civil rights bill to Congress, but black leaders felt that he was getting cold feet due to resistance from southern politicians who felt things were moving too fast. Kennedy, for his part, felt that a march would endanger the legislation. So, much like his predecessor, he called black leaders to the White House to dissuade them from marching.[2]

Yet 1963 was not 1941. Randolph was no longer a lone labor organizer, but the dean of a powerful movement that included the "Big Six" of Martin Luther King Jr. and his Southern Christian Leadership Conference (SCLC), John Lewis of the youth-driven Student Nonviolent Coordinating Committee (SNCC), Roy Wilkins of the National Association for the Advancement of Colored People (NAACP), James Farmer of the Congress of Racial Equality (CORE), and Whitney Young of the National Urban League (NUL). While the group acknowledged to President Kennedy that it was possible the march would cause him problems, they told him in no uncertain terms that they would have even bigger problems with their members, who had struggled and suffered for civil rights, if they did not march.[3]

The march was unlike anything anyone had ever seen before. Over 100 organizations were represented, including not only black activist groups, but also organizations like the AFL-CIO and the American Jewish Congress—Randolph called it a "coalition of conscience"—and almost 250,000 people in all would attend.[4] Anybody who expected to see a caucus of angry militants would be terribly disappointed. The protestors were well dressed, well behaved, and of all colors, creeds, and social classes.

The highlight was Martin Luther King Jr.'s "I Have a Dream" speech. As in the remarks he gave eight years earlier at the start of the Montgomery Bus Boycott, King appealed not only to racial grievances but to quintessential American values, and invoked the founding documents of the republic. "In a sense, we've come to our nation's capital to cash a check," King announced to the crowds in front of the Lincoln Monument. "When the architects of our republic wrote the magnificent words of the Constitution and the Declaration of Independence, they were signing a promissory note to which every American was to fall heir. . . . Now is the time to make real the promises of democracy."[5]

The most memorable portion was, of course, when King talked about his dream, which envisioned a more inclusive, peaceful, and prosperous America that was true to the principles upon which the country was founded. "I still have a dream," he declared. "It is a dream deeply rooted in the American dream. I have a dream that one day this nation will rise up and live out the true meaning of its creed—we hold these truths to be self-evident that all men are created equal."[6]

The "I Have A Dream" speech was an enormously powerful moment. For many, it encapsulates the struggle for civil rights, and it is widely credited with spurring the passage of the Civil Rights Act of 1964. Yet its significance is often misunderstood. Massive demonstrations have become *de rigueur* for modern-day movements seeking to make an impact. Today, with the wonders of digital technology and social media, it is far easier to mobilize large numbers, so it would seem that forging change has become easier. Yet that is largely a mirage.

The March on Washington in 1963 did not create change because it attracted so many to join in. Its power was derived from the culmination of years of successful legal initiatives, sit-ins, bus strikes, and other actions. In effect, the civil rights movement didn't become powerful because the March on Washington was successful; the March on Washington was successful because the civil rights movement had become powerful. It was part of the end game, not an opening move.

As Clayborne Carson, who edited Martin Luther King Jr.'s posthumously published autobiography, wrote, "In assessing the summer's events, some observers have tended to diminish the achievements by treating the demonstrations as an end in themselves. The heroism of the march, the drama of the confrontation, became in their minds the total accomplishment. It is true that these elements have meaning, but to ignore the concrete and specific gains in dismantling the structure of segregation is like noticing the beauty of the rain, but failing to see that it has enriched the soil. A social movement that only moves people is merely a revolt. A movement that changes both people and institutions is a revolution."[7]

All too often a moment is misunderstood to be a movement. As we saw in Chapter 3, a cascade ensues when an idea breaks through higher and higher thresholds of resistance. Ideally, that is because linkages have been built from the passionate early adopters into the mainstream through years of painstaking work to widen and deepen connections. Yet sometimes, a triggering event can reduce thresholds enough to produce the same cascading effect. The financial crisis brought out thousands to support Occupy's message of "We are the 99%," just as the election of Donald Trump brought out masses of people to march on Washington.[8] Yet without a network in place and a unifying cause that forges shared purpose and shared consciousness, the moment passes and little changes.

Modern communications technology and social media cuts both ways. It can help mobilize support, but it also may awaken opposition and spur a countermovement. That's essentially the trap that modern-day change efforts like Occupy and Black Lives Matter fell into. They looked to gather maximum attention before doing crucial groundwork. Successful movements don't start by rousing crowds, but by formulating a clear objective and building out from there. As with any journey, you start with where you want to end up and then figure out how you're going to get there.

That's what a plan is.

THE SPECTRUM OF ALLIES

There are two tools that nascent movements can use to develop plans to make change happen. The first is called the Spectrum of Allies (Figure 5.1), which outlines the groups from which you can expect active or passive support, neutrality, and active or passive opposition. As Srdja Popović of Otpor and CANVAS put it to me, "Sun Tzu wrote 'know yourself, know your enemy and know the terrain.' The Spectrum of Allies is the terrain."[9]

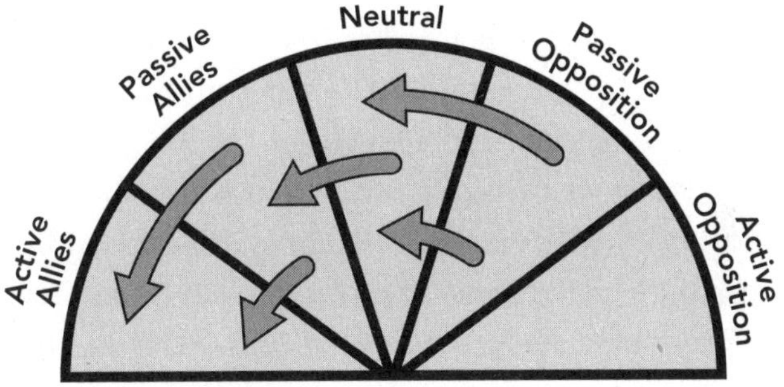

FIGURE 5.1 The Spectrum of Allies

Just as a military strategist studies maps to understand how the battle will flow, where his own forces' strengths lie, and how to exploit the enemy's weaknesses, the Spectrum of Allies marks the path of the cascade that a movement will have to take if it is to attain its objectives. It is only through understanding where the thresholds of resistance lie that you forge the connections you need to push through them.

We've already seen how Gandhi navigated the spectrum of allies in the struggle for Indian independence. While he played an active part in the Indian National Congress and helped mobilize its base of active allies, he also did much to bring those Indians, such as the peasant and non-Hindu population, who were passive and neutral into the fold. Yet some of his most fervent efforts were made toward the British themselves. The essence of Satyagraha was not to defeat your opponent, but to show him the error of his ways. That may seem like a terribly naive approach, but Gandhi proved that it can work time after time.

Consider the remarks of General Jan Smuts, who was Gandhi's chief adversary in his South Africa Satyagraha. After it was over, he said, "It was my fate to be the antagonist of a man for whom even then I had the highest respect. . . . For me—the defender of law and order—there was the usual trying situation, the odium of carrying out the law, which had not strong popular support." Smuts had not only been defeated; he had been won over and lost any rationale to keep fighting.[10] In a similar fashion, after Gandhi's death, the Mahatma was mourned all over the world, but especially in Great Britain, the empire he had fought so long and hard against.

Now, Gandhi was unique, and it wouldn't be realistic to expect the most ardent defenders of the status quo to all of a sudden see the light and join your ranks. However, you should act in such a way that they have the option to do so, because while victory does not require you to win over all of those who resist change, you do need to erode the support of your opposition. Smuts, it must be said, was a vigorous and sometimes brutal antagonist, but in the end he had to choose between giving in to Gandhi's demands, which in the final analysis not only cost him little but actually raised his stature, or lonely intransigence.

That's why plans that are focused solely on rallying the faithful are doomed to fail. The only thing you will accomplish is to harden the support of those who oppose your vision of change. So when you see change as a zero-sum game, you are mobilizing your opponent's forces as much as you are your own. Nobody wants to lose, but everybody wants a better tomorrow.

"You are not trying to impose your vision," Srdja Popović told me. "You are sharing it, you are listening, and you are respectful to those who don't hold the same views as you. But above all, you are clear and everybody knows where you stand."[11] A struggle for change is not a debate. You don't have to win every argument. What you do need to do is win support from those who don't necessarily agree with you from the start.

Make no mistake, you will not win everybody over, but it is also a grave misapprehension to see your opponents as monolithic or to dehumanize them. I remember after the Orange Revolution when Viktor Pinchuk, the son-in-law of President

Kuchma and a powerful oligarch in his own right, was asked what he thought about the protests. He said he was worried about violence, because his own children were down on the Maidan. In the final analysis, nobody, except a true sociopath, wishes to do evil. They may rationalize the situation and see themselves as just being "practical," or, in some cases, view the situation as a classic prisoner's dilemma and believe that it is best to look after their own interests. Yet none of that makes them evil, blind to reason, or impervious to persuasion.

It doesn't mean that your opponents will give in willingly, either. As we saw in Chapter 1, while Ukraine's Orange Revolution ended peacefully, the Euromaidan protests in 2014 were met with a much more forceful and deadly response. First, Interior Ministry troops were sent to beat the protestors. Activists were kidnapped from their homes, taken out to the woods, and tortured. In some cases, they were killed. Finally, the Yanukovych regime ordered snipers to open fire on the protestors. In the end, nearly a hundred people were left dead.

Yet these harsh actions did little more than weaken the government's hand. In fact, Mustafa Nayyem, a key leader of the Euromaidan protests and later a member of the Ukrainian Parliament, told me that the regime's brutality against peaceful protestors was its biggest mistake, and not only because it bolstered support for the protestors within the country.[12] International condemnation quickly followed, and the United States threatened sanctions that would have isolated the oligarchs allied with President Yanukovych from the international financial system. Anybody who was seen to be supporting the regime's heinous acts would lose their right to buy luxury villas abroad and send their children to prestigious schools in the West.[13]

The intense international pressure forced the Yanukovych regime to come to the negotiating table. He agreed to hold free and fair elections later that year, but things never got that far. The night before the agreement was to be signed, his allies in the Party of Regions met in the Rada, Ukraine's parliament.

After seeing their citizens slaughtered on the street and Ukraine being treated as a pariah nation, they too had had enough. They wanted Yanukovych out of their lives.[14]

The next day, President Yanukovych met with the opposition politicians and signed the deal that the international negotiators had brokered. But as the group left the room, Yanukovych's security detail seemed to just melt away. Without allies even in his own government, the former strongman had no choice but to flee. He rushed to his residence, gathered some things, and boarded a helicopter. Yanukovych was never seen in Ukraine again and, within a few days, was unanimously impeached from office. In the end, he was done in not by the protestors, but by his most ardent supporters. At that point, to be seen as allied with Yanukovych was to become a pariah.

Let's return to the civil rights movement. Its leaders had spent years mobilizing support from southern blacks and liberal whites. During those earlier protests, mainstream America had witnessed scenes on the televisions in their living rooms that they could not imagine happening in their own country. Ordinary citizens were being beaten for exercising their right to speak and to vote. Children were being attacked by snarling dogs and fire hoses. It was unconscionable. Few wanted to be associated with such brutality and injustice.

The March on Washington was designed not to rally the faithful, but to appeal to those in mainstream America who had been watching those enormously powerful scenes unfold on their televisions—those in the middle of the Spectrum of Allies—and to shift some passive opponents to a more neutral position and active opponents to a more passive position. Surely, in the end, it didn't convince everybody, but it did enough to win civil rights and bring important changes about.

The same strategic approach can be put to use within an organization. The military reformer Colonel John Boyd knew that he would face fierce opposition to his efforts to reform wasteful spending in the Pentagon, which had become endemic by the 1980s. Costs were ballooning, and budgeting was so slipshod that a colleague had calculated that President Reagan's defense buildup was being underestimated by $500 billion, an enormous sum even in the context of federal budgets.[15]

At the same time, it was in many people's interests for the profligate spending to continue. Certainly, the defense contractors who made fat profits on expensive weapons systems didn't want things to change. It also benefited the generals and the admirals, who earned prestige from overseeing big projects and, not uncommonly, cushy, lucrative jobs consulting for the defense industry after retirement.[16] They were, understandably, resistant to change, but especially contemptuous of aspersions being cast by a mere colonel.

Another challenge was that the military is a profoundly hierarchical organization in which orders are not to be questioned. Senior officers in the military are accorded a level of deference unlike anything in the private sector. They are also surrounded by junior officers and staff who depend on their evaluations to get promoted. It's not like an army officer can just go out and take a job with a competitor. One black mark can send a once promising career spanning decades into oblivion, so subordinates are wary of speaking out of turn.[17]

With all this in mind, Boyd was careful not to brief the generals directly, at least not at first. He started out briefing a small circle of confidants, known as the Acolytes, who would help check facts, streamline logical arguments, and hone the message. Once he was confident that his argument was unassailable, he would start presenting to junior officers. After he had gained some momentum and polished his pitch some more, he moved on to congressional staffers, who were always receptive to ideas that they could take to their bosses. He then moved on to elected officials, many of whom relished the opportunity to push for reforms. Boyd moved on to the top generals last, only when he had already gathered far too much support to be ignored.

Make no mistake. The only way to create change is to gather support, and the Spectrum of Allies maps your path to victory. If, for example, you are an employee at a major corporation and you want to push for change, camping out with a few confederates outside the CEO's office would achieve little more than losing your job and being led out of the building by burly security guards. If, on the other hand, you built allies and worked to recruit others, especially those with somewhat higher thresholds of resistance, your chances of achieving something worthwhile would markedly increase.

Still, while mobilizing support is absolutely essential, it is far from sufficient. Attracting adoring crowds might feel good, but that's not what brings change about. Institutions are what do. And that brings us to the second element of strategy: the Pillars of Support.[18] Every tyrant, no matter how powerful, needs others to carry out his or her bidding. Without those, even the mightiest empire will crumble. Successful movements identify these pillars—not to knock them out, but to draw them in.

THE PILLARS OF SUPPORT

Every political regime needs institutions such as the police to keep order, bureaucracies to administrate policies, business groups to manage commerce, and others to carry out crucial functions of governance. In a private organization, leaders need to maintain the support of a variety of different stakeholders, including shareholders, customer groups, partners, various functional departments, and others. Every situation is different, but one thing is always constant: nobody rules alone. No regime is a monolith.

Figure 5.2 shows what the pillars might look like in a typical nonviolent revolution like the ones we have seen in Serbia and Ukraine. Otpor's tactics were cleverly designed to bring institutions over to their side. Their pranks were funny and exposed the hypocrisy of the regime, which made great copy for the media. Even arrests were seen as an opportunity to build personal relationships with police officers, some of whom sympathized with the protestors and were receptive to their good-natured banter. Business leaders were already unhappy with the years of war and economic isolation that Milošević's reign had wrought.

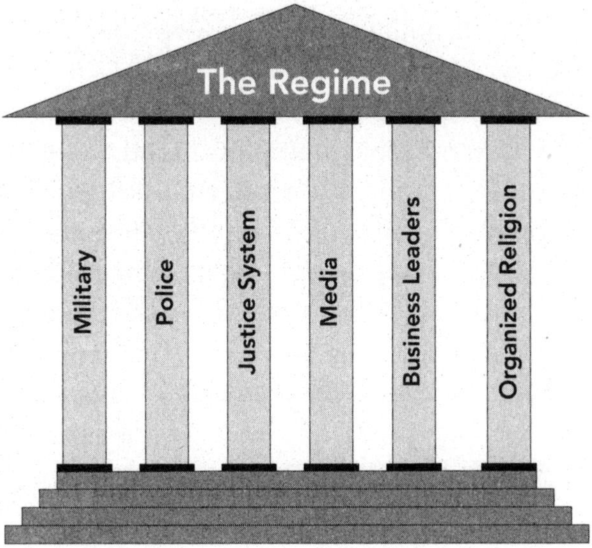

FIGURE 5.2 The Pillars of Support

All of these would eventually become decisive in the end game, when Milošević refused to honor the results of the election he lost. Support from the business community proved essential to help organize and supply the protests. Police and security forces were forced to decide whether to shoot into the crowds or obey the will of the people. They chose the latter. Professional journalists were needed to report events to the Serbian people—and the world. Otpor activists, for all of their energy, savvy, and talent, could have done little of this alone.

Although we didn't know it at the time, a similar dynamic played out during Ukraine's Orange Revolution in 2004. As we stood in the freezing cold on the Maidan hoping for a new future for Ukraine, 10,000 Interior Ministry troops were gathering outside Kyiv to crush the protests. Armed with live ammunition and tear gas, they were fully mobilized and ready to strike. Martial law was to be declared in Ukraine.

The events that came next were fit for a John le Carré novel. The Ukrainian security service, the SBU, moved to thwart the Interior Ministry's efforts. They informed the opposition leaders of the impending danger and then conferred with the army. As C. J. Chivers later reported in the *New York Times*, a message was relayed to the Interior Ministry that they "'are on the side of the people, and will defend the people, and that the M.V.D. [the Interior Ministry] will have to deal not only with unarmed people and youth if it comes to Kiev, but with the army' and the special forces inside the intelligence agencies." The troops were turned back and no action took place.[19]

In his quest to reform the Pentagon, Colonel Boyd also recognized the importance of the pillars of support. Notice how while building his Spectrum of Allies, which represented increasing thresholds of resistance, from close allies, to junior officers, to congressional staffers, to elected officials and political appointees, he was also skillfully navigating the institutions that supported corruption within the military.

He actively leveraged his Spectrum of Allies to win support of officials in both the legislative and executive branches of government, both of which had constitutionally mandated authority over senior military leaders. Talk of the findings of Boyd and his "Acolytes" eventually found its way to the media, and unclassified briefings were prepared for journalists. One of these, termed the "Spinney Report," landed on the cover of *Time* magazine in 1983 with the seductive headline, "U.S. Defense Spending: Are Billions Being Wasted?"[20] A few years before that, a young journalist named James Fallows spent hours interviewing Boyd and his Acolytes, which led to a story in the *Atlantic* entitled "The Muscle-Bound Superpower." It was read widely, led to further articles, and eventually a book, *National Defense*, which won numerous awards and launched Fallows's career as one of America's premier journalists. Other media outlets also began covering the story of America's "hollow military," which led to congressional hearings and drove real change at the Defense Department.[21] Popular support is essential, but to drive through change you need the institutions that make up the Pillars of Support.

Boyd and his small band of followers had taken on the Pentagon, one of the most powerful and change-averse institutions on the planet, and won. At the heart of his movement was the notion that first you need to subvert your ego to the cause. "To *be* somebody or to *do* something," he would tell his Acolytes. "In life there is often a roll call. That's when you will have to make a decision. To *be* or to *do*? Which way will you go?"[22] Boyd chose to do, and that meant mobilizing his Spectrum of Allies to influence the Pillars of Support with a laser-like focus on creating the change he wanted to see. He wasn't interested in just making a point; he wanted to make a difference.

"You need an institutional shift," Srdja Popović told me, "It's not only a mind shift." When he works with activist movements in his capacity as executive director of CANVAS, Srdja walks groups through an exercise called "power graph," in which they chart where key institutions stand related to the vision for change as the movement progresses and see what influences their attitudes. "It's a dynamic exercise," he explained, "in which you say, 'This is the change I want to achieve, these are the constituencies I want to talk to, and these are my early allies and these are my later allies. . . . And these are the pillars that the status quo is standing upon,' and then you need to ask yourself, 'what influences the change in the pillar?' You are still examining the battlefield; you are not fighting yet. You are still learning about your opponent. You are still learning about the terrain. You need to understand which social groups you need to pull and which pillars you need to change."[23]

On the other side of the coin, we have already seen how John Antioco at Blockbuster had his plans thwarted because he failed to gain the support of powerful institutions connected to his organization, such as the franchisees and the shareholders. He won a battle against Netflix by formulating a shrewd market strategy, and in doing so he won some favor with customers, but when it came to the battles within his own organization, he didn't make the same effort. When I talked to him, it seemed to me that his earlier success overcoming critics, such as when he switched to the revenue sharing model for acquiring movies at Blockbuster, had convinced him that if he just kept pushing through everybody would see the wisdom of his plan and everything would be okay. After all, his approach had proven successful time and time again. Unfortunately, things didn't work out the same way this time. Uncertainty about his plan crushed the stock price, which attracted the corporate raider Carl Icahn. That led to the compensation dispute and his departure from the company.

Now imagine how different things could have been if the Occupy protestors, instead of rushing to take over Zuccotti Park, had instead courted local Chambers of Commerce (there are roughly 3,000 in the United States)[24] whose members had been harmed by the malfeasance of large banks. Or if instead of disrupting political rallies, the Black Lives Matter movement had worked to gain the support of even a few dozen of the over 15,000 police departments in the United States,[25] or forged a common purpose with organizations like the National Organization of Black Law Enforcement Executives.

Criminal justice reform is not just important for the minority communities most directly affected, but has serious consequences for the nation as a whole. Consider that today, amid a serious labor shortage that hamstrings major industries, 6 to 7 percent of prime working age males have a history of incarceration,[26] which renders them all but unemployable, often due to minor, nonviolent convictions. Or that it costs tens of thousands of dollars a year to incarcerate an inmate (estimated to total about $80 billion in expenditures and $1 trillion in indirect costs for the country as a whole),[27] meaning that our overly aggressive criminal justice system means fewer cops on the beat and teachers in classrooms.

Or, as President Harry Truman put it, "We have learned that nations are interdependent and that recognition of our dependence upon one another is essential to life, liberty and the pursuit of happiness of all mankind. So long as the basic rights of men are denied in any substantial portion of the earth, men everywhere must live in fear of their own rights and security."[28]

Gathering the support of law enforcement officials sympathetic to their cause, making the argument for the common cause of economic competitiveness, and invoking the words of a revered president—Black Lives Matter had the opportunity to do all of these and many other things. Sure, none of that would have been as thrilling as holding a public demonstration and denouncing the powers that be, but it would have helped inoculate them from being portrayed as anarchists or antipolice and might have pointed the way to a strategy that could actually make a difference.

A successful strategy matches the key constituencies in the Spectrum of Allies and the key institutions that make up the Pillars of Support with the tactics that are most likely to bring them into the fold. That's how you win and bring about the change you want to see.

Let's return to our corporate example. Once you've decided not to camp outside the CEO's office and begin to recruit allies, your attentions would turn to the various stakeholders that support the business, such as internal departments, shareholders, customer groups, and so on. Which ones stand to gain from the change you want to see? Which stand to lose? How can they be convinced that change is in their best interest or, at the very least, so inevitable that resistance is futile? If you want to make change happen, these are the questions you need to ask.

Successful movements recognize that the Spectrum of Allies and the Pillars of Support intersect because, after all, institutions derive their power from people. Otpor saw the inevitable arrests they had to endure not merely as an inconvenience, or even as a way to test their courage and conviction, but also as an opportunity for infiltration. They recognized that the policemen were, ultimately, just people with a job to do, not necessarily malevolent figures. So they used their time in police stations to build relationships with the officers, while also gathering the media outside the police station and gaining more exposure. It was these relationships that became crucial in the end game, when police had to make the decision of whether to shoot into the crowds to keep Milošević in power or throw in with the protestors.

As we saw in the last chapter, when Paul O'Neill was named CEO at Alcoa and set out to turn around the struggling company, he started by putting worker safety first. His efforts not only led to a better workplace and improved product quality, but also forged a common purpose between managers and workers. By winning over these constituencies in his Spectrum of Allies, he made inroads into important Pillars of Support, such as the unions and the media, which helped him also pull in other pillars, like customers and shareholders. After all, who could argue with better safety? What O'Neill understood was that the same culture and practices that promote a safer workplace could also lead to operational excellence and a much more profitable company.

Look at any successful movement for change, and it contains the three elements we've discussed: a clear vision for fundamental change, breaking through increasing thresholds of resistance within the Spectrum of Allies, and institutional shifts within the Pillars of Support. Those are the building blocks of strategy through which you design your tactics.

To understand how this all works, let's take a close look at one of the lesser-known, but still crucial, campaigns in the struggle for civil rights, the Nashville sit-ins.

HOW A STRATEGY COMES TOGETHER

It was 1958 and John Lewis was a sophomore at the American Baptist Theological Seminary in Nashville, Tennessee, when he met James Lawson. Thirty years old, but worldly beyond his years, Lawson had already been to jail for refusing to report for the draft. Although he would have been eligible for a ministerial or student deferment, out of principle he never sought to obtain one and entered captivity willingly. After being released from prison, he went to India as a Methodist missionary, where he studied the principles of Satyagraha with several of Gandhi's disciples. He came to Nashville with the dual purpose of pursuing a doctorate at the Vanderbilt Divinity School and serving as a field secretary for the Fellowship of Reconciliation (FOR), a pacifist organization active in the civil rights movement.[29]

Lewis was immediately taken in by Lawson and began attending his Tuesday evening workshops, which indoctrinated students in Gandhi's methods. Before long, Lewis convinced his friend Bernard Lafayette to join the slowly growing coterie that included future civil rights luminaries such as Diane Nash, James Bevel, and Marion Barry. Eventually, the students organized themselves into the Student Movement. They wanted to make a difference through a direct nonviolent action, but what kind of action they would undertake was still unclear.[30]

As young, passionate, and idealistic students, many from out of town, they were clearly on the far left side of the Spectrum of Allies, with little connection to the other groups with higher thresholds of resistance. To a large extent, they had no voice in Nashville affairs, few ties to the community, and little shared consciousness with the people that did. Whatever action they took, it had to be one that would mobilize their passive allies and make inroads into those neutral and even passively opposed to the issue of racial integration. What they could not afford was to do anything that would make them appear to be out-of-town rabble-rousers, inspire resistance to change, and set the movement back.

Lawson, already an experienced organizer by this point, met regularly with local church, business, and social groups in Nashville's black community in search of a unifying issue that could form the basis for fundamental change. As he did, one grievance stood out from the rest—the downtown department stores, where black women would shop and spend money, but still be denied the right to sit down at a lunch counter, rest their feet, and get some nourishment. Anybody who has ever gone shopping with their kids can empathize with how maddening, inconvenient, and humiliating the situation was. If the Nashville Student Movement targeted the lunch counters, they were sure to win allies among Nashville's established black community.[31]

So at the end of November in 1959, the students began scouting out local department stores. They would show up smartly dressed, in suits and ties for the boys, and skirts and blouses for the girls. They would then buy a small item to establish themselves as paying customers and ask to be served at the lunch counter. When they were refused service, they politely asked to see the manager. A few minutes later, the manager came out and informed them, "it is our policy not to serve colored people here." They left quietly, with little commotion except for a few hushed whispers among the patrons. The next Saturday, a similar test run was performed with identical results.[32]

After the Christmas break, training began in earnest. By this time, the attendance at Lawson's workshops had swelled. The novice activists took turns sitting on chairs while the others hurled vicious epithets at them. Their resilience and dedication to Gandhi's principles would be tested thoroughly before any of them would be allowed to join any active protest. Specific directions were given for every aspect of their conduct, from how they would sit and talk to what they should bring and what they needed to be prepared for. If the sit-ins were to fail, it wouldn't be for lack of preparation.[33]

The campaign began in earnest on Saturday, February 13, 1961. The night before, a half foot of snow had fallen on

Nashville, which Lewis took to be a good omen. The protestors made their way to First Baptist Church, where they were divided into five groups of 25 students or so. At eleven o'clock they marched out in double file a few blocks till they reached Fifth Avenue, Nashville's main shopping area, where they split up, each group going into the store to which they'd been assigned.[34]

Lewis's group entered Woolworth's, where each activist made a small purchase. From there they made their way to the lunch counter, sat, and asked to be served. "We don't serve niggers here," they were told. Then the lunch counter was promptly closed. The students pulled out their schoolbooks, began to study, and waited for whatever came next.[35]

Before long, a group of young white men showed up and began spewing insults, but the protestors did not respond and kept their eyes straight ahead. At around 6 p.m., a runner from the First Baptist Church came to tell them it was time to go. The students calmly stood up and left in an orderly fashion. When they met the other protestors back at the church, all hugged and cheered. They had made their first strike, and it had all gone off just as planned.[36]

Sitting in a café with the lights off and calmly doing your schoolwork may seem like a minor victory, but nonetheless a Rubicon had been crossed. Black activists had taken action, and the white community had no idea what to do about it. The activists were well dressed, well spoken, polite, and refrained from raising their voices even when provoked. No laws had been broken. They had even made purchases at the store. A neutral onlooker would have to ask, "What's the problem? Why would a business turn away a paying customer?"

As the sit-ins continued, the stores began to take countermeasures. Managers at a few of the stores began to stack lampshades, wastebaskets, pots, pans, and other items on the lunch counters so the students could no longer study as they sat. Still, neither black nor white customers could be served. The department stores were losing money, and the sit-ins continued without any sign of abating.[37]

At one point, it became clear that the segregationists had reached their wit's end. Word came back to the activists at the First Baptist Church that any further actions would result in arrests. There were also credible rumors swirling that violence was about to break out and that the police would do nothing to stop it. Forewarned, John Lewis and Bernard Lafayette printed out leaflets with the following instructions:

DO NOT:
1. Strike back nor curse if abused.
2. Laugh out.
3. Hold conversations with the floor walker.
4. Leave your seat until your leader has given you permission to do so.
5. Block entrances to stores outside nor the aisles inside.

DO:
1. Show yourself to be friendly and courteous at all times.
2. Sit straight; always face the counter.
3. Report all serious incidents to your leader.
4. Refer information seekers to your leader in a polite manner.
5. Remember the teachings of Jesus Christ, Mahatma Gandhi and Martin Luther King. Love and nonviolence is the way.

MAY GOD BLESS EACH OF YOU[38]

As the activists made their way into town the next day, they were met by a group of young white men shouting, "Go home, nigger! Go back to Africa!" Police officers stood idly by as the students were pushed and shoved on the street. When the students finally made their way into the stores and sat down at the lunch counters, the young white toughs continued hurling insults at them and began to get physical. Lewis was punched in the ribs and knocked off his chair. He calmly got up and sat back down again. In other stores, students had mustard and ketchup poured on them. One white activist, Paul LaPrad, was beaten particularly viciously. After a short while the police showed up and made a point of ignoring the attackers. The officers arrested the protestors, who were led away in handcuffs as they sang "We Shall Overcome."[39]

That day proved to be a turning point. Nashville, at least by southern standards, was a moderate city. Film crews had captured the beating of Paul LaPrad, and many had seen the mistreatment of the clean-cut student activists firsthand. The black community was enraged, and many whites were feeling very uncomfortable with the turn of events. Looking to defuse the situation, bail for the arrested protestors was dropped from the usual $100 to $5. They refused to pay, a practice among activists that went back to the women's suffrage movement, and began to chant, "Jail without bail!" At a loss for what to do, the authorities ordered the students released on their own recognizance later that night. The next day they appeared in court and were each ordered to pay a $50 fine. They refused to pay that as well, much as Gandhi had done in a similar situation.[40]

By this point, older, more conservative blacks (up to this time, passive allies) had moved decidedly into the fold and actively supported the young activists. Footage of Paul LaPrad being kicked by the white toughs had been aired on national news, and telegrams of support from luminaries such as Eleanor Roosevelt and Harry Belafonte began to arrive. The "respectable" citizens of Nashville were now beginning to feel even more uncomfortable. They just wanted the problem to go away.[41]

To defuse the situation, the mayor of Nashville, a moderate named Ben West, ordered the students released. He also announced a biracial committee to investigate the issue of segregated lunch counters and make recommendations. While the committee was deliberating, the protestors agreed to a short moratorium on sit-ins. Things began to settle down.[42]

Yet the avid segregationists, those on the far right of the Spectrum of Allies, soon thwarted these efforts. James Stahlman, the staunchly conservative editor of the *Nashville Banner*, an influential local newspaper, wrote an editorial denouncing James Lawson as an "outside agitator" who was responsible for stirring up all the trouble. Under pressure, Lawson was expelled from the Vanderbilt Divinity School, and he was arrested two days later.[43] It would, much like the violent response to the nonviolent Euromaidan protests in Ukraine, prove to be the demise of the status quo.

We can assume that the segregationists expected that Lawson's jailing would quell the protests, but they were wildly off the mark. The students' brave, yet reserved conduct at the sit-ins had made them heroes on campus. Many of their classmates, who were once reticent about the protests, now wanted to join them. The older black citizens, who at first didn't want to get involved, now called for a boycott of the downtown stores. White shoppers also began to steer clear. Some simply wanted to avoid the unpleasantness, but others marched into the stores and turned in their credit cards as a show of solidarity with the activists. Downtown Nashville became a ghost town. Except for the protestors, no one wanted to be seen there. Much like with Yanukovych in Ukraine, anyone associated with the policies of the lunch counters risked being seen as a pariah.

As the Spectrum of Allies began to shift, Pillars of Support were pulled in as well. Media outlets, both local and national, were actively covering the events, often in terms favorable to the black activists. Future Pulitzer Prize winner David Halberstam, then a young reporter for the *Tennessean,* wrote some of his first big stories about the Nashville sit-ins. At black churches, ministers openly encouraged their parishioners to support the boycott. Black radio stations broadcast announcements to spread the word, "Don't Buy Downtown." Even some of the store owners themselves remarked that being able to serve black customers everywhere in the store except for the lunch counters didn't make much sense to them either.[44]

With support for the movement growing seemingly by the minute, the segregationists made one last-ditch effort to stop it in its tracks. They bombed the house of one of Nashville's most prominent black citizens, Z. Alexander Looby, a well-respected lawyer and city councilman. The act horrified almost everybody. Within hours, thousands were marching to City Hall to confront Mayor West. He came out to meet the crowd and made a plea for peace. "We are all Christians. Let us pray together," the mayor said. "How about eating together?" came the reply. Then Diane Nash, who would go on to become a major figure in the civil rights movement, came to the front with a series of questions that had been prepared in advance.

DIANE NASH: "Will you use the prestige of your office to appeal to the citizens to stop racial discrimination?"

MAYOR BILL WEST: "I appeal to all citizens to end discrimination, to have no bigotry, no bias, no hatred."

DIANE NASH: "Do you mean that to include lunch counters?"

MAYOR BILL WEST: "Little lady, I stopped segregation seven years ago at the airport when I first took office, and there's been no trouble since."

DIANE NASH: "Then, Mayor, do you recommend that the lunch counters be desegregated?"

MAYOR BILL WEST: "Yes."

The crowd erupted, and West almost immediately began to backtrack. "That's up to the store managers, of course," he said, but it was too late. The newspaper headlines the next day read "INTEGRATE COUNTERS—MAYOR." By that point, everyone was relieved to resolve the situation. In the subsequent weeks, the store owners and the activists met to plan an orderly transition. Lunch counters would begin to be integrated on May 10, but only a small number of black patrons would ask to be served at first. Before long, the stores in downtown Nashville were thriving again.[45]

The Nashville sit-ins were a decisive victory, but still just one battle in the middle of a long war. The Montgomery Bus Boycott was more than four years earlier, and the major Civil Rights

Acts of 1964 and 1965 were still a long way off. For all their savvy and discipline, the members of the Nashville Student Movement could do little more by themselves. They needed to embed themselves into a larger network if they were to have an impact on a national scale.

With that in mind, a number of the student leaders, including Diane Nash, John Lewis, Bernard Lafayette, James Bevel, and Marion Barry, went on to help form the Student Nonviolent Coordinating Committee (SNCC). Jim Lawson continued to support the civil rights movement as a pastor and academic. He would eventually return to Nashville, decades later, to become a valued faculty member at Vanderbilt University, the same school where he was once expelled during the sit-ins. Marion Barry would go on to be a four-time mayor of Washington, D.C. John Lewis was elected to represent Georgia's 5th district in the US House of Representatives in 1987. Today, he is often referred to as the "conscience of Congress."

The civil rights movement was one of the most dramatic series of events in history, and it is easy to get awed by the heroism of the individual actors. The heroism of Rosa Parks, Martin Luther King Jr., Jim Lawson, John Lewis, and so many others who made such major contributions can blind us to the fact that they had absolutely no power to implement change themselves. They were, in the final analysis, nodes in a network. A movement, as the term suggests, is kinetic. It must travel from where it began to be effective. That's what a cascade does.

So whatever change you want to make, whether it is in your community, your company, your industry, or throughout society as a whole, you must start with a plan to mobilize specific constituencies in the Spectrum of Allies to influence specific institutions in the Pillars of Support. If you want to make a difference and not just a point, you must make a plan. A movement without a plan is nothing more than a revolt.

CHAPTER 6

Networking the Movement

It takes a network to defeat a network.

—GENERAL STANLEY MCCHRYSTAL

In 1979, Rick Warren was finishing up his master's degree in divinity at Southwestern Baptist Theological Seminary in Fort Worth, Texas. With a pregnant wife and less than $2,000 in the bank, he wanted to start a new congregation, but wasn't quite sure where. He began to pore through census records in search of a suitable place and finally hit on the Saddleback Valley outside Los Angeles. Although it was one of the fastest-growing communities in the country, it had relatively few churches. He did some more research and discovered that while many residents identified as Christians, they didn't attend services regularly. It seemed like he had found just the kind of place he was looking for.[1]

So in December of that same year, with his wife and four-year-old daughter, Warren packed his things into a U-Haul, headed for Orange County, and began looking for a place to live. He walked into a real estate office and introduced himself to the first agent he found, a man named Don Dale. Dale asked Warren the usual questions, what he did for a living, how much money he had to spend, and so on. Warren happily replied that he was an unemployed minister, without a congregation, and had little money. Dale found him a place to rent that day and became the first member of Saddleback's congregation, which, of course, didn't actually exist yet. Rick Warren just had that kind of effect on people.[2]

He also had big dreams. He wanted to build a congregation like no other. Yet much like Mahatma Gandhi when he returned to India from South Africa or Jim Lawson before the Nashville sit-ins, Warren didn't start planning his campaign immediately, but first set out to carefully survey the terrain. He spent three months going door-to-door, introducing himself in his own friendly way and asking people why they didn't like going to church. The people he met said the services were boring, irrelevant to their daily lives, and lacked adequate programs for kids. They also hated the outdated organ music, the formal dress, and the fact that churches were always asking for money. Warren took careful notes and began to formulate a plan to build his flock among the "unchurched" residents of Orange County.[3]

He began holding prayer groups in his small living room with sermons that focused on real, everyday problems, like how to handle discouragement, deal with stress, feel good about yourself, and take care of your family. His direct, plainspoken, and easygoing style began to attract followers, and before long he was renting out school auditoriums. He continued to dress casually, and instead of the regular hymns and organ music, his services featured an electric guitar. During the week, he tended tirelessly to his flock, making himself available for counseling in congregants' homes and on the phone. Before the end of the year, his congregation had grown to 200 members.[4]

Eventually, the long hours got to him. He collapsed right in the middle of a service. "I'm sorry, folks, I'm going to have to sit down," he told the congregation. He had been suffering from anxiety and depression for years, but the long hours and the struggle to build his church had finally gotten to him. He drove to Arizona to recuperate for a while. When he returned, he assigned everyone in the church to a small group that met every week to take over some of the load he had been bearing himself. Surprisingly, what started out as a laborsaving strategy to preserve his sanity turned out to be a hit with the congregation. As it turned out, the members loved the groups.[5]

"Now when people come to Saddleback and see the giant crowds on weekends, they think that's our success," Warren told *New York Times* reporter Charles Duhigg. "But that's just the tip of the iceberg. Ninety-five percent of this church is what happens during the week inside those small groups. The congregation and the small groups are like a one-two punch. You have this big crowd to remind you why you're doing this in the first place, and a small group of friends to help you focus on how to be faithful. Together, they're like glue. We have over five thousand small groups now. It's the only thing that makes a church this size manageable. Otherwise I'd work myself to death and 95 percent of the congregation would never receive the attention they came here looking for."[6]

In other words, the Saddleback Church is a *small world network*, just as we saw in Chapter 2. Small groups, loosely connected, but united by a shared purpose. The weekly groups build strong personal bonds. They study the Bible together, but also support each other through problems at home and at work. They visit each other when they or a family member is sick. That's what drives them to the weekend services, where they interact with other groups. And all of it is driven by the principles in Rick Warren's sermons and in his books. Warren's magnum opus, *The Purpose Driven Life,* published in 2002, has sold more than 30 million copies.

The model that arose out of Warren's collapse has also propelled his church from a local community to a global phenomenon. While the California congregation attracts upwards of 20,000 parishioners to weekend services at its 120-acre campus, his message is also being carried throughout the world. "Building the church was the first challenge," says Warren, "and we did that with small groups. Saddleback wouldn't work without our small groups—that's where people get excited about God, where church becomes really relevant for them, that's where people spring into action. But then we were given a new vision. We started to teach others how to plant churches and make them grow. Eventually our whole focus came to be summed up by this word 'purpose' and that has taken me through two books and a world-wide ministry network, training pastors and other church leaders, into a much more global orientation and a preoccupation with putting an end to poverty and AIDS in Africa and throughout the world."[7] Small groups, as it turns out, are almost infinitely scalable.

AnnaLee Saxenian has noticed a similar trend in the technology industry. While her first book, *Regional Advantage*, chronicled how Silicon Valley's network-driven economy propelled it past Boston's more hierarchical structure in the 1980s, her follow-up, *The New Argonauts*, written almost 20 years later, explains how it became a global phenomenon. The Bay Area's culture of openness and meritocracy made it an ideal place for immigrants to thrive. Many of them maintained deep ties to the region even when they returned to their home countries and started businesses there.

These linkages proved incredibly valuable on both sides, leading to profitable licenses and partnerships for the entrepreneurs returning home and opening up new markets for the US-based technology companies. Over time, some of these countries, such as India, China, Taiwan, and Israel, became particularly adept in certain technical areas and began to specialize. The links back to Silicon Valley proved to be a crucial element of success, providing a ready market, a wealth of technical expertise, and, in some cases, finance. These nascent technology hubs benefited Silicon Valley as well, providing access to new sources of talent and ideas, while spreading much of the Valley's unique cultural attributes and values. As Saxenian puts it, the "brain drain" has become a "brain circulation."[8]

Saxenian also pointed out to me that, after decades researching the entrepreneurial ecosystem in Silicon Valley and in other tech hubs across the world, she has never seen a new ecosystem form "de novo." As she sees it, the Silicon Valley ecosystem arose out of a unique set of preconditions. Unlike Harvard and MIT in Boston, universities like Stanford and UC Berkeley, where she has been on the faculty since the eighties, didn't have large established companies to collaborate with. So reaching out to nascent firms may have been more an act of necessity than design. Also, because the entire Bay Area was, in a sense, itself a start-up, there was a tendency to band together. "Everybody worked for the same company—Silicon Valley," she told me. Since then, all of the tech hubs that have sprung up around the world, from Bangalore to Beijing and Taipei to Tel Aviv, have done so, to a greater or lesser extent, through connections to the Bay Area.[9]

It's an interesting observation that explains a lot. We often hear of various regions that bill themselves as "the next Silicon Valley." They invest in technology campuses, offer generous incentives for companies to locate there, and support many initiatives designed to mimic Silicon Valley, like technology incubators, accelerators, and coworking centers. Still, they never seem to pan out, and Saxenian's insight explains why. First, by trying to build a technology hub from scratch, they miss the most important asset—Silicon Valley. It is the informal ties among entrepreneurs that make new technology centers thrive. Second, the new ecosystems that link back to Silicon Valley tend to further reinforce the Bay Area's network centrality—and primacy.

This point also exposes a crucial flaw in recent social movements such as Occupy Wall Street and Black Lives Matter. In their quest to upend the establishment, they shunned any ties to existing institutions. Instead of pulling in Pillars of Support, they actively pushed them away. As Joe Nocera observed in his *New York Times* column before the 2012 election, "ultimately, Occupy Wall Street simply would not engage with the larger world. Believing that both politicians and corporations were corrupt, it declined to dirty its hands by talking to anyone in power. The takeover of the park—especially as the police threatened to force the protestors out—became an end in itself rather than the means to something larger. Occupy was an insular movement, whose members spoke mainly to each other."

In the same 2012 column Nocera explained that the Tea Party did just the opposite. "It, too, believed that politicians were venal," he wrote, "but rather than turning away from politics, its adherents worked to elect politicians who believed in the same things they did. Yes, the Tea Party had wealthy benefactors, but their money would not have succeeded without enormous grass-roots support. Two years ago, 87 new Tea Party-elected candidates showed up in Washington. Much as you or I may not like it, they have largely succeeded throwing sand in the wheels of government. That was their goal."[10]

The Tea Party, incidentally, also shared some important attributes with the Saddleback Church. Like Saddleback, from the outside it looked monolithic, able to rally huge numbers of people to support or oppose a particular issue. There were large conferences and national spokespeople on cable TV. However, much like Saddleback's weekend services, all that is somewhat of a mirage that distracts us from the real power of the Tea Party movement.

In a study of the Tea Party in America, researchers Theda Skocpol and Vanessa Williamson found that what most motivated activists were issues in their own communities, and they banded together with other local groups who felt the same way. Their leaders were largely people of comfortable means, many of whom owned their own businesses. Often they were retired, semiretired, or homemakers. Many had previous experience in organizing community events. Inspired by CNBC commentator Rick Santelli's now famous on-air rant, these people set up groups in local cafés, community centers, libraries, and places of worship. Meetings, which often involved a speaker on a particular issue, a group discussion, or, in some cases, a movie night, were promoted with e-mails, flyers, and Meetup sites. They were largely financed by bake sales, collection plates, and other small-scale activities, As one Tea Party leader put it, "It's like being a Girl Scout mom."[11]

Once again, we see the same pattern: small groups, loosely connected, but united by a common purpose leading to real change.

WHAT MAKES A NETWORK EFFECTIVE?

A Broadway musical, like a movement, needs to attract people to it. To do so, the producers must find the right mix of tune, message, artistic expression, and commercial appeal to both engage audiences in the theater and impress critics enough to get good reviews. Millions of dollars depend on keeping people in the seats. So, if you were going to invest in a musical, what would you look for?

You might say, go with a proven team like Rodgers and Hammerstein, who produced such hits as *Oklahoma!* (1943), *South Pacific* (1949), and *The Sound of Music* (1959), all of which were Broadway legends that ran for years. Yet their 1955 production of *Pipe Dream*, performed in the heart of their creative prime, flopped. Or you might say that you need a great story, but bestselling novels like *Breakfast at Tiffany's* and *Carrie*, both of which became blockbuster movies, failed to attract audiences on stage.[12] Or maybe it's the acting, but bankable stars like Al Pacino and Bruce Willis have had horrendous failures on stage.[13] So what determines whether a Broadway musical becomes a hit or goes down in flames has long been something of a mystery.

Two researchers, Brian Uzzi and Janet Spiro, decided to unravel the puzzle. They analyzed 474 musicals that were performed between 1945 and 1989. What they found was startling. Even when controlling for factors such as competition, marketing budget, production budget, economic conditions, and the track record of the cast and crew that worked on the play, what best determined the success of any particular Broadway musical was the structure of the networks of the cast and crew.[14]

Using a metric called "Q," which measures the "small worldliness" of a particular network, they found that if very few people among the cast and crew had previously worked together, the play performed poorly in terms of both critical recognition and financial results. However, if too many people had worked together and the connections were too dense, results were similarly bad. Top performers had combinations of both, people who knew each other well and new blood that could take the team in new directions. In other words, small groups, loosely connected, but united by a common purpose are key to success on Broadway as well, and this can be represented by a measurable quantity. Similar results were found in a wide array of studies, including ones that focused on engineers at Bell Labs,[15] currency traders,[16] and the German automotive industry.[17]

This is an enormously helpful insight if we want to create a movement for change. Clearly, if connections are too loose, it will be hard for people to coordinate action. For a long time, the LGBT movement suffered from this problem. Lesbian and gay groups were diverse in geography, makeup, and their aspirations, which made it hard for them to coordinate actions. On the other hand, groups like Occupy Wall Street and the Indian National Congress were both highly dense networks, and they failed to connect with the larger populace. In the latter case, Gandhi was able to provide a bridge between the elites and everyday Indians, but Occupy seemed to revel in their disconnection, and that made it hard for them to recruit a Spectrum of Allies. For any movement to succeed, you need to have deep, personal ties among activists, but also make sure that you keep nodes open for others to connect to. That's how a movement grows and stays relevant.

Since Watts, Strogatz, and Barabási did their seminal work in the late nineties, researchers have also found that mapping networks can reveal power relationships. As Anne-Marie

Slaughter, who served as the director of policy planning in the US State Department under Hillary Clinton, has noted, "Power in networks flows from connectedness: the number, type, and location of connections a node has. . . . The most central nodes have the most connections and the highest likelihood of gaining more."[18]

In fact, shortly after the 9/11 attacks, a network scientist named Valdis Krebs was able, using publicly available data culled from newspaper reports, to determine the leadership structure of the hijackers, by determining which of the terrorists had the highest "network centrality" scores.[19] Like the "Q" metric, these are measurable quantities that we can determine by assessing how many connections a particular node has, to which other nodes it is connected, and where it is positioned in the network.[20]

For example, a high-powered CEO might sit at the top of a hierarchy but be relatively unconnected to important parts of the network (like franchisees in Blockbuster's case), and so might not be as powerful as his formal position implies. Meanwhile a subordinate, by being connected to both the CEO and crucial stakeholders within the organizational network, might wield much more influence than her position would imply.

This is what General McChrystal realized in Iraq. He saw that by virtue of being at the top of the hierarchy he had enormous authority, but often lacked the ability to influence events on the ground with the speed and agility he needed to win. That's why he put so much emphasis on increasing horizontal connections in his network, so that those lower down on the totem pole with important information could create their own information cascade and bring the required resources to bear. In a similar vein, by keeping networks open, Silicon Valley was able to connect to new ideas forming in the marketplace and adapt to them, while the much denser networks along Boston's Route 128 closed themselves off and paid the price.

The results of network studies yield important insights for any movement that seeks to create transformational change.

First, you need to create strong bonds within individual groups. That's how you build trust and operational effectiveness. Yet at the same time, you must also keep your network open, not only so that you can keep the movement growing, but so that new information and insights can flow through.

Also, to gain power, nascent movements must work to position themselves in the center of the networks around them. This has nothing to do with ideology. Many movements, including the struggles for independence in India and South Africa, and more recently, the LGBT movement, took what would once have been considered extreme positions. Yet by continually making new connections, they were able to shift the center of networks and gain influence.

HOW OTPOR WEAVED ITS NETWORK

In 1992, when Serbia's war in Bosnia was already raging, Srdja Popović was 19 years old, a freshman biology student at the University of Belgrade, and a bassist in a rock band. "At the time," he told me, "being a part of the rock community meant that you were against the war. It was very much like the identity of the sixties in the US and the war in Vietnam. Both of my parents were top journalists, so were really aware, and they were very unhappy with what was going on."[21]

It was almost inevitable that Popović would get involved when demonstrations broke out at his university to protest against the war in June of that year. The students occupied Belgrade University for 26 days and demanded Milošević's resignation, but it didn't amount to much. The protests began on the very last day of school, and pretty soon the summer beckoned, the demonstrations broke up, and the students went their separate ways.[22] As Popović remembers, "These were very 'Occupy' type of protests where we occupied the five biggest universities and lived there in our little islands of common sense with intellectuals and rock bands while the rest of the country was more or less supportive of Milošević's idea. And this is where we began to understand that staying in your little blurb of common sense was not going to save the country."[23]

Soon after, a friend convinced him to cut an organic chemistry class to attend a meeting of the center-left Democratic Party. Before long, he formally joined the party, became president of its youth organization, and met Zoran Djindjić, the leader of the Democratic Party. A former dissident who earned a PhD in philosophy while in exile in Germany, Djindjić's combination of an informal but direct style and a powerful intellect had an immediate effect on Popović.[24]

"I learned so many things from Djindjić," Popović remembers. "He was a Western type politician. He knew a lot about campaigning. He understood why it is so important to build networks on the ground. He was an organizational freak, in terms of that he was obsessed with structures and organizations and having little cells in every community. . . . He understood that it is not only the software, which is the ideology, that is important, but the hardware, which is the machinery. So this is how we started to understand the structures and activities on the ground and why it is important to have an organization on every corner."

Djindjić also indoctrinated Popović into what he called his RAT triangle: Recruit-Train-Act. The idea is that when you first recruit an activist, you want to immediately invest in the skills of that person. You want to teach the recruit how to campaign, how to organize, how to fundraise, and how to design actions. Most of all, you want to get that person immediately involved, because when people take action, they begin to take ownership and feel that the movement belongs to them, too. Eventually they become recruiters and bring new people in, and the process becomes self-perpetuating.[25]

Djindjić took Popović under his wing and encouraged him to run for city parliament in 1996. Although he was contesting a seat representing a district he had never lived in, Popović ran a vigorous campaign, personally meeting over 3,000 out of

11,000 constituents, and, at 23 years old, became the youngest person ever to win an election in the Belgrade city government. "That was the first time the opposition was united and Milošević was caught off guard. That was the first time I understood the value of unity," he remembers.[26]

Shocked by the defeat of his party, Milošević had the election results annulled, and protests erupted once again. Marches were held every evening, and Popović took a central role in organizing student protests, many of which were immensely creative. As the journalist Tina Rosenberg would later report, "A Belgrade art student made a large puppet of Milošević in prison stripes that was carried through the streets. (The student was arrested and badly beaten.) Students did street theater with bodies outlined on the ground, as at a crime scene. They poured detergent on the ground to clean up the streets after a pro-Milošević rally. When state media called the protests destructive, students built a brick wall in front of the Parliament building to argue that they were, in fact, constructive."[27] These were a foreshadowing of the tactics that Otpor later became famous for.

The student protests and the party marches were separate but coordinated. If the party march was at 3, the students would demonstrate at 1 or at 5. It went on for 100 days and was the largest mobilization in Serbian history. "This is where you needed to think about a new tactic every day to keep people busy. And you are talking about a very cold December in Belgrade," Popović remembers. So the actions they devised had to be engaging and fun for people to participate in. "This is where basically we learned the tactics; . . . 1996 was Otpor before Otpor," he told me.[28]

Eventually, Milošević bowed to public opinion and to international pressure. On February 11, 1997, he agreed to honor the elections. Opposition officials took office all over Serbia, even in Belgrade, where Djindjić became mayor. It was an enormous triumph, but soon the coalition of parties that had coalesced during the elections, called Zajedno ("Together"), descended into infighting and fell apart, much like what would happen later in Ukraine after the Orange Revolution. One of the major opposition politicians in Serbia, Vuk Drašković, even entered the Milošević government as deputy prime minister.

As soon as the heat was off, Milošević began cracking down once again. Seeing that the universities and the media could be fervent hotbeds of protests, he passed laws to bring them into tighter government control, even going so far as to fire professors who would not pledge loyalty to the regime. He also played up nationalist sentiment, convincing Serbians that the world was against them and posing himself as their only protector, while at the same time he deftly played the opposition parties against each other—they were soon lambasting each other in the media. Before long, the Serbian strongman's hold on power was greater than ever before.

Yet Popović and his friends were beginning to build a learning curve. In 1992, their protests looked much like the Occupy demonstrations that would spring up in 2011. They voiced grievances within the confines of their universities, but didn't reach much further than that. Despite their initial failure, however, the Serbian students began to understand that if you want to really make a difference, instead of just making a point or "building awareness" for your cause, you need to create traction outside of your immediate context. In Serbia, it wasn't enough to rile up some students in the major cities—you had to reach out into the rural, less educated masses from which the regime drew its strength. If you could take these away from Milošević, his power would be greatly diminished.

In 1996, the activists that went on to form Otpor learned the value of organization and unity to win elections. They also began to realize that if Milošević lost an election, he would attempt to steal it, and that could be a trigger for a mass mobilization of people from all walks of life. As Popović would later explain, "We began to understand that if we combine opposition unity, elections, large turnout, election fraud, and demonstrations, then we will get to victory. So this is when the formula was pretty much set." They also learned the value that international pressure could have. In fact, when Milošević finally validated the results of the 1996 elections, he cited the authority of the Organization for Security and Cooperation in Europe (OSCE) rather than any local constituency or authority.[29]

While Milošević was undertaking a successful counterattack against civil society, there were also increasing signals indicating that he intended to start a new war, this time in Kosovo, to rile up nationalist spirit and tighten his grip on power. The situation made Popović and his friends increasingly depressed. "It was smelling like a new war, with a very strong autocratic tendency, combined with a complete apathy in society and the opposition falling apart," Popović remembers. "This was our 'Rivendell' moment, like in *The Lord of the Rings*—everybody is quarreling and Sauron [the villain in the story] is coming. Frodo Baggins steps in and says, 'I will take the ring to Mordor, but I do not know the way.' "[30] In the famous book, that's how the "Fellowship of the Ring" that defeated the evil empire of Sauron was formed, and that's how Popović and his friends saw themselves.

In the autumn of 1998, they met in a coffee shop and decided to start anew. "We wanted to create a replica of the student protests of 1996–1997, but we also came up with the idea that we would make it a little mysterious,"[31] Popović told me. They wanted to build a strong brand and settled on the clenched fist design, patterned off of the World War II Serbian antifascist partisans, that evoked strong feelings among their fellow citizens. Their aim was to duplicate the cultural and political conditions of the student protests, but without an immediate political goal. Instead, they had a longer-term plan to build a network to fill the vacuum that the disintegration of the united opposition had left in its wake. They knew that a new election was coming in just two years, and if they could mobilize the populace and create a huge turnout, Milošević would try to steal the election and they would have a chance to create a massive uprising. That was the plan all along.

So they created a "vision of tomorrow" that encompassed three principles. The first was civil rights, such as freedom of speech, freedom of assembly, free and fair elections, independent universities, and an independent media. The second was peace with neighbors. Popović and his compatriots understood that whenever Milošević encountered a crisis at home, he would create a war abroad. Clearly, this was an unsustainable situation, and Serbia could never prosper as long as it persisted. The third was to adopt European values, such as economic liberalization and the rule of law.

Each of these was targeted at a different segment of the Spectrum of Allies, although the Otpor activists were not yet aware of the formal concept. The idea of civil rights resonated with their most active supporters, who would rally behind abstract concepts like freedom of expression. The second was targeted at the other side of the spectrum, specifically the military and Serbian veterans from failed wars in Croatia and Bosnia. If they could undermine the case for constant war among Milošević's constituents, they would rob him of a crucial base of support. The third principle, economic liberalization and European values, was designed to gain traction among small businesses that were mostly in the neutral column. As a rule, these people were more conservative and not as politically active, but they understood how the kleptocracy Milošević had installed and the economic isolation it created was robbing them of their livelihood. They also understood how their counterparts in places like Poland, Hungary, the Czech Republic, and the Baltic States were benefitting from EU ascension.

A month later, the Otpor founders met with representatives of five major student organizations at the offices of a student newspaper called *Buka* (*Noise*), where they discussed the three principles and published a document, *Declaration for the Future of Serbia*, based on them. One of those in attendance, a student at the technical university, took the additional step of posting the document on the Internet, even though few in Serbia had access at the time. Later, as it turned out, it would help mobilize support among Serbian students studying abroad and become an important asset.

At the original coffee shop meeting there were only five people present. A day later, six of their friends joined them. Together they made up the 11 founders of Otpor. Each of them brought their own affiliations. They were from varied student groups and supported different parties. "But we made a decision that the party people go on the back bench," Popović told me. They wanted to create something new that would be distinct from the history of infighting and failure that the political parties represented. "A lot of people wanted to act, but a lot of people didn't have a relationship to the political parties," he noted.

It was a move made out of desperation, but from a network perspective, it was a stroke of genius. By freeing themselves of party loyalties, but retaining their connections, the Otpor activists moved themselves to the center of the opposition movement, and, as we already know, the center of the network is where the true power lies. Moreover, because many of the university students were from rural towns, focusing on the student organizations also gave them crucial connections into the heart of Milošević's most important constituencies.

With a core group on board, Otpor's nascent movement began to act. Their first action was a graffiti campaign. They took stencils and began spray-painting the clenched-fist logo all over Belgrade. "Then, a miracle happened," Popović remembers. "Four students were arrested for putting graffiti on the walls, which was unusual . . . I don't even know why they arrested them." The young activists were sentenced to 10 days in jail.[32] It was a silly, brutish error and gave Otpor an enormous opening. That the regime made such a show of cracking down on such a small infraction gave Otpor a remarkable public relations coup.

In response, the largest opposition newspaper, *Dnevni Telegraf*, printed a copy of Otpor's clenched-fist logo along with the mission statement that the activist group had printed out on its leaflets:

RESISTANCE IS THE ANSWER!
There will be no other way.
It will be too late
When someone you know starves to death,
When they start killing in the streets,
Turn off the last light
And poison the last water well . . .
It will be too late.
This is not the system,
This is a disease,
Bite the system!
Get yourself together,
Live
THE RESISTANCE![33]

The newspaper was hit with a draconian fine. This, however, only fanned the flames further. Other media outlets actively reported the arrest of the four students, the manifesto, and the harsh penalty the newspaper endured for printing it. The movement, which only numbered about 30 at the time and didn't even have an office, looked like a powerful new force on the political scene. That was the start, and it would end in Milošević's downfall.

From there, Otpor followed the blueprint that Djindjić had supplied them with. Recruit-Train-Act. Street theater and pranks, like putting Milošević's face on a barrel and supplying a stick to hit it with, gained attention and brought people in. They would be trained and given the opportunity to act. Those further actions attracted more people to join them, who they would train to undertake further actions and recruit more activists. The regime's attempts to crack down would only create more unrest, leading to more recruitment and accelerating the cycle. As the links in the network metastasized, the process became self-perpetuating.

A splinter group, the Otpor Mothers, emerged to protest the harsh treatment of their sons and daughters in the movement. The regime's harsh treatment of mothers, in turn, only undermined its support among the general populace and won even more support for Otpor. Because many of the university students had rural roots, the movement gained crucial footholds in even Milošević's strongholds, the villages and towns far away from the sophisticated intellectualism of Belgrade. Abstract concepts like "freedom," "independence," and "economic liberalization" might lack emotional resonance, but the jailing of a student or the oppression of a mother is something that everyone can understand on a visceral level.

Otpor succeeded because it understood a few basic truths about networking a movement. To grow, you have to connect, and the more you connect, the more central you become. The more central you become, the more power you have. And with enough power, you can bring change about.

THE NEW ROLE OF LEADERS

When we think of great movements for change, we usually distill them down to the acts of a single charismatic leader. The Indian independence movement will always evoke images of Mahatma Gandhi, just like the civil rights movement will always be associated with Martin Luther King Jr. To a lesser extent, the corporate turnarounds at IBM and Alcoa are hard to separate from the leaders that drove them, Lou Gerstner and Paul O'Neill, respectively.

While it is true that these were all inspirational leaders that were indispensable to the incredible accomplishments that their movements achieved, we often mistake their effectiveness for control. We imagine them as chess masters, deftly moving pieces around the board, but that couldn't be further from the truth. In fact, they were master weavers of networks, deftly managing coalitions and forging new connections.

One leader that exemplifies this approach is Talia Milgrom-Elcott, executive director of 100Kin10, an organization that was set up to train 100,000 STEM teachers in 10 years. As a program officer at Carnegie Corporation focused on education programs, she got a wake-up call when she set up a communications training session for grantees. While those who attended found the curriculum stimulating and valuable, they were most excited about the opportunity to meet each other, compare notes, and share ideas. "How was it that so many skilled professionals, working in the same field and on many of the same issues, in some cases for decades, had little prior contact with each other?" she thought. They were, essentially, islands unto themselves.[34]

So when she set up 100Kin10, she didn't just establish yet another program with yet another approach, but rather a platform for collaboration for nearly 300 partner organizations. "Complex problems tend to have multiple interconnected roots that require multiple interconnected solutions and can benefit from a networked approach based on shared values." Milgrom-Elcott told me. "We don't offer our own ideas, we create opportunities for programs to connect with each other, share ideas, and learn together, so that a great idea in one place can cascade through the network and expand its impact."[35]

In much the same way that Milgrom-Elcott is building an ecosystem to train STEM teachers, IBM is building one to support a futuristic technology, called quantum computing, through its Q Network. Although quantum computing is still years away from practical applications, the company is already building formal links to top research organizations like Oak Ridge National Laboratory, the University of Oxford, and others on one side and future developers and users of quantum applications like JPMorgan Chase and Daimler on the other.

It has also made some of its early prototypes available to the public through its "Quantum Experience" program. "There is already a research community around quantum computing, and they're already working on things like basic quantum algorithms and quantum games," IBM scientist Jerry Chow told me. "The Quantum Experience helps support those users, but also extends the community into those who are just getting to learn about quantum computing. We're training a new generation."[36] When building a network for mobilization, it always pays to start early.

The Institute for Healthcare Improvement took a similar approach to its "100,000 Lives Campaign," which sought to enlist 1,600 hospitals in its program to implement six evidence-based procedures that would reduce needless deaths through medical error. Knowing that they couldn't train and indoctrinate that many facilities at once, the team set out to build a network approach. "We had to figure out how to support their learning. So we identified certain facilities that could act as nodes that could help support local initiatives for improvement. That's how we built scale. It was less about broadcasting information and more about harvesting the good work that was going on," Joe McCannon, who led the campaign, told me.[37] Within 18 months, more than 3,100 hospitals joined the effort and well over 100,000 lives were estimated to have been saved.[38]

At Wyeth Pharmaceuticals, which sought to transform its operations through implementing lean manufacturing methods at 16 plants encompassing 20,000 employees, it was clear to leadership that a simple dictate from the top would not get the job done. So they planned to do it in stages, creating "mini-transformations" in two or three areas at eight of the plants and then using network effects to cascade early successes throughout the organization as a whole.

Michael Kamarck, then president of Wyeth's manufacturing group, described the process this way:

> We copied the way viruses infect. We started small. We infected groups, individual groups, but then we brought in people from the other sites, who hadn't yet gotten started. We pulled them forward into the process, if you will. So, we made them part of the mini-transformation

> so that they could get infected and take the infection back. And so, first of all, we phased the 16 sites. We had early and late adopters, basically, and we used pull-forwards to seed the late sites, so they didn't feel like they were left out. In fact, some of the people from the late sites made real contributions to the process in the early sites.[39]

By pursuing a strategy of small groups, loosely connected, but united by a common purpose, replicating, in many ways, Rick Warren's prayer groups at Saddleback and the tent cities on Kreshchatyk in Kyiv and other cities in Ukraine, Wyeth was able to transform its business.

In much the same way, Gandhi connected the Indian National Congress, mostly made up of elite Hindu nationalists, with other facets of Indian society, such as Muslims, Sikhs, and untouchables. As head of the Southern Christian Leadership Conference (SCLC), Martin Luther King Jr. was only one of the "Big Six" which included A. Philip Randolph, James Farmer of the Congress of Racial Equality (CORE), John Lewis of the Student Nonviolent Coordinating Committee SNCC, the National Urban League's Whitney Young Jr., and Roy Wilkins of the National Association for the Advancement of Colored People (NAACP). Each of these had hundreds of individual chapters and affiliates. Nobody creates transformational change alone.

General Stanley McChrystal likens the role of leader to that of a gardener. During his time in Iraq, he learned that the role of leader can no longer be "that of a controlling puppet master, but that of an empathetic crafter of culture." He goes on to say that he needed to shift his focus "from moving pieces on the board to shaping the ecosystem."[40] Srdja Popović and his comrades in Otpor came to a similar conclusion, realizing that if they were ever going to make a difference, they needed to reach into all aspects of society, not just fellow students at elite universities that were early adopters of their philosophy.

Strategy, in other words, is no longer a game of chess, but a matter of widening and deepening connections. Especially today, when the world is connected as never before, power no longer lies at the top of hierarchies, but at the center of networks. In a movement for change, the role of leaders is not merely to plan and direct action, but to inspire and empower belief. So to create positive change, movements need more than shared purpose; they also need shared values. As General McChrystal wrote, "An organization should empower its people, but only after it has done the heavy lifting of creating shared consciousness."[41]

CHAPTER 7

Indoctrinating a Genome of Values

The revolutionary sees his task as liberation not only of the oppressed but also of the oppressor.

—STEPHEN BIKO

Nelson Mandela was an unlikely revolutionary. Born into a royal Xhosa family in the South African region of Transkei, he was raised by the chief with the intention of him becoming a tribal councilor. However, when he learned that a marriage had been arranged for him without his knowledge, he ran off with his cousin to Johannesburg, where he became a clerk at a law firm, in 1941.[1]

It was in Johannesburg that his involvement with the African National Congress (ANC) began. He met a variety of people associated with the movement, including Walter Sisulu, who would become a lifelong friend and colleague, as well as Oliver Tambo, with whom Mandela would become a partner in a law firm after he finished his studies. This too would become a lifelong association rooted in both the law and the revolutionary struggle.

The 1940s would be a period of transformation for both Mandela and the ANC, which, much like the Indian National Congress of Gandhi's time, was largely made up of educated elites who sought to bring about change within the system. Mandela, along with Sisulu and Tambo, as well as a number of other young activists, such as Anton Lembede and A. P. Mda, formed the African National Congress Youth League, which was far more African nationalist in nature than the older organization.[2]

"I was sympathetic to the ultra-revolutionary stream of African nationalism," Mandela would later write. "I was angry at the white man, not at racism. While I was not prepared to hurl the white man into the sea, I would have been perfectly happy if he climbed aboard his steamships and left the continent of his own volition."[3]

These views would be tempered in time. Much like Gandhi, Mandela would have to learn to conquer himself before he could overcome his enemy. Still, his views were in keeping with the zeitgeist of the moment. As the Afrikaner regime became more repressive, a stronger brand of resistance was increasingly seen to be necessary.

Life for blacks would take a turn for the worse in 1948, when the National Party, led by Dr. Daniel Malan, prevailed over the more moderate United Party led by Jan Smuts. During World War II, the United Party, which had ties to Great Britain, supported the Allies, while the National Party openly sympathized with Nazi Germany, and in the 1948 campaign it ran on a white supremacist platform of Apartheid. Its victory was, much like Donald Trump's in the 2016 American election, wholly unexpected. Nevertheless, the white Afrikaner Nationalists would dominate South African politics for almost half a century.[4]

The National Party began to implement its policy of Apartheid, which included putting restrictions on trade unions, disenfranchising the already limited political power of Indians, Coloureds (mixed race), and native Africans, outlawing mixed marriages and sexual relationships between races and mandating that races live in different areas. As this was underway, Mandela and his comrades stepped up their efforts as well. The Youth League drafted a document that called for a "Program of Action," which included boycotts, stay-at-homes, strikes, and other actions. This program was later adopted by the ANC as a whole, making direct action the official policy. Whatever hopes for working within the system had remained were now gone for good.[5]

In the years that followed, Mandela maintained his African nationalist leanings and was skeptical of building links to other insurgent elements, such as the South African Indian Congress (SAIC, which Gandhi helped found), the Coloured People's Congress (CPC), and the South African Communist Party (SACP), which he saw as a potential source of disunity and disempowerment among his people. It wasn't that he bore animosity toward any of these groups, but he felt that they diluted the power of the ANC. His friend Walter Sisulu, however, vehemently disagreed and Mandela was outvoted.[6]

Over time, as Mandela began to see the wisdom and value of collaboration he became a driving force behind the Congress of the People, a mass meeting of diverse groups that met in 1955. Over 2,000 organizations were invited, including liberal white activist groups like the Congress of Democrats (COD), which advocated for full equality among the races, including the right to vote. In June, the Congress adopted the Freedom Charter, which Mandela called a "revolutionary document precisely because the changes it envisioned could not be achieved without radically altering the economic and political structure of South Africa. . . . In South Africa, to merely achieve fairness, one had to destroy apartheid itself, for it was the very embodiment of injustice.[7]

In other words, the Freedom Charter encapsulated the movement's vision of tomorrow. It was far more than a statement of grievances. It called for fundamental change in how the affairs of state were handled. The Charter proudly stated, "only a democratic state, based on the will of the people, can secure to all their birthright without distinction of colour, race, sex or belief." Yet it also did more than that. It set down a clear set of values:

- The People Shall Govern!
- All National Groups Shall Have Equal Rights!
- The People Shall Share in the Country's Wealth!
- The Land Shall Be Shared Among Those Who Work It!
- All Shall Be Equal Before the Law!
- All Shall Enjoy Equal Human Rights!
- There Shall Be Work and Security!
- The Doors of Learning and of Culture Shall Be Opened!
- There Shall Be Houses, Security and Comfort!
- There Shall Be Peace and Friendship![8]

While to modern eyes, these may seem like fairly anodyne statements, they were, in fact, values that constrained the anti-Apartheid movement in important ways. The Freedom Charter called for universal rights, including not only for the other downtrodden races, but also for the white oppressors. It was also somewhat controversial at the time. As Mandela would remember, "Some in the ANC, particularly the Africanist contingent, who were anti-Communist and anti-white, objected to the charter as being a design for a radically different South Africa from the one that the ANC had called for throughout its history.[9]

Yet it was those constraints that made the Freedom Charter such a powerful document. Rather than a mere statement of grievances coupled with a call to overthrow the oppressors, it envisioned a society that most people throughout the world would recognize as just (and international institutions would prove to be a key Pillar of Support that the anti-Apartheid movement would learn to leverage over time). Also, because it had broad-based support, it represented shared values and shared consciousness among the entire network of organizations opposed to Apartheid. Sure, it would have been written differently if the ANC had created it alone, but values, if they are to be more than platitudes, always cost you something.

In the years and decades that followed, much of the power and respect that Mandela would gain, both in his own country and throughout the world, stemmed from the fact that he adhered to the values laid out in the Freedom Charter even when they were not to his immediate advantage and convenience. In fact, in future years when Mandela was often accused of being a communist, an anarchist, and worse, he always proudly pointed to the Freedom Charter and would note that nobody needed to guess what he believed in or was fighting for because it had been written down in 1955.

In 1962 Mandela was arrested and charged with "inciting workers through strikes and leaving the country without permission."[10] He was, of course, guilty of that and much more. A year before he had set up, along with Walter Sisulu and Joe Slovo, the leader of the South African Communist Party, a military wing of the ANC called Umkhonto we Sizwe ("Spear of the Nation" or, more commonly, "MK").

The shift from nonviolence to violence was not taken lightly, but was seen as unavoidable after a number of recent events, including the notorious Sharpeville massacre, in which police opened fire—without any warning—on thousands of unarmed civilians, killing 69 and wounding more than 400, including women and children. Although there were only 75 officers, over 700 shots were fired. Many of the demonstrators were shot in the back as they were running away.[11] The plan for violence was also constrained to sabotage and sought to avoid casualties, but increase the economic costs of Apartheid.

At trial Mandela didn't even try to defend himself. As he would later write, "It was indisputable—and in fact I did not dispute—that I was technically guilty of both charges."[12] Yet he still did all he could to make the trial work to his advantage by giving voice to the values of his cause. In court, he insisted on wearing a traditional kaross rather than European dress, and upon entering and leaving the court he would raise his fist and say "Amandla!" (Power!), to which his many supporters in the crowd would reply "Ngawethu!" (To the people!).

In his statement to the court, he explained, "there comes a time, as it came in my life, when a man is denied the right to a normal life. . . . I was driven to this situation, and I do not regret the decisions that I did take. Other people will be driven in the same way in this country, by this very same force of police persecution and of administrative action by the government, to follow my course, of that I am certain."[13] He went on to declare, "I have done my duty to my people and to South Africa. I have no doubt that posterity will pronounce that I was innocent and that the criminals that should have been brought before this court are the members of the government."[14]

He was, of course, proven right. Today, few can remember Mandela's oppressors, but his name is revered throughout the world because, like Gandhi, he committed himself not only to the struggles of his people, but to the values of his cause, which helped him to be considered a man of vision, rather than one solely of grievance.

In the years and decades that would follow, he put those values above his own personal despair during imprisonment, when he had little reason for hope, as well as during his years of triumph, when those same values would limit the power he had won and lead him to act against the wishes of many of his most ardent supporters. It was his commitment to those values, in both despair and triumph, that allowed his movement to not only prevail, but to survive victory and achieve transformational change for the long term.

Mandela would be found guilty and sentenced to five years in prison, but that would be just the beginning of his travails. Nine months into his five-year sentence, South African police raided Liliesleaf, the farmhouse that served as the headquarters for MK, the militant wing of the ANC that Mandela had helped to found, and captured its high command as well as hundreds of documents filled with plans and operational details.

The result was the famous Rivonia trial, in which Mandela and nine others were charged under the Sabotage Act. Once again, there was little doubt that Mandela, and most of the others due to their leadership in MK, were guilty (although two that had been caught up in the net were eventually acquitted), and Mandela, resigned to his fate, once again wanted to make a statement that put the blame squarely at the foot of the regime. He spoke from the dock for three hours, concluding with the lines that would become famous, "I have cherished the ideal of a democratic and free society in which all persons live together in harmony and with equal opportunities. It is an ideal, which I hope to live for and to achieve. But if it needs be, it is an ideal for which I am prepared to die."[15]

Nelson Mandela was sentenced to life in prison. He would serve 27 years, and during his incarceration, his statements were banned from public consumption. The Apartheid regime thought that by imprisoning both his body and his ideas both would eventually die out.

They were wrong on all counts.

Stephen Biko was still a college student during the Rivonia trial and its aftermath. With Mandela in prison and the ANC a banned organization, there was no national movement for him to join, no prevailing ideology for him to grasp onto, and no mentors to take him under their wing. So Biko would start anew, establishing the South African Students' Organisation (SASO) and the Black Consciousness Movement.

Whereas Mandela and the ANC had worked to free black South Africans from physical and legal oppression, Biko sought to free them from the psychological oppression brought on by decades of being treated as inferior beings in which they had learned to "feel that there is something incomplete in your humanity, and that completeness goes with whiteness."[16] This was, incidentally, an affliction that even Nelson Mandela himself suffered. On a trip abroad to gather support among African nations for MK, he boarded a flight on Ethiopian Airlines and found himself alarmed to find that the pilot was black, before chiding himself for falling into an "Apartheid mind-set."[17]

Much like Gandhi a half century before, Biko saw that in order to change the world, he and his compatriots would first have to change themselves. Unlike the ANC, the Black Consciousness Movement did not call for strikes, stay-at-homes, or other forms of conventional protest. Instead, much in the mold of Saul Alinsky, it focused on development through its Black Community Programs (BCPs), which ran self-help and literacy classes, managed health clinics, and undertook other projects that would directly benefit its constituents.[18] Another difference is that while much of the ANC's work was done underground, Biko insisted that his organization, the Black People's Convention (BPC), would only operate openly.[19]

These were Biko's values, and even after his death in police custody in 1977, they held great sway in South Africa and internationally as well. They were also, of course, somewhat different than the values put forward by Mandela and the ANC, but they were not at all mutually exclusive or even inconsistent, a point that Biko readily acknowledged. "While the BPC is nonviolent, it should not be forgotten that we are part of a movement which will be confronted with new situations that may require different strategies. We begin with the assumption that rapprochement is necessary. The BPC is not a third wing among the blacks, next to the ANC and the PAC [Pan Africanist Congress, a splinter group that broke away from the ANC]."[20]

In other words, while Biko was by no means a member of the ANC, he readily acknowledged that he shared values with others in the anti-apartheid movement, and those shared values constituted a bond that transcended the differences in their approaches. This is a recurrent theme among movements that succeed. Many of the organizations involved in the civil rights movement resented the center stage afforded to Martin Luther

King Jr. and his SCLC, but all worked together to achieve common goals. When the American Federation for Equal Rights (AFER) announced that it would seek to bring a court case to overturn Proposition 8, the amendment to the California Constitution that banned same-sex marriage, it initially encountered hostility from traditional gay rights groups.[21] When the case became a reality, though, everybody pitched in and helped.

Movements for change always feature strong personalities with varied opinions and approaches. The successful ones learn how to transcend those differences. The key is to recognize values for what they are, not dictates and not plans, but rules for adaptation that can be combined and recombined as the environment shifts, without losing their power or provenance.

VALUES AS RULES FOR ADAPTATION

Our DNA is not a blueprint or a technical specification. In fact, our genome contains only about 1.5 gigabytes of data, barely enough for a full-length movie. Its genius is that rather than specifying detailed features of our biology, it provides us with rules for adaptation—first, for chemical gradients in the womb and later for the outside environment. Genetic codes are also not monolithic, but contain various influences from different ancestors and can express themselves differently when exposed to different environmental factors.

Successful movements for change operate on a similar principle, providing genomes of values that act as rules for adaptation. For example, both the ANC and the Black Consciousness Movement had similar ancestors—namely Gandhi's Indian independence movement and the civil rights movement in the United States—but expressed those influences very differently. Nevertheless, they were—and considered themselves to be—part of the same family, much like the various organizations in the civil rights movement, such as Martin Luther King Jr.'s SCLC, John Lewis's SNCC, the NAACP, CORE, and others, despite being distinct efforts, were part of the same movement and were able to collaborate effectively.

The need to express values is obviously critical in a political or social movement, although as we have seen, many movements lack the discipline to adhere to the values they profess to hold. What is less obvious is the important role that values play in a corporate context where, just like in a political or social movement, various constituencies and institutions need to be woven together into a coherent network. Make no mistake, however—values are absolutely critical to success. For example, Irving Wladawsky-Berger, whom we met in Chapter 4, stressed to me how central values were both to IBM's decline and to Lou Gerstner's historic turnaround in the 1990s.

"At IBM we had lost sight of our values," he remembers. "For example, there was a long tradition of IBM executives dressing formally in a suit and tie. Yet that wasn't a value, it was an early manifestation of a value. In the early days, many of IBM's customers were banks, so IBM's salespeople dressed to reflect their customers. So the value was to be close to customers. Lou reminded us of that, and we realized that if our customers now wore khakis, it was okay for IBMers to also wear khakis."

"IBM had always valued competitiveness, but we had started to compete with each other internally rather than working together to beat the competition. Lou put a stop to that and even let go some senior executives who were known for infighting. He thought we should be open to ideas from the outside instead of thinking, 'if it was a good idea, we would already have done it.' He pushed these values constantly, through personal conversations, company e-mails, you name it. Eventually it all stuck."

Every effort to create transformational change is, to a certain extent, unique, with its own "vision of tomorrow" as well as its own particular Spectrum of Allies and Pillars of Support. However—and this is a crucial point—every movement must be true to itself, and that requires that it be faithful to certain values and maintain discipline.

A high level of organization and discipline can be an asymmetric advantage because it makes anything that seems like a brutal response by the powers-that-be backfire. Police beating peaceful protestors becomes impossible to characterize as "troublemakers getting what they deserve" because the movement has so clearly displayed a high level of morality and courage. Brutality is seen for what it is, the last resort of a corrupt regime. Yet movements that don't display that kind of discipline are fairly easy to discredit.

The apparent disorganization of the Occupy movement, along with the filth of its camps and the vulgarity of some of its members, turned off many in the mainstream who shared its concerns about economic inequality and the greed of financial firms. When Black Lives Matter protestors disrupted political rallies, they attracted attention to their cause, but also turned off many potential supporters. During the 2016 presidential election, a faction of Bernie Sanders supporters, branded "Bernie Bros" in the media, did great harm to their cause with their obnoxious behavior. In many cases, it only takes a few rock throwers among a cast of thousands to discredit an entire movement. Anarchy isn't a value, but simply a lack of discipline.

That's why instilling a genome of values is so crucial for success. Most activists come to their cause with the best of intentions, but in the heat of the moment, when they are insulted or violence is perpetrated on them, it's easy to fall into the trap of yelling out an epithet or picking up the nearest rock and throwing it at antagonists. It feels good to reply to a snarky social media post with one that tops it. Yet the second you respond in the moment, you risk all of the work that has come before (which is one reason that successful political movements often avoid large demonstrations until the end game).

So a crucial feature of any successful movement is training activists to internalize the genome of values so that it becomes second nature. In preparing for the "Freedom Rides" of 1961, the activists did more than just recruit volunteers, organize logistics, and set up media coverage: they held a weeklong training camp in which the volunteers were prepared for the travails ahead. They were insulted, intimidated, and denigrated, and the very real dangers that lay before them were clearly spelled out. By the end of the week the activists were ready to face hostility with restraint and dignity.[22]

CANVAS provides an entire curriculum online, including guidebooks and videos that explicitly spell out its principles. Srdja Popović told me that he considered these materials to be the organization's "unique selling proposition" and a key part of its success, along with the workshops it does with activist groups.[23] There are many who can incite a crowd and fuel passion, but very few that can provide a genome of values that will lead them to success. However, providing this backbone is crucial. In the Orange Revolution, for example, I personally felt enormous social pressure to act in accordance with the movement's values. Everyone else seemed to feel the same way.

The principle of building a genome of values is not at all limited to the political sphere, but is important to any organization. Facebook runs a six-week "Bootcamp," which every engineer, regardless of experience or expertise, must complete. It does so for many of the same reasons that the "freedom riders" set up their intensive training camp—to indoctrinate and maintain values even as the company continues to grow at a rapid pace.

"Beyond the typical training program, at our Bootcamp new engineers see firsthand, and are able to infer, our unique system of values," says Eddie Ruvinsky, an engineering director at Facebook who is deeply involved in the Bootcamp program. "We don't do this so much through training manuals and PowerPoint decks, but through allowing them to solve real problems, working with real people who are going to be their colleagues. We're not trying to shovel our existing culture at them, but preparing them to shape our culture for the future."

Incidentally, Facebook's "Bootcamp" has another added benefit. During the course of the six weeks, new employees build close bonds with each other and often maintain those bonds as they spread throughout the company, which not only provides a support system but also helps to create the "small world effect" that Duncan Watts discovered in his research. That, in turn, not only helps new information and best practices to cascade throughout the company, it also helps reinforce values. We had a similar training program at our company in Kyiv and noticed many of the same things. It is through building those kinds of informal relationships that you can transform a diverse organization from a collection of varied business units and functional departments into a true "team of teams."

In their book *Scaling Up Excellence*, Robert Sutton and Huggy Rao, both professors at Stanford's Graduate School of Business, explain "Catholic" vs. "Buddhist" approaches to values. "Catholic" organizations seek to create a strict doctrine of beliefs and practices. "Buddhist" ones are more open-ended, providing guiding principles but leaving details open to interpretation. They tend to be able to travel across cultures much more effectively, because it is the values that are being evangelized, not a rigid set of procedures.[24]

Moreover, Sutton and Rao show how taking a "Buddhist" approach can be crucial to success in today's business climate, in which the ability to adapt to a changing context can be decisive. For example, they tell the story of how Home Depot flopped in China because it stuck to its "do it yourself "strategy, which did not appeal to Chinese customers. IKEA, on the other hand, understood that its genome of values wasn't a rigid set of rules, but principles for adaptation, and encouraged local managers to make necessary adjustments. Its stores in China, which its Western customers would still recognize as quintessentially IKEA, are thriving.[25]

However, Sutton and Rao also explain that in reality, things are rarely so clear-cut, and most organizations take a Catholic approach to some things and a Buddhist approach to others. The highly successful Cheesecake Factory restaurant chain, for example, has the same menu in each of its locations, but each dish is cooked according to which ingredients can be freshly procured. McDonald's, known for its highly standardized business practices, also has a long history of successful local experiments, which resulted in hit products like the Big Mac and the Egg McMuffin. *Cosmopolitan* magazine, with 64 international editions published in 110 countries, is the most successful periodical publication in the world. Its brand book, which every local market must adhere to, clearly divides its guidelines into "must have," "can have," and "don't." CANVAS takes pains to recognize that every movement is different, but loads its training manuals with specific advice like "Break down a campaign into small and concrete tasks"[26] and "Adopt the backward planning process for creating a campaign calendar."[27] It further advises, "You need to give volunteers simple and achievable tasks that lead initially to small successes and victories."[28]

Values, it should be noted, are not solely a shield, but can also be wielded as a sword. For example, in the struggle for women's suffrage, which in many ways was the prototype for all change movements that came after, Alice Paul's band of "Silent Sentinels" picketed the White House with phrases lifted from President Wilson's own book, published just a few years earlier. How could he object, without appearing to be a tremendous hypocrite, to signs that read, "LIBERTY IS A FUNDAMENTAL DEMAND OF THE HUMAN SPIRIT" and "WE ARE INTERESTED IN THE UNITED STATES, POLITICALLY SPEAKING, IN NOTHING BUT LIBERTY," when he was, in fact, the very author of those same words?

Later, when he declared war against Germany and its allies, the suffragists once again carried Wilson's words, "WE SHALL FIGHT FOR THE THINGS WHICH WE HAVE ALWAYS HELD NEAREST OUR HEARTS—FOR DEMOCRACY, FOR THE RIGHT OF THOSE WHO SUBMIT TO AUTHORITY TO HAVE A VOICE IN THEIR OWN GOVERNMENTS." It was an inspiring message for a country to join a war, but was just as strong an argument for the women's voting rights that the president was neglecting to support.[29]

In much the same way, Apple CEO Tim Cook often speaks out about data privacy and supports the principle that consumers should own their own data. This is, by all indications, a deeply held personal and corporate value. However, as many observers have noted, it is also a potent weapon against competitors like Google and Facebook, both of which have businesses based on monetizing their customers' data.[30]

To create fundamental change, what is crucial is that values are tied to an affirmative vision of tomorrow rather than merely targeting grievances. You may, for example, think banks are greedy, but unless you have a practical plan for replacing the global financial system without causing severe economic havoc, closing them down is not an option. There are literally millions of people who work in banking, most of them good, civic-minded people. What values do you share with the best of them?

Police brutality is a horrific abuse of power, but the vast majority of law enforcement officers risk their lives every day to make us all safer. What hopes and dreams do you share with those brave, admirable people? You may believe that inefficiency stems from laziness, but unless you can present a clear plan for improvement, like the executives at Wyeth Pharmaceuticals did in their movement to implement lean manufacturing principles across the company, don't expect things to change. There are many people who can see flaws in any system, but far too few who are willing put in the hard work to actually make things better. That requires you to adapt to the hard truths of the real world, but maintain your values nonetheless.

There are few injustices in the world that can compare with the Jim Crow laws in the American South. Yet Martin Luther King Jr., in his famous "I Have a Dream" speech at the March on Washington, spoke not to black grievances, but to common values. He said, "When the architects of our republic wrote the magnificent words of the Constitution and the Declaration of Independence, they were signing a promissory note to which every American was to fall heir. This note was a promise that all men, yes, black men as well as white men, would be guaranteed the 'unalienable Rights' of 'Life, Liberty, and the pursuit of Happiness.'"[31]

Later, before the historic march from Selma to Montgomery, he declared, "I say to you this afternoon that I would rather die on the highways of Alabama than make a butchery of my conscience. . . . I'm asking everybody in line, if you can't be nonviolent, don't get in here. If you can't accept the blows without retaliating, don't get in line. If you can accept it out of your commitment to nonviolence, you will do something for this nation that may well save it. If you can accept it, you will leave those state troopers bloodied with their own barbarities. If you can accept it, you will do something that will transform conditions here in Alabama."[32]

Nonviolence and dignity were core values of the civil rights movement, but what made them powerful was that they were inextricably tied to King's vision for fundamental change: civil rights. In much the same way, when Paul O'Neill announced his vision "to make Alcoa the safest company in America," that was also inextricably tied to certain values, such as respect for employees and a passion for excellence. These, in turn, produced further changes that helped to make the turnaround at Alcoa one of the most successful in history.

For example, when workers were encouraged to suggest changes to increase safety and those changes were implemented, they started to suggest changes in other realms as well. One worker had an idea for grouping painting machines together so that the company could more nimbly respond to changes in demand for aluminum siding. Within a year, profits in the division doubled.[33] When O'Neill required that every Alcoa office throughout the world link up to an electronic network to share safety data and practices, an unusual practice in the early 1990s, they began sharing other information too, such as changes in local market prices to help the company respond, which resulted in even more profits.[34]

Values are how an enterprise honors its mission, so ends cannot be divorced from means. A crucial feature of any successful movement is training adherents to internalize the genome of values so that it becomes second nature. Successful revolutionaries are warriors, but they are also educators. Once "I Have A Dream" devolved into "Any Means Necessary," progress stalled, because values are not salves for the far left side of the Spectrum of Allies, designed to rile up the most active supporters, but are vehicles of shared purpose and shared consciousness that allow you to connect even to those who are not committed to your struggle and may even be passively opposed.

SHARED VALUES AND SHARED CONSCIOUSNESS

Values, if they are to be anything more than empty platitudes, always come with costs. To be true to the values of a just society, Gandhi had to instill among his compatriots the importance of treating Muslims and outcastes as equals, which to many meant a loss in status for themselves. In fact, as we have seen, they could not be successful until they had fully internalized the values of Satyagraha. At the Saddleback Church, Rick Warren stresses the importance of service to others and tithing earnings. Martin Luther King Jr. preached the importance of remaining nonviolent even when horrific violence was perpetrated on his people. Srdja Popović and Otpor realized early on that in order to create real change in Serbia, the band of passionate student activists needed to take into account the viewpoints of their fellow citizens in rural areas who did not share their cosmopolitan sympathies. Paul O'Neill insisted on putting safety first, to the consternation of many market observers. Lou Gerstner preached the gospel of the customer, even though that may have meant settling for less on a particular sale. To make transformational change a reality, the mission always has to come first, and the mission cannot be divorced from the values that sustain it.

That's never an easy sell, so values and their costs always need to be tied to the fundamental change that will make a positive vision of tomorrow a reality. There must be, above all, the will to make a real difference rather than just to make a point, and to do that every movement for change must overcome gaps of trust that exist along the Spectrum of Allies. That is the role that a genome of values plays.

As we discussed in Chapter 4, in every endeavor there exists a classic Prisoner's Dilemma in which the immediate gains to defection will always surpass those of trustful cooperation, even though the payoffs to building trust are always greater in the end. Values, if they are adhered to, are what help to bridge that gap. Paying the costs associated with values by appealing to deeper truths creates the shared purpose and shared consciousness that lead to empowerment. It also signals to those outside your movement that you're serious, not just an undisciplined band of rabble-rousers.

Perhaps most important, values are most powerful when they speak to shared human experiences. When, during the struggle for civil rights, the American public saw the scenes of well-dressed, well-mannered black activists being beaten by vulgar white bigots on the TV screens in their living rooms, they couldn't help but feel commonality with those who were being oppressed. That's what Martin Luther King Jr. meant when he said he was there to "cash a check" written by the founding documents of the Republic. When Nelson Mandela was accused of being a radical and a communist, he pointed to the Freedom Charter, which espoused values that any free country would recognize. When Paul O'Neill wanted to create change at Alcoa, focusing on the value of safety created a sense of shared mission among workers and management, just as Lou Gerstner's commitment to the customer helped to restore IBM to its former greatness.

At the same time, as we have also seen, when movements for change are unable to articulate a clear sense of shared values, they fail to make much headway. Occupy, by its very name, implied you needed to be willing take over public spaces to be a full-fledged member of its movement. The filth of many of its camps and the conduct of many of its members did not remind people of friendly neighbors that you'd want to barbecue with, but of a loud-mouthed nephew who wouldn't shut up at Thanksgiving dinner. John Antioco's strategy to take on Netflix was formulated and executed among a relatively small cadre of executives. While their strategy was effective, other stakeholders weren't committed to it, which is part of the reason that his successor, Jim Keyes, was able to reverse course so easily. The LGBT movement floundered for decades trying to make the American public understand what it was like to be gay, but became ascendant when it made clear that most gays want the same things that everybody else wants, to be in a committed, loving relationship and, often, to raise a happy family.

It is the assertion of shared values that leads to shared purpose and shared consciousness across the Spectrum of Allies and allows a movement to influence the institutions in the Pillars of Support that have the power to drive changes through. The way you communicate those values is through platforms and tactics, which is what we turn to next.

CHAPTER 8

Building Platforms for Participation, Mobilization, and Connection

Start doing the things you think should be done, and start being what you think society should become. Do you believe in free speech? Then speak freely. Do you love the truth? Then tell it. Do you believe in an open society? Then act in the open. Do you believe in a decent and humane society? Then behave decently and humanely.

—ADAM MICHNIK

By 1969 the Polish government's promises of creating a worker's paradise were beginning to ring hollow. It was becoming increasingly clear that the Polish economy was hitting the skids. To close the budget gap, a series of austerity measures were announced, including cuts in healthcare, housing, and wages. A year later, it was decreed that food prices would also be increased. Despite efforts to defy the basic laws of economics, even a planned economy eventually must make the numbers add up, and the regime intended to do that by squeezing the workers from both ends.[1]

The next year, in December 1970, the employees at the Lenin Shipyard in Gdansk decided to walk out on strike in order to protest the austerity measures. They stopped work and marched to the provincial party headquarters in the center of the city chanting, "We want bread! Down with Gomułka!" (Communist Party boss Władysław Gomułka). The next day, they returned in even greater numbers, and before long, the demonstration turned into a riot. The workers first began throwing stones and, later, Molotov cocktails at the party headquarters, setting it ablaze before returning to the shipyard. By this time the regime had had enough and sent the army in, and soldiers shot into the crowd, killing 4 workers and wounding 15. The ones that survived barricaded themselves in the shipyard and vowed that they would remain until their demands were met.[2]

It was, as Srdja Popović would say about the 1992 anti-war protests in Belgrade, an "Occupy moment." Much like the early version of the Serbian movement, the striking workers in Poland had grievances, but no real vision for what change should look like. Sure, they wanted higher wages and lower prices, but who doesn't? They also neglected to make a clear plan. There were no efforts to identify a keystone change, mobilize a Spectrum of Allies in order to influence Pillars of Support, build a genome of values, or network the movement. They simply expected that by causing a commotion they could achieve their aims. Their efforts, perhaps not surprisingly, failed.

Over the next decade, discontent in the country grew. An intellectual movement, led by Jacek Kuron, an ejected party official, Karol Modzelewski, a university professor, and Adam Michnik, a student at Warsaw University, began to envision a new path for change. Instead of fighting the regime directly, they aimed to mobilize the Polish people against it. "The immediate task of opposition intellectuals," Michnik wrote, is to build "a real day-to-day community of free people."[3] They also recognized, much as Popović and his friends at Otpor would later on, that there was little intellectuals and students could do by themselves. Change would only come when they built an alliance between the disaffected elites and the workers. To attract the workers, they would also need the Catholic Church, which even after decades of Communism remained tremendously influential in the country. Based on those crucial insights, the contours of a plan began to form.

The intellectuals formed the Workers Defense Committee, known by its Polish acronym, KOR, to act as a platform for collaboration with their Spectrum of Allies and to attract constituencies with higher thresholds of resistance to change. When strikes broke out in the latter half of the decade, instead of ignoring them as they did in 1970, the intellectuals pledged solidarity with the workers and opened a new front in the struggle. Knowing the regime was sensitive to its global image, they also began courting allies in the international community, giving interviews to foreign journalists, and establishing committees made up of Polish expatriates living in cities like London, Paris, and New York. Another action they undertook was to establish a "flying university" that would hold lectures to help indoctrinate a genome of values among its growing dissident network. Before long, KOR was achieving small victories, proving itself to be effective at mobilizing allies and pulling in pillars to build increasing political clout.[4]

By 1980, the regime was in deep trouble. It had borrowed money from abroad in order to placate the demands of the workers and was now deeply in debt. At the same time, productivity had plummeted, capital was scarce, and corruption among officials was rampant. The Polish government, after decades of mismanagement, had become both financially and morally bankrupt. Once again, food prices were raised to cover the debt, and the regime braced itself for the inevitable public discord. Strikes immediately broke out and, thanks to the Western media allies that KOR had built up over the years with outlets such as Radio Free Europe and the BBC, the unrest was widely publicized throughout Poland.[5]

The underlying forces had been building for years. The incompetence of the communist regime and the now extensive linkages between the workers, the intellectuals, and the Catholic Church had created the conditions for a network cascade to erupt. All that was needed was a trigger to set things in motion, and it was about to come from an unlikely and unexpected place.

Anna Walentynowicz arrived in Gdansk as a war orphan in 1945 and began working at the Lenin Shipyard in 1950. She was a hard worker and well liked, but she also had a rebellious streak, helping to organize the ill-fated strikes in 1970 and tirelessly advocating for her fellow workers on issues both large and small. In 1978 she joined a group of activists who were working to establish private trade unions (previously, all unions were controlled by the Communist Party). Over time, she emerged as a nexus between the disaffected workers and the nascent dissident movement.

It's not exactly clear why the regime chose, with tensions already running high in 1980, to fire Walentynowicz in August of that year after 30 years of service. Maybe the officials thought that by removing her from the picture they would break the link between the workers and the activists. Or maybe she just finally wore out their patience. Whatever the reason, it was a foolish blunder and one the Communist Party would quickly regret.

Over the next few days allies of Walentynowicz began planning a strike. This time, they would avoid many of the mistakes made in 1970. Instead of rashly walking out, they made sure to prepare the ground beforehand, quietly building support and printing out thousands of leaflets detailing Walentynowicz's years of service, explaining the injustice of her dismissal, and underlining the need for workers to advocate for themselves. "Anna Walentynowicz has become unacceptable," the text read, "because she defended others and could organize her co-workers." It then continued, "If we are not able to resist this, there won't be anybody who will speak out against raising work quotas, breaking safety regulations, or forcing people to work overtime."[6]

When the strike began, many of the workers wanted to march down to the party headquarters in the center of Gdansk, but the organizers had learned from their experience in 1970 that would lead them nowhere. Instead, they announced that everyone would remain in the shipyard. Delegates would be elected to form a negotiating committee, and no further work would be done until they got satisfaction. Their first demands were that Walentynowicz would be brought to the shipyard (in the director's car), and that the negotiations would be broadcast to the workers through the public address system. Lech Walesa, an electrician who, like Walentynowicz, was fired for political reasons, would lead the negotiations.[7]

It was to be the trigger that would set a cascade in motion. Unlike during the ill-fated strikes of 1970, the workers were no longer an island unto themselves, but linked into a larger network. They immediately notified Jacek Kuron and the KOR in Warsaw, who quickly got the word out to foreign journalists. The news was then broadcast back to Poland through Radio Free Europe, Voice of America and the BBC, which allowed the movement to navigate around government censorship. They had also identified a keystone change: instead of merely asking for better working conditions, higher wages, and lower prices, they demanded the creation of their own trade union to represent them. They were no longer just shouting for bread, but demanding justice for all Polish workers.[8]

It resonated. As the news filtered out, thousands of workers began striking to support their brethren at the Lenin Shipyard. At first, it was mostly among neighboring factories in the Gdansk region, but before long workers in other cities, following developments closely on international media, started walking out too. As the dominoes began to fall and the regime was confronted with a nationwide strike, it was forced to negotiate. Outmatched by a united opposition and an already crippled economy, it had no choice but to give ground. The Solidarity trade union would be established, first in Gdansk and then throughout Poland, with Lech Walesa as its chairman.[9]

In the years that followed, Solidarity grew in power. As its membership swelled, it began to include not only industrial workers, but also professionals, such as doctors, teachers, engineers, and even police officers. By calling a nationwide strike, it could paralyze the entire country. This was an unprecedented situation in the Eastern Block, which undermined Poland's party leaders with their overlords in Moscow and created a delicate situation for Solidarity's leaders.

Beyond Poland's borders, the Soviet tanks always loomed large. If the trade union pushed too hard, it risked an invasion, like those that had already taken place in Hungary in 1956 and Czechoslovakia in 1968. Yet at the same time, after feeling the first taste of political power in decades, its membership was constantly agitating for better conditions and more freedoms. Eventually, Solidarity's constant push for greater reforms proved to be too much, and on December 13, 1981, the regime declared martial law. Public gatherings and strikes were banned, most of Solidarity's leadership, including Walesa, were arrested, and the ones who somehow eluded the authorities were forced to run and live in hiding.[10]

The flame sparked by Solidarity could not be extinguished entirely. Although the trade union could not operate openly, it retained its moral power and was able to continue many activities surreptitiously. An underground press sprang up. Church groups formed secret committees that would help maintain a dissident infrastructure, and the "Flying University" began its lectures once again. The activists also turned to a new weapon, boycotts, which were focused on the unions that the regime formed to replace Solidarity as well as the government-run media.[11]

The media boycott proved to be problematic. It called for people to protest the government's propaganda and lies by not watching the evening news. But ordinary Poles sitting at home with their TV sets turned off could achieve little. Sure, it might give them some personal satisfaction, but it lacked the power to signal their disapproval to their neighbors or to the regime. It also did nothing to build connections, and without connections, there could be no cascade.

Yet the residents of the small city of Świdnik found an ingenious way around these constraints. Every night when the newscast started at 7:30, they went for a walk and placed their TV sets in the window facing out so that everybody could see that they were refusing to watch. Others took the idea even further and brought their TV sets with them in baby strollers and wheelbarrows, which added to the fun, satirical spirit of the protest. No signs were held and no chants rang out, but the message being sent was unmistakable. It was a quiet "walking protest," and it was fun, cost little, and had minimal risk of provoking a crackdown by the regime. After all, who could object to getting a little fresh air? Certainly, it was not a prosecutable offense, even under martial law.

Before long, similar "walking protests" spread across the country, and the country's rulers began to look ridiculous. With thousands of its citizens openly mocking it, eventually the government felt it had to respond, moving the evening curfew from 10 p.m. to 7 p.m., before the evening news came on. Yet that made an already weak regime seem even more hollowed out and illegitimate. Who could be afraid of a regime that was scared of people going out for a leisurely evening stroll?

"If the resistance is done by underground activists, it's not you or me," one of the Solidarity supporters would later say. "But if you see your neighbors taking their TV for a walk, it makes you feel part of something. An aim of the dictatorship is to make you feel isolated. Świdnik broke the isolation and built confidence." These and similar protests, such as people switching their lights on and off to signal that they were listening to outlawed Solidarity radio broadcasts, kept the movement going during the dark days of martial law. Poland's communist regime finally crumbled in 1989.[12]

PLATFORMS FOR PARTICIPATION AND MOBILIZATION

In their book-length study comparing 323 violent and nonviolent resistance campaigns between 1900 and 2006, Erica Chenoweth and Maria Stephan found that nonviolent activists are nearly twice as likely to achieve their goals as violent ones. At first glance this seems implausible or, at best, naive. How could a bunch of hippies in T-shirts outperform hardened and committed rebels carrying AK-47s?[13]

Yet take a closer look, and it becomes clear that nonviolent activists have distinct advantages over armed rebels. First, an armed group is mostly limited to men of fighting age, which greatly reduces the number of people who can actively participate. Those who do join the struggle must also have an extremely high level of commitment. Not only do they need to be willing to risk physical harm and even death, they also forgo the ability to participate in daily life. Unlike nonviolent activists, they can't regularly go to work, take care of their families, or meet with friends. They also face moral barriers. Violent campaigns kill people. Those people have families and others that love them who will actively work to sway public opinion against the movement. Finally, armed resistance movements are far more limited in their actions. While nonviolent campaigns have a wide array of tactics available to them, including boycotts, street theater, marches, strikes, and many others as well, violent campaigns are mostly limited to military confrontations, which, given the superior resources of a nation state, they are unlikely to win.[14]

Nonviolent campaigns have very few barriers to participation. Everybody, from the youngest child to the meekest senior citizen, can join in. I personally witnessed this on the

Maidan in Kyiv in 2004. Nobody hesitated to bring their families to demonstrations and, in fact, many wanted their young children to see history unfold. Pensioners would eagerly bring blankets and food to the "tent city" located just a few hundred yards from the Maidan. Middle-class professionals would attend protests when they could and then run back to the office to get work done. As I noted in Chapter 1, during the height of the Orange Revolution, many companies allowed employees to attend the protests in shifts, with half of the office going out to the streets and then returning so that the other half could participate. Those who didn't sympathize with the movement had to sit and work quietly in a corner, feeling left out and isolated.

In the final analysis, it is this participation advantage that proves to be decisive. In fact, Chenoweth and Stephan show that "a single unit increase of active participants makes a campaign 10 percent more likely to achieve its ultimate outcome."[15] That's why successful change efforts work hard to make it as easy as possible to join in. Clearly, deep commitment is essential for any change effort. However, before you can have commitment, you must have participation.

Let's return to the Institute for Healthcare Improvement (IHI) and its "100,000 Lives Campaign" that was discussed in Chapter 6. The healthcare industry, populated as it is with high-status professionals and often conflicting stakeholders, is famously resistant to change. So a key part of IHI's strategy was to lower barriers to participation, so that early adopters could not only join its movement but also easily recruit their friends and colleagues. It did so by identifying and eliminating points of friction.

First, rather than requiring an extensive application process, a simple fax from the hospital CEO, along with a commitment to share mortality data, was enough to join the movement. Instead of including every improvement it had identified during its years of research, IHI narrowed the list down to six procedures, which were chosen not only for impact, but ease of implementation. For each of these, IHI provided "change kits" complete with how-to guides. And the participating hospitals were not even required to adopt all six procedures, but were free to choose those best suited to their organization.[16]

A lot of thought was also put into the procedures themselves, and in some cases, simple but ingenious solutions were contrived. For example, one of the procedures that the team identified was to keep the heads of patients on ventilators elevated at a 45-degree angle to reduce the risk of pneumonia. The change kit suggested drawing a line on the wall behind the patient's bed so that it would be obvious when it dipped below that level. That enabled not only doctors and nurses, but families, orderlies, and even janitors, to monitor the 45-degree standard.[17] Much like in Świdnik during the Solidarity movement, you didn't need any special abilities or supreme sacrifice to help make change happen.

As the work of Chenoweth and Stephan suggested, IHI didn't focus on recruiting hard-core healthcare warriors for its battle against preventable medical errors—it recruited everybody, and it worked. After the 100,000 lives goal was achieved, IHI launched a campaign to save 1 million lives and then 5 million lives. Simple things can sometimes have enormous impacts.

Or consider England's National Health Service (NHS), a truly mammoth organization with 1.3 million employees serving 54 million citizens. Transforming an organization of that scale presents unique challenges. With that in mind, a group of change activists within NHS established a "Change Day," on which employees pledge to do one thing to improve the lives of patients. When it was established in 2013, it immediately became a roaring success. In that first year there were 189,000 pledges for action, and that figure rose to 800,000 in the second year. Many of these actions were small. For instance, employees who work with older people at University Hospital Leicester wore continence pads for a day to see how it feels for their patients. Staff at Countess of Chester Hospital decided to change the paint on the walls to colors that would be more comforting to dementia patients. Each initiative made a small difference, and multiplied by hundreds of thousands, it created a real impact.[18]

Change Day was, in many ways, in much the same spirit as the Recruit-Train-Act strategy Otpor used to build the movement that resulted in the ousting of Milošević. Encouraging people to act, even if those actions are small, allows people to internalize and take ownership of a movement for change. Or, as Helen Bevan, Chief Transformation Officer for the NHS Horizons team, put it to me, "Programmatic methods have their place, but if you want to create change on a truly massive scale, a top-down approach on its own doesn't work so well. You need to get people invested in change. They have to own it."[19]

Another initiative at NHS is the "School for Change Agents," a free five-week online course addressing subjects like, "How to Rock the Boat and Stay in It," "How to Tell Your Narrative," and "Rethinking Resistance to Change." Free to anyone who wants to enroll—whether they are employed by NHS or not—the course attracted 8,000 students in 2018. Each of those students can then recruit their friends and colleagues to contribute to initiatives or, even better, start their own. That's how you create the conditions in which a cascade can arise.

In a sense, this all may seem fairly obvious. The notion that to have a popular uprising you first need to be popular is so tautological that it borders on the ridiculous. Still, a surprising number of change efforts voluntarily forgo their participation advantage by adopting tactics that exclude wide swaths of potential supporters.

Consider again the Occupy movement. Besides being unable to articulate a vision for the change it wanted to see, its very name implied that participation was limited to those who were willing to sleep in a park. If you weren't willing to "Occupy," then how could you really be a full-fledged member of the movement? It also somewhat limited its actions to a single tactic. You couldn't very well start handing out leaflets in neighborhoods and expect to get support (especially from those with a park nearby). Nobody wants a bunch of activists occupying their neighborhood. To openly show support for Occupy might have seemed tantamount to an invitation!

Further, as we saw in Chapter 3, when Congressman John Lewis asked to participate at an Occupy rally, he was refused. The reasons given were varied, from the fact that he was part of the "two-party system" to that he failed to follow the arcane rules of the movement's events. Any way you slice it, the message was clear: only the anointed belong, all others are not welcome.

It's also not clear what the activists expected to achieve by their actions. Occupy's choice of tactics represented a massive investment in time and effort—millions of man-hours if you count all 951 cities—but cost their opponent little. Why would a banker sitting in a comfortable, air-conditioned office care if a bunch of crazy people wanted to sleep on the street? Maybe some felt a bit uneasy as they passed by Zuccotti Park carrying their morning coffee from Starbucks, or perhaps when the car service happened to drive by on their way to an expensive lunch to entertain clients, but for the most part they went about their business unfettered. The protestors, on the other hand, were greatly restricted from taking part in everyday life because they had to occupy the park. Eventually, their numbers dwindled and the park was cleared. Not a single Wall Street executive got so much as a parking ticket in the process.

Other recent movements, such as Black Lives Matter and the Bernie Sanders political campaign, fell into similar pitfalls. Instead of reaching out, they seemed to revel in sticking their fingers in the eyes of potential allies, because to them only the most pure of heart belonged. Any deviation from strict doctrine was apostasy. That may rile up the most faithful supporters, but it alienates the rest of the Spectrum of Allies, and by limiting participation, greatly reduces the likelihood of success.

In order for a movement's tactics to be effective, they must focus not merely on making a point, or "raising awareness" of an issue, but on actually making a difference. They must be part of a larger strategy to mobilize constituencies in the Spectrum of Allies to influence institutions in the Pillars of Support. Also, especially in the beginning, tactics must be designed to be cheap, low risk, low involvement, and easy to replicate to maximize potential for participation.[20]

Consider once again Otpor's "barrel prank" from the Introduction of this book. The activists took a rusty barrel and painted Milošević's face on it along with the words "Bash his face for a Dinar!" It cost them next to nothing. It happened at a time and place of their choosing, so it was relatively low involvement. It was also low risk—the activists were nowhere near the barrel, but down the street sipping coffee at a café the whole time—and it was easy for passersby to participate. They just needed to put a dinar in the barrel (about two cents) and whack away. What's more, it was fun—and funny! It didn't make people feel angry, it made them feel empowered.

The barrel prank was also designed to work as part of a larger strategy. The street they chose was full of fashionable shops and cafés, exactly the type of place where they would find people who either passively supported or were neutral to their movement and who would have been unreceptive to a rowdy band of young activists marching and shouting slogans and epithets, but were entertained by the clever bit of street theater that the barrel prank represented. By alerting key media outlets of their plans, which allowed them to capture the scene of out-of-shape cops struggling to wrestle the rusty barrel into their tiny squad car, they also pulled in a key Pillar of Support. Throughout the two-year campaign that led to the "Bulldozer Revolution" that ousted Milošević, journalists faithfully covered Otpor's every move. One of the reasons was that they always made great copy.

"You either disrupt, you mobilize, or you draw people from the middle of the spectrum. These are the three purposes of every tactic," Srdja Popović of Otpor and CANVAS told me.[21]

The barrel prank achieved all three. Ordinary citizens bashing Milošević's face on a barrel was certainly disruptive to the regime, which is why the police came and wrestled the barrel into a squad car. It mobilized the people who took a swing, and it amused those who watched but weren't quite ready to participate. Surely some went home that night and regretted not joining in.

Occupy's takeover of Zuccotti Park, on the other hand, was certainly disruptive, but to ordinary citizens, not the bankers they sought to overthrow. It may have helped to mobilize supporters, but not for long. Nobody is content to sleep in a park forever. As for those in the middle, they were not won over in the slightest. Many, in fact, were turned off. Worst off all, it was incredibly resource intensive: those who occupied the park could not effectively hold down a job, care for a family, or maintain friendships outside the relatively small band of protestors. Once the occupation failed, so did the movement. Occupy was never really taken seriously again.

Today, of course, the Internet is a major asset for mobilization, especially social media sites like Facebook and Twitter. Although often denigrated as "slacktivism" by critics, Internet campaigns meet all of the requirements of a successful platform for mobilization. Internet-based tactics tend to be low-risk, low involvement, cheap, and easy to replicate. They can also be enormously constructive.

Zeynep Tufekci, a longtime activist and academic, describes several particularly successful initiatives in her book *Twitter and Tear Gas*. One, called 140journos, used citizen journalists to get around the Turkish government's censorship and report on events around the country.[22] Another effort, @TahrirSupplies, coordinated medical supplies for the protests in Cairo. Run by four Egyptians who had never met each other in person and only two of whom were in Cairo, it proved remarkably efficient in getting resources to where they were needed most. At one point, it raised over $40,000 for some much-needed surgical equipment in less than five hours.[23]

Yet the mobilizing power of the Internet and social media is both a blessing and a curse. On the one hand, it is an incredibly efficient way to get a message out. On the other, it is so successful at attracting admirers that it's easy for nascent movements to forget that it is only the first part of the recruit-train-act triangle. If you only recruit people, but don't get them to act, then there isn't much use in recruiting them in the first place. If they do act, but haven't been trained and indoctrinated into the genome of values, the results can be even worse, because they will be likely to act in ways that discredit the movement.

Make no mistake. Movements, as the name implies, must be kinetic to be successful. They need to start in one place and end up somewhere else, evolving and changing along the way. Every tactic needs to be a platform for participation, mobilization, and connection. It also must target specific constituencies in the Spectrum of Allies in order to influence institutions in the Pillars of Support.[24] Perhaps even more important, a movement for change needs to realize that the battlefield is always shifting and that their own tactics will often alter it in ways that don't necessarily favor them.

ACTION AND REACTION

In President Bush's 2004 State of the Union Address, he took a hard line on the issue of gay marriage, criticizing Massachusetts's recent decision to allow same-sex unions. It seemed like a smart move. Protecting the idea that marriage was to be strictly defined as a sacrament between a man and a woman was popular at the time, and many people believed that activist judges were ignoring the popular will by ruling in favor of LGBT plaintiffs. Yet Bush's remarks were to have unintended consequences that would set a series of events in motion that no one could have predicted.[25]

Gavin Newsom, then the young and charismatic mayor of San Francisco, happened to be in attendance and was appalled that the president of the United States, in the middle of fighting two wars, was taking time to condemn gay citizens and deny their right to marry. Incensed, he resolved to do something about it. When he returned to San Francisco, he began performing same-sex weddings at City Hall. As soon as word got out, there were lines down the street of couples waiting to tie the knot.[26]

For gay rights groups, it was seen to be an enormous victory. "The dams were bursting," exclaimed Susan Sommer of Lambda Legal, a gay rights group.[27] "The Newsom thing made everybody feel that the battle was on," echoed Mary Bonauto, a prominent civil rights lawyer at the Gay & Lesbian Advocates & Defenders.[28] Yet the triumph was to be short-lived. Within a month the California Supreme Court halted the San Francisco marriages, and in 2008 the state passed Proposition 8, a constitutional amendment specifically outlawing same-sex marriages by referendum. It seemed like Newsom's actions had backfired. Instead of giving the idea of gay marriage a boost, he had inadvertently mobilized the forces against it.[29]

Yet if the Newsom marriages led to a setback, Proposition 8, ironically, proved to be a boon to gay marriage advocates. It's one thing to oppose altering the sacrament of marriage; it is quite another to deny couples who love each other the right to spend their lives together and to sanctify that union. That is, of course, a subtle distinction, and in fact, both amount to largely the same thing. Still, it proved to be decisive. One gay activist even went so far as to call Proposition 8 "the greatest thing that could have ever happened."[30]

As it turned out, the conservatives opposing same-sex marriage had misread the polls and overreached. Yes, most people, when asked, weren't crazy about the idea. It seemed unnatural. Everybody who had grown up with the idea of marriage as a union between a man and a woman didn't see any good reason for that to change. At the same time, however, most people didn't have strong feelings about the issue either, and most of the opposition tended to lie closer to the center of the Spectrum of Allies than to the extreme.

The combination of seeing perfectly respectable same-sex couples getting married in Massachusetts, San Francisco, and elsewhere, along with the harshness of Proposition 8, seemed not only unjust, but downright cruel, and shifted opinion in the opposite direction. The United States Supreme Court ruled in favor of gay marriage in 2015.

One of the lead attorneys arguing in favor of the LGBT activists was Ted Olson, a prominent conservative Republican attorney.[31] In a *Newsweek* op-ed, he laid out his case. Olson wrote that legalizing same-sex marriage wasn't strictly a gay issue, but would be "a recognition of basic American principles." Allowing gays to marry, he argued, wouldn't weaken the institution of marriage, but strengthen it by extending the right to make a covenant to more American citizens.[32] The argument was eerily reminiscent of Martin Luther King Jr.'s call to make good on the promises of the Declaration of Independence and the US Constitution. In the final analysis, the assertion of commonality, not difference, made marriage equality a reality. Lasting change can only be made on the basis of shared values and shared consciousness.

Unfortunately, the cycle of revolution and counterrevolution does not always end so happily. As we have already seen, the internal backlash against John Antioco's bold strategic moves to invest heavily in a digital platform and to cut late fees created the tensions that ultimately led to his departure from the company. His successor, Jim Keyes, reversed the strategy, focused efforts on reviving the retail operation and lost further ground. The once dominant company never recovered.

PLATFORMS FOR GOVERNANCE, COHESION, AND COORDINATION

Movements for change tend to be decentralized, with various factions and interests. To prevail against the British, Gandhi often needed to act as a broker between elite Hindus, peasants, outcaste "untouchables," Muslims, and Sikhs. The coalition behind the civil rights movement was known as the "Big Six,"[33] each of their leaders representing different constituencies and interests. In the struggle against Apartheid in South Africa, Nelson Mandela's African National Congress led an alliance of seven distinct organizations,[34] all of which signed the Freedom Charter. In each case, the various components within the coalition had their own factions, local chapters, and tensions.

Obviously, the decentralized nature of movements raises serious issues of governance and coordination that can cause things to spin out of control. In some cases, a wise and charismatic leader like Gandhi or King can, largely through force of personality and charisma, help hold things together. However, all too often, things devolve, and that usually spells disaster for the movement.

That was exactly the problem that General Stanley McChrystal faced in Iraq. As Commander of Special Forces, he had enormous authority over the units under his command, but little ability to compel action at partner agencies, such as the CIA, the State Department, law enforcement agencies, and others. To be successful, he realized that he needed to be able to establish some semblance of governance and coordination.

He found one part of the solution in liaison officers. Usually, these roles were given to officers nearing retirement or simply substandard officers who weren't fitting in. However, McChrystal realized that by upgrading liaison officer positions and awarding those roles only to his best people, he could build linkages and weave a network that could engender trust and help information cascade to where it needed to go.[35]

Since leaving the military, his consulting firm, the McChrystal Group, has implemented similar practices at civilian organizations. Every executive today complains about "silos" in his or her enterprise that restrict the flow of information. Yet the real problem isn't silos—which are somewhat inevitable—but how they are connected.

One of McChrystal's clients, Eastdil Secured, is an investment bank that puts together complex real estate transactions. To succeed in a high-value, ultra-competitive market, it must adapt quickly to constantly changing investment conditions and respond with clarity. By installing highly respected liaisons at each of its offices that are responsible for helping information to flow, the emergence of a new trend in one market can immediately be transmitted to other offices so that they can be on alert for signs of similar things happening with their clients.

Another platform that McChrystal used to weave connections is the Operations and Intelligence (O&I) forum. These are meetings, usually held among a core set of people but open to anybody in the wider organization through videoconference. Meetings are held regularly, usually daily or weekly, and are made up of short briefings on anything important that is going on. The O&I forum is designed to ensure maximum communication across a diverse set of actors. It is not run by the highest-ranking officer, but by a meeting coordinator, and it is composed of five-minute updates.

In the military version, thousands would tune into daily O&I meetings, including a wide array of partner agencies as well as military officers and frontline soldiers in the field. However, in *One Mission: How Leaders Build a Team of Teams*, Chris Fussell, McChrystal's former aide-de-camp and currently president of his consulting group, explains how the format has also been implemented at organizations as diverse as Under Armour, Intuit, a state agency in Oklahoma, and the Eastdil Secured real estate investment bank mentioned above. It works in the private sector for many of the same reasons it worked during the Iraq war: at the speed at which events move today, agility and interoperability often trump careful, deliberative planning, so we need to infuse traditional bureaucratic hierarchies with network mechanisms. Fussell calls this the "hybrid model."

Unlike a traditional meeting, the purpose of the O&I forums is not to make decisions, but to widen and deepen linkages and cascade information to where it needs to go in an operational cadence. So, for example, if some of those tuning in find one of the briefings relevant to a present issue they are facing, they can follow up offline, get more details, and act accordingly. "The [traditional] meeting structure is based on an outdated bureaucratic model," Fussell told me. "We need to reimagine meetings around a network model, where the goal is not to necessarily make decisions, but to share information so that decisions can be made and executed at the tactical level."[36]

Otpor had its own version of the O&I forum that it called networking meetings. As the movement grew, branches of the activist group sprung up in cities across Serbia. At first, these were larger population centers with large universities, like Novi Sad and Kragujevac, but then they spread to smaller cities with strong opposition sentiment, like Čačak and Subotica and finally to even smaller towns in areas traditionally loyal to the regime. At its height, Otpor had as many as 70 chapters and needed a platform to provide some form of governance and cohesion, which is what the networking meetings were designed to do.[37]

Unlike McChrystal's O&I forums, these were very low-tech affairs. Serbia is a small country, and even the farthest-flung village is no more than a three-hour drive away from Belgrade. So every two weeks, two or more representatives from each Otpor chapter would make the trip and meet either at the Otpor office or, more often, at a law office where Nenad Konstantinović, who coordinated the meetings, worked.

Networking meetings would begin with an overview and update of the strategy, so that everybody was informed on what was being done centrally, including what constraints were being imposed and what was being done with the major opposition parties. Then each chapter would begin its own updates. Everything was directed at comparing notes and building horizontal connections, rather than giving top-down orders. If one branch came with an idea that proved successful, the other branches would quickly adopt it. Srdja Popović called this practice "horizontal copy-paste."

For example, in Niš, Serbia's third-largest city, police arrested some activists for wearing Otpor T-shirts, which outraged the town because these were star pupils at the local high school. So the mayor of the town went to the police station in an Otpor

T-shirt demanding that the students be released or that he be arrested for the same offense. Immediately upon hearing about it, other Otpor chapters decided to talk to their mayors and explain to them how they could win political points by doing the same.

In other cases, successful local initiatives could be adopted nationally. One of the challenges that Otpor faced was that the regime was portraying them as unpatriotic. An activist from Niš suggested that they take steps to position Otpor as the voice of true patriotism, and 100,000 posters declaring "Resistance Because I Love Serbia" were printed up and distributed around the country. It was to be one of Otpor's largest and most successful mobilization campaigns. In many ways, it was very much the same as when one lone McDonald's franchisee created the Big Mac, which eventually became emblematic of the organization as a whole.

Platforms for governance and cohesion like the O&I forum and Otpor's network meetings transform decentralized chaos into a network for adaptation. A seemingly random event, when connected to similar events in other places, allows information to cascade, forms a trend, and gives the opportunity to take action far earlier than would otherwise be possible. It is this ability to adapt and evolve that often makes the difference between success and failure. As the challenges of the marketplace evolve, you need to continually empower change from within.

Participation matters. In fact, as Chenoweth and Stephan's research shows, it is often decisive. That's probably why every successful change effort I studied, whether it was 100Kin10's movement to train 100,000 STEM teachers, the Institute for Health Improvement's campaign to cut down on medical errors, or Wyeth Pharmaceuticals' drive to implement lean manufacturing techniques across 16 production sites encompassing 20,000 employees, put serious thought and effort into designing effective platforms to build the participation, cohesion, and governance that allows information to cascade.

SCHWERPUNKT

In his efforts to reform the Pentagon, Colonel John Boyd emphasized the German Blitzkrieg concept of *Schwerpunkt*, or focus on action as both a military doctrine and a means of driving change. The idea is that instead of trying to defeat your enemy with overwhelming force generally, you want to deliver overwhelming force and win a decisive victory at a particular point of attack. Boyd's prescription for uncovering the most favorable *Schwerpunkt* was the Observe-Orient-Decide-Act or OODA loop, which allows you to continually adapt to a changing environment.[38]

For example, Otpor's barrel prank made good use of the *Schwerpunkt* because it focused on an unprotected, high-value target: a fashionable street where people somewhat sympathetic to the movement were concentrated. The Tea Party focused on the sparsely attended town halls held by Republican candidates, where they could fairly easily make up an overwhelming force.

Yet *Schwerpunkt* is a dynamic, not a static concept. A successful action or campaign shifts the battlefield and forces the opponent to adopt countermeasures. So the success of any particular action renders that action less powerful the next time around. That's where the OODA loop comes in. You need to be constantly observing and reorienting yourself in order to make decisions and take actions that are best suited to current conditions. That's why internal platforms like McChrystal's O&I forum and Otpor's networking meetings are so important. You need to continually use the reach of your network to allow information to cascade and be able to determine the next focus of your actions.

As sociologist Doug McAdam observed, during the civil rights movement activists continually innovated their tactics, first focusing on boycotts like the Montgomery Bus Strike to use the economic power of the black community to force change. Their opponents, however, soon learned to adapt to these actions, by intimidating and sometimes jailing participants as well as changing bus rules in such a way as to give the appearance of compliance but keeping the status quo intact. With the effect of economic boycotts nullified, sit-ins, which required far less participation, became preeminent. With just a few dozen activists, an entire commercial district could be disrupted. Yet the more sit-ins were successful, the more local communities learned to take them in stride. After that came "Freedom Rides," community actions, mass marches, and so on.[39] The power of any particular action or tactic diminishes over time, so you continually need to evolve.

What you want to avoid is getting locked into any particular *Schwerpunkt*, because its effect will soon be diminished and ultimately negated, as in the case of Occupy as well as similar movements like the Gezi Park protests in Istanbul. In both cases, activists failed to develop effective internal platforms of governance, cohesion, and coordination and soon found that their tactics were nullified by those who supported the status quo. In the end, it didn't matter how effective they were at mobilizing supporters, whether that was through social media or elsewhere, because they were unable to observe, orient, decide, and act effectively.

Successful movements for change understand that you can't simply create change because you don't like things as they are. They are based on values, not on any particular demographics or issues. That's why they are always focused on pushing outward, not simply catering to a base of impassioned supporters. Every action is focused on mobilizing a Spectrum of Allies in order to influence Pillars of Support. Perhaps most important, they recognize that none of this is an end in itself, but a means to an end. It is preparation for victory, not victory itself.

Every successful movement for change has three phases. The first is an emergent phase, in which a keystone change is identified, constituencies on the Spectrum of Allies are mapped out, and institutions within the Pillars of Power are determined.

The second phase, or the engagement phase, is when tactics are designed to target particular constituencies and institutions for mobilization. The last phase, or the victory phase, is typically triggered by an outside event, which lowers resistance thresholds and sets a cascade in motion.[40] An election is falsified, a regime's brutality is exposed, a new technology is introduced into the market, a chief executive fires a well-liked employee (or an FBI director) without cause, or maybe crucial intelligence is acquired on a key terrorist.

Sometimes the trigger is planned in advance. In the case of Otpor, the activists knew, from their experience after the 1996 elections, that if they mobilized a high turnout for the 2000 elections, Milošević would cheat and try to steal a victory and that would be their trigger. Similarly, Paul O'Neill knew that his safety program at Alcoa would, once it was taken seriously, be itself a trigger for creating operational excellence in the once sclerotic firm. On the other hand, the LGBT movement was initially crushed by the passage of Proposition 8 in California. Only later was it realized how it galvanized supporters and that the subsequent lawsuits would lower resistance thresholds and become a trigger to change public opinion.

If mobilization builds numbers and pulls in the needed constituencies and institutions, linkages are built between disparate groups, and a genome of values keeps the network focused on the vision of tomorrow, a cascade will ensue. The existing regime defending the status quo usually doesn't even see it coming. They, embedded in their own networks and ecosystems, usually fail to notice that the Spectrum of Allies and the Pillars of Support have shifted away from them until it's too late.

Yet final victory, as I and so many others have found, can still be elusive, because every revolution inspires a counterrevolution. The vanquished will not simply disappear, but will immediately begin plotting their return. This too must be part of the plan, as we will see in the next chapter.

CHAPTER 9

Surviving Victory

I dare not linger, for my long walk is not yet ended.

NELSON MANDELA

I remember sitting in the living room of my Kyiv apartment one night early in 2005, drinking whiskey with my friend and colleague Vitaliy Sych. As the editor in chief of *Korrespondent*, Ukraine's most popular newsmagazine, Vitaliy was one of the most prominent journalists in the country and one of the best people to talk to if you wanted to get a sense of the zeitgeist of the nation.

We had developed a great working relationship in the office, but what I really treasured was to get a few quiet hours to sit and talk with my friend. Apparently, *New York Times* columnist Thomas Friedman felt the same way, because upon meeting Vitaliy in 2014, his next column focused largely on him.[1] Vitaliy has that effect on people. Straightforward and direct, while at the same time thoughtful and insightful, he is someone that immediately commands attention in his own quiet way.

On this particular night we were still basking in the afterglow of the Orange Revolution. The old order had been defeated and a new era was dawning. *Korrespondent*'s sales were soaring, and the future seemed to be ripe with opportunity. We talked and poured some whiskey and then talked some more. Eventually, after we had drunk the requisite amount of whiskey to broach the subject in earnest, we got around to discussing what the future might hold for Ukraine.

As both an outsider and someone who had lived in Poland during its intense years of reform, Vitaliy was interested in my opinion. I told him that I thought EU and NATO ascension would be key to securing the country's future. It was only through external structures such as these, I thought, that the necessary reforms could be accomplished. Vitaliy had other ideas. He favored a more "Finnish-style" solution in which Ukraine was neither in the Russian camp nor part of NATO or the EU. He just wanted his homeland to be left to find its own way.

As usual, Vitaliy captured the mood of the country. Ukrainians had just taken to the streets to stand up to injustice, and they had won. Now, they just wanted to be able live normal lives once again. It was to be a terrible mistake. What came next should have been predictable, but as best as I can recall, nobody saw it coming. I certainly didn't.

What happened first was a breakdown of the political alliance between Viktor Yushchenko, now President of Ukraine, and Yulia Tymoshenko, the Prime Minister. Yanukovych's Party of Regions regrouped and obstructed all that they could. The Russians cut off the gas supply, and infighting soon broke out between the various ruling factions. There was a scandal involving Yushchenko's son, increasingly erratic behavior from Tymoshenko, and before long we all felt betrayed by those we had gone through such pain and privation to support.

The financial crisis hit at the end of 2008. The hryvnia, Ukraine's currency, plummeted by 45 percent, and GDP fell by 20 percent. It was the final straw. When the presidential elections came around in 2010, Viktor Yanukovych was politically reborn. His image and message newly polished by the

American political consultant Paul Manafort, he seemed to many Ukrainians a more stable choice than his scandal-ridden opponent, Yulia Tymoshenko, despite her well-earned reputation for competence. He seemed to many just the man to make Ukraine great again. He wasn't. And soon the country would descend into turmoil once again.

THE DANGERS OF VICTORY

The events that unfolded in Ukraine after the Orange Revolution are far from uncommon. As we have seen, the Zajedno coalition of Serbian opposition parties that won elections in 1996 collapsed soon after their victory, and Milošević only tightened his grip on power. After Hosni Mubarak was ousted in Egypt during the Arab Spring, the Muslim Brotherhood rather than the pro-democracy protestors took power. Their leader, Mohamed Morsi, was then overthrown in a military coup and was replaced by Abdel Fattah el-Sisi. The Egyptian government today remains at least as repressive as it ever was. The incredible triumph of Barack Obama in 2008 gave way in 2016 to Donald Trump's successful campaign, which vowed to reverse many of his policies. His strident actions and rhetoric, in turn, led to a Democratic wave in the 2018 midterms and broke his party's almost decade long dominance of the House of Representatives. Power today, as Moisés Naím put it, does seem to be easier to get but harder to use or keep.

As we have also seen, the backlash from San Francisco Mayor Gavin Newsom's initiative to perform same-sex marriage ceremonies at City Hall led to Proposition 8, which constitutionally banned gay marriage. The law was so harsh, however, that it led to renewed efforts among LGBT activists that led the US Supreme Court to rule that such marriage bans were unconstitutional under the Equal Protection Clause of the Fourteenth Amendment. John Antioco's digital initiatives at

Blockbuster Video led his successor to retrench the company in physical retail. Countless change efforts, in every sphere, fail almost as soon as they attain their initial objectives, precisely because they awaken and embolden the forces supporting the status quo. The victory phase, Srdja Popović stressed to me, is often the most dangerous phase of any movement.[2]

As Saul Alinsky has noted, every revolution inspires a counterrevolution. Yet Alinsky also points out that anticipating this challenge is the key to overcoming it. "Once we accept and learn to anticipate the inevitable counterrevolution, we may then alter the historical pattern of revolution and counterrevolution from the traditional slow advance of two steps forward and one step backward to minimizing the latter."[3]

If Black Lives Matter had anticipated that their opponents would paint them as anti-police anarchists, they could have built alliances with law enforcement institutions sympathetic to their cause. In much the same way, if John Antioco had taken into greater account the backlash against his digital initiatives from the franchisees and shareholders, he might have sought to make inroads with them sooner, and his "Total Access" initiative and nascent efforts to build an online video streaming service could have won the day.

Yet all too often, we have our minds so set on what we need to win that we neglect to think about what comes the day after the victory we seek. We are so focused on beating our opponents into submission that we fail to realize that they will eventually rise up again, learn the lessons of their failure, and return to the fight with renewed vigor. That's why we so often succeed in making our point, but fail to make a difference.

The problem is not that the world is too corrupt or that the status quo is too ingrained, as we have seen positive change often can and does prevail, even against seemingly insurmountable odds. Rather, you must take responsibility for the change you want to see if you want to truly make a difference and not just score debate points. As Gandhi is often quoted as saying, "If you want to change the world, start with yourself."

BECOMING THE CHANGE YOU WANT TO SEE

By 2000, when the endgame against Milošević was approaching, the Serbian activists had learned from earlier mistakes. They understood that democratic reformers, once in power, could soon be corrupted. Yet they also had learned the importance of values. "It's about the vision, not persona," Srdja Popović would later tell me. "It was not about bringing down Milošević, but bringing about democracy, free and fair elections, European Union, and open economy in Serbia. That means we won't stop until we make the new government to deliver. . . . You don't proclaim the game over when the immediate goal has been achieved. You build till your values become a permanent change. That means you not only plan your strategy for your initial victory, you plan to make your victory permanent."[4]

So as soon as the new government in Serbia took power, hundreds of billboards went up around Belgrade that read, "We are watching you!" and others warned, "There are 4,500 bulldozers in Serbia and about 4 million potential drivers."[5] Srdja Popović and other activists entered the parliament to begin the long, hard task of reform far away from crowds and excitement. When he did, his old friends in the Otpor movement gave him hell whenever they felt that his efforts didn't meet their expectations.

"Stable democracy is about strong institutions, but also about people keeping those institutions accountable," Popović told me. The goal of a movement, as he sees it, is not to preserve the excitement of the heady days of struggle, but to become mainstream, to be mundane and ordinary. If you are successful it should be difficult to explain what was won because the previous order seems so unbelievable.[6]

The one thing Srdja constantly stressed to me is the importance of values for surviving victory. That's why in the run-up to the victory phase in Serbia, opposition politicians were pushed to sign a "contract with the people" that bound them to actions they were to take after the election. "It created a sense of obligation among the new leaders," he said, "and a sense of ownership among the people." The idea was to show to the new leaders that whatever mandate they had was only borrowed and that they were expected to live up to their promises. Otpor made the transition from a revolutionary movement to a watchdog group.

The years that followed lacked much of the romance of the early days. Four out of the original 11 members of Otpor joined the Serbian Parliament. Some went into business. Otpor grew into a prominent NGO, launching anti-corruption campaigns and ensuring that the promises of the revolution were kept. In October 2011, more than 10 years after the downfall of Milošević, Serbia became an official candidate for EU ascension. It is not a perfect country today, and it still has many flaws and challenges to overcome, but it is a stable and increasingly prosperous democracy.

Every movement for change starts with an immediate goal to be achieved. A wrong needs to be set right; a problem needs to be solved; or an unmet need has to be addressed. That's why when Talia Milgrom-Elcott found herself inspired by President Obama's call to train 100,000 STEM teachers in 10 years, she answered the challenge by setting up 100Kin10. Today, seven years on, the objective is within reach and, at the current pace, will be achieved on time.

Yet she has also learned that her journey must extend beyond that initial ambition. "About halfway in we began to see that, although we were likely to achieve the goal of 100,000 teachers, many of the core challenges would still remain," Milgrom-Elcott told me. "So we started to delve deeper and get down to the root problems of recruiting and retaining great people for education. Solving those will be harder than reaching the 100,000 goal. As we get closer to achieving our initial target and set our sights on even bigger challenges, we are increasingly realizing how pivotal the founding values of our effort are: the importance of collaborating and connecting, sharing solutions and expertise, and building a common vision. It is those values, and the sense of trust and shared purpose that they foster, that will fuel us to achieve the next goal, and the one after that."[7]

In a similar vein, Irving Wladawsky-Berger stressed to me how important values were in continuing the initial success of the Gerstner years at IBM. "The Gerstner revolution wasn't about technology or strategy, it was about transforming our values and our culture to be in greater harmony with the market," he remembers. "That's what enabled IBM's strengths to come through, as they had in previous decades, and we didn't want to go back to failing again. Because the transformation was about values first and technology second, we were able to continue to embrace those values as the technology and marketplace continued to evolve."[8]

In the years since Gerstner stepped down as CEO in 2002, the company has faced many challenges and has had no shortage of ups and downs. Nevertheless, it has remained consistently profitable. Nobody talks about breaking up IBM anymore. If the turnaround had been centered on Gerstner himself, rather than the values he sought to instill, that would likely not be true. Very few of the top technology companies in 2002, when Gerstner stepped down, are still relevant today. Perhaps like no other, it is an industry that demands you constantly adapt to change. That's why, when Barry Libenson set out to move Experian to the cloud, he focused on more than just the company's technological infrastructure. He also worked to bring about a shift in values and skills, so that the heavy lifting that was done during the transition to the cloud would carry over to new challenges, such as implementing artificial intelligence applications.

"We need to debunk the 'heroic leader' myth. If we believe in mountaintop leaders, we end up centralizing our organizations around the mountaintop instead of pushing accountability to people who are closer to the problems." Chris Fussell, General McChrystal's former aide-de-camp, told me.[9] Yet it's so easy to look at a larger-than-life persona like Gandhi, Mandela, Martin Luther King Jr., or Lech Walesa and think that if only Occupy or Black Lives Matter had a leader of sufficient charisma, they could have achieved more. For many of the same reasons, it's easy to fall into the trap of believing that, with just the right strategy, a failing company can become great once again. It's much more comforting to assume that if Blockbuster had embraced the Internet earlier, it would have been able to stave off Netflix, than to accept that it had not only formulated a viable strategy, but executed it competently—and still failed.

What should be clear by now is that successful movements create transformational change through shared values. It is that easy and that hard. Clearly, the American Revolution would not be considered the great success it is today without the Declaration of Independence and the US Constitution. In fact, the founders created and then adopted the Constitution, more than five years after the British were defeated in the Battle of Yorktown, precisely because it had become clear that without shared values the whole experiment was unworkable.

Yet maintaining a commitment to values is a challenge even in the best of circumstances. It's always easier to act in the moment or to prioritize an immediate need or desire than it is to sustain discipline and live up to the values you profess to believe in. As Pulitzer Prize–winning historian Jon Meacham explained in his book *The Soul of America: The Battle for Our Better Angels*, America has struggled, throughout our history, to uphold the values upon which the country was founded:

> For all of our darker shortcomings, and for all of the dreams denied and deferred, the experiment begun so long ago, carried out so imperfectly, is worth the fight. There is, in fact, no struggle more important, and none nobler, than the one we wage in service of those better angels who, however besieged, are always ready for battle.[10]

The quest for change is always a journey, never a destination. It is with that thought that, before I end, I would like to return to where we began, to my friends in Ukraine who, after so many hard lessons, have learned important truths and have continued their struggle, with somewhat better success.

THE STRUGGLE GOES ON

I now live on the opposite side of the world from my friend Vitaliy, so we don't get to talk nearly as often as I'd like. But recently, we had the chance to speak over Skype about events since the Euromaidan protests and how they compared to how things were back when we had that earlier conversation in my apartment.

Much has changed in the years that have passed. Our company, KP Media, was sold to an investment group led by the chocolate tycoon Petro Poroshenko and Boris Lozhkin, the owner of a rival media company. Vitaliy built a positive working relationship with both men, although there were some tensions when *Korrespondent* came out with stories that made the regime uncomfortable, particularly when bombshell pictures of President Yanukovych's ostentatious estate, Mezhyhirya, were published.

Nevertheless, they never interfered with Vitaliy's editorial independence, beyond some occasional grumbles. Yet over time, the pressures increased, and in the summer of 2013, just months before the Euromaidan protests began, Poroshenko received a generous offer from allies of President Yanukovych to buy the company. Always a savvy operator, Poroshenko saw the writing on the wall and agreed to sell.[11] Roughly 18 months later, in a dramatic turn of events after Yanukovych was ousted, Poroshenko would be elected president of Ukraine and choose Lozhkin to serve as his chief of staff.

As the sale went through, Vitaliy was given a contract to sign by the new owners. The first point was a ban on criticism of five individuals: Yanukovych, his son, and three others close to the regime. They also wanted to review all editorial content, including advertising, before publication. Vitaliy refused. They told him if he didn't comply, his career would be essentially finished. He told them, "Then I guess I'll have to find something else to do, but there is no way I can agree to these things. There are some things I can't do for any amount of money, and even if I could, my journalists wouldn't accept it." So he left the company, and a significant portion of the editorial staff joined him. They would later establish a new newsmagazine and website, *Novoye Vremya*, with the backing of independent investors. As of this writing, its readership far surpasses that of *Korrespondent*.

When I asked Vitaliy how the Euromaidan protests, or what Ukrainians have come to call The Revolution of Dignity, were different than what we experienced together in the Orange Revolution, he told me, "In 2005 everybody just disappeared and let Yushchenko do what he wanted. They thought he was some kind of magician and things were going to happen right away. But then nothing happened and they thought, 'something is brewing, he's getting something ready,' but then it became clear that nothing is getting ready and nothing is going to happen."

"But this time [after the Euromaidan protests], nobody believed that things would change by themselves," he continued. "People went to the legislature, went into government. For the first time, lots of top managers [in the private sector, such as the former general manager of Microsoft Ukraine Dmytro Shymkiv] took ministerial posts. They thought they had to take part as well." He also pointed out that the new officials had a much more international perspective. "In Yanukovych's cabinet only 2 out of 20 people spoke English. Now, only 2 out of 20 don't speak English. It's a totally different type of people."

When I spoke to Mustafa Nayyem, the journalist and activist whose Facebook post sparked the Euromaidan protests, he voiced similar sentiments. "In 2005 it was a very political protest," he said. "The only goal we had was that Yushchenko be President. He was the hope that everything would change. But it was not about social mobilization. It was not about political mobilization. We hoped that these people will change the country if we elect them. In 2005, people tried to change the country through politics. In 2014, they did it themselves." The Orange Revolution ultimately failed because it was about putting people in power, not about changing the values by which the country was governed.

He also explained that most of the protestors during Euromaidan were those who had been disappointed during the Orange Revolution, and they had learned from the experience. "Even today, you can't say who were the leaders in 2014," he remembers. "It was not a revolution done by politicians, it was a revolution done by activists, journalists, and middle-class professionals. In 2014 we were fighting for an idea. That's why 2014 was different. In 2005 people just went home [after the protests were over]. The social mobilization was very low and we lost our chance to push the government to make some changes. In 2014, people stayed angry. They stayed active. They kept pushing. And this spirit of protest is still proceeding." Nayyem himself was elected to Parliament and continues to push for reforms.

Much like in Serbia, the activists learned to take a more active role. They not only mobilized the populace, they also organized institutions. Independent organizations like Chestno (Honesty), the Anti-Corruption Action Center, and others, which were funded in large part by international foundations like George Soros's Open Society Foundation and US AID and staffed by experts, sprung up and not only advocated for change, but put forth specific programs to be adopted. "NGO activity exploded after Euromaidan," Nayyem told me, "because many saw that it was possible to put pressure on the government."

I spoke to a leader of what has perhaps been the most impactful NGO in Ukraine, Vitaliy Shabunin, head of the Anti-Corruption Action Center, which began operations two years before the Euromaidan protests took place. Shabunin, a former political operative, founded the organization with his friend, Daryna Kalenyuk, after she returned from receiving a law degree in the United States and doing a short stint at Transparency International. They both saw the need for a watchdog group to investigate wrongdoing and advocate for reforms.

Their respective backgrounds led them to the realization that while journalists could investigate, any complaints needed to be submitted according to legal procedures or they would simply be cast aside. So they set out to not only document transgressions, but to present them in a way that they could not be so easily ignored. One of their first initiatives, which was financed by a grant from The Global Fund to Fight AIDS, Tuberculosis and Malaria, was to investigate how HIV medicines were being procured by the state medical service. Their work not only uncovered massive malfeasance, but suggested reforms that would make medical procurement more transparent and efficient.

That early work led to a formula, which became the Anti-Corruption Action Center's modus operandi. First, they would thoroughly investigate corruption and "name and shame" those who were responsible for misusing state resources. However, this wasn't an end in itself, but only a means to an end. The goal was to formulate and suggest specific reforms based on their investigations and then leverage key institutions, especially international organizations, a key Pillar of Support.

Shabunin continually stressed to me how important it is to do the groundwork early, long before a window of opportunity opens up, to drive the reforms through and make them a reality. It is that early work that helps you build up expertise so that you are able to propose detailed, viable reforms and win the credibility to gain support from both internal stakeholders and international institutions.

That window of opportunity for Ukraine opened up once the new government was elected and installed after the Euromaidan protests. The country no longer had Vladimir Putin's Russia as a patron. In fact, after the annexation of Ukraine's Crimea province and the "hybrid" invasion of the eastern regions of Donetsk and Luhansk, it was now a sworn enemy, and that strengthened the resolve of the populace. At the same time, Ukraine was bankrupt, at war, and highly dependent on international institutions for survival.

Now, Shabunin and the other NGOs had three significant levers to force through reforms. The first was IMF loans, which the country needed desperately. The second was the possibility of a visa-free regime with the European Union, something that the citizens of Ukraine desperately wanted. It would be a sign that Ukraine had begun its ascent into the community of free nations and had started out on its path to become a "normal" country. Third, after the presidential elections, new parliamentary elections loomed. "It was not only us and the internal pressure we put on Parliament, it was also the IMF, which made it a condition for the loan. There was also an election coming up, and Parliament needed to show that they accomplished something. So it was a confluence of mechanisms that led to the passage of major reforms," Shabunin told me.[12]

Those reforms, which included an Anti-Corruption Bureau within the government, a law that required all officials to disclose their assets (so that when an official or judge on a small government salary owns three Bentleys and a large estate he or she must explain where the wealth comes from), criminal liability for a false declaration, and human rights legislation, all had significant impact. Perhaps the most popular reform, borrowed from the Georgian Republic's earlier revolution in 2003, was a complete restructuring of the traffic police. All former officers were dismissed, and a new cadre, with higher recruiting standards and training provided by a team of police from Reno, Nevada, proved to be a considerable improvement in daily life. No longer could law-abiding citizens be arbitrarily shaken down on the whim of a corrupt officer.[13]

Still, many challenges remain, and after the pressure from the need to win financing from the IMF and the visa-free regime from the EU abated, little was done. As further needed reforms lingered, Petro Poroshenko quickly became a disappointment.

In the past few years, his approval ratings have fallen through the floor. A new presidential election will be held in 2019, just before this book is published, and he will likely lose. (And, in another case of political revival, Yulia Tymoshenko is a key frontrunner.)

"The window of opportunity has closed, because Ukrainian politicians have gotten all they need from the West," Shabunin told me. Now that the visa-free regime has been installed and Ukraine is no longer desperate for loans from the IMF, much of the impetus has dissipated. Nevertheless, just as he did before the Euromaidan protests, Shabunin continues to prepare for the next window of opportunity that can trigger more comprehensive reforms. "Our long-term strategy is to create a situation in which it will be impossible not to do anti-corruption reforms. We are working to ensure that these reforms will be done, either by these politicians or by another, because they will lose their office if they don't do these reforms."

So the struggle continues, but the forces for change have far more advantages than we did back in 2004. Russia has lost its influence, most probably for generations to come. Vitaliy Sych and other journalists continue to do hard-nosed reporting on corrupt officials and inept policy, Mustafa Nayyem and his compatriots inside the Ukrainian government continue to agitate for better governance, and NGOs like the Anti-Corruption Action Center continue to investigate and develop proposals for new legislation that can help move the country forward. Kuchma, Yushchenko, and Yanukovych have all long disappeared from the scene and, most likely, Poroshenko soon will too. Yet the struggle continues and, hopefully, Ukraine will prosper because of it.

AFTERWORD

Leading Toward Common Ground

It always seems impossible until it's done.

—NELSON MANDELA

Everybody has something they want to change, whether it is something in their community, their organization, their industry, or throughout society as a whole. However, not everybody wants the same change. What excites and inspires some, others fear. No change affects everyone equally. That's why, as Saul Alinsky pointed out, every revolution sparks a counterrevolution. One person's win is often another's loss.

We've seen this dynamic throughout this book. Whether it is a movement to lift up the oppressed, to improve healthcare or education, to turn around a failing company, or to advocate for a new corporate initiative, change of any kind threatens the status quo, which never yields its power gracefully. There will always be a backlash. That is the physics of change. Every action provokes a reaction.

It was President Kuchma's corrupt regime that led to the Orange Revolution in 2004, which, along with the failures of the

Yushchenko government, set the stage for Yanukovych's startling comeback. That, in turn, led to the Euromaidan protests, which swept him from power and led to Ukraine's break with Russia. In a similar vein, it was President Bush's full-throated condemnation of same-sex marriage in his State of the Union Address that led then San Francisco Mayor Gavin Newsom to perform weddings for gay and lesbian couples at City Hall. The ensuing backlash resulted in Proposition 8, which was considered so harsh that it gave new life to the same-sex marriage movement. John Antioco's investments in a digital platform at Blockbuster Video led his successor to retrench the company in physical retail. The list goes on.

In my research of change movements throughout the world and throughout history this pattern is remarkably consistent, and the tennis match of ideologies can go on for years or even decades. What is also remarkably consistent is what it takes to end the cycle: the forging of a new agenda based on shared values.

What I hope you've learned in this book is that you don't need any special abilities to create transformational change that endures. In his early years, Gandhi was so shy that he could hardly bring himself to speak in court. Martin Luther King Jr. was far from the obvious choice to lead the Montgomery bus strike. Nelson Mandela began as an angry nationalist. Lech Walesa was just a simple electrician. Srdja Popović thought he would spend his life playing bass guitar in a rock band. Mustafa Nayyem told me he didn't have any special plans when he posted the message on Facebook that sparked the Euromaidan protests; he just did it out of anger and frustration.

Nevertheless all of the successful changemakers we have seen in this book learned along the way and were able to lead their movements to common ground that didn't exist when they started out. Gandhi created his philosophy of Satyagraha and indoctrinated his Indian followers. Martin Luther King Jr. built his movement based on the founding documents of the American nation, the Declaration of Independence and the

US Constitution. Nelson Mandela's anti-Apartheid movement created the Freedom Charter. Paul O'Neill made safety in the workplace the platform from which he would launch his campaign for operational excellence. General Stanley McChrystal led his forces from failure to success by forging a true "team of teams."

What's perhaps most striking is how dramatically things can shift when a movement for change turns its focus from highlighting differences to indoctrinating shared values. The Euromaidan protests achieved far more than the Orange Revolution ever did because they aimed to do more than just bring about a change in leadership, but to instill the norms of their European neighbors. The LGBT movement foundered for decades, but public opinion shifted sharply when it began to assert same-sex marriage as a "recognition of basic American principles." Alcoa and IBM remain, even today, decades after their historic turnarounds, profitable companies.

Make no mistake, successful movements do not overpower, they attract. If you are simply out to prove yourself right and others wrong, you are destined to fail. It's not enough to just want to make a point, you have to actually want to make a difference, and that means making change work for everybody.

There are many injustices in the world and many other things that can be improved. That's why it's so easy for a passion to improve the world to devolve into blind opposition to those who don't see things the same way you do. All too often, that frustration leads us to self-righteous indignation and we end up preaching to the choir instead of venturing out of the church and mixing with the heathens. That's how movements fail.

The salient point here is that movements that succeed do things differently than others. Cascades obey scientific principles that govern their behavior, and successful movements learn how to harness them. That's why those that prevail end up looking so much alike. As we have seen throughout this book, starting out with very different challenges, philosophies, and personalities, those that rose to meet the challenges and overcome seemingly insurmountable odds all eventually arrived at surprisingly similar principles. That's what enabled them to achieve the change they sought. They learned from early failures, made adjustments, and continued to work toward their vision of tomorrow. Those that fell short failed to learn those lessons, and lacked the discipline to harness cascades to build common ground with other key stakeholders. Inevitably, they blamed their lack of progress on those that opposed them, rather than on their own inability to win support.

I hope you have learned that change is truly possible and that you can help to make it happen. Whether you are a senior executive at a major corporation or at a nonprofit organization, a political leader, a community activist, or simply someone who seeks to make things better for your family, friends, neighbors, and coworkers, you can do more than just tilt at windmills or sink into angry despair. You too can embrace the principles of successful movements and go out and make your own brand of transformational change a reality. You can work to reshape your community, your organization, your industry, or even your entire society. The world we live in today was built on change and so will be the one we leave to our children and our grandchildren. However, those changes seldom come easy or happen by themselves.

So let's return to the six principles for creating transformative change that I've outlined in this book and examine how each one represents a crossroads where you will be tempted to make a point, but if you want to really make change happen, you will have to refocus your efforts on making a difference through building common ground.

1. IDENTIFY A KEYSTONE CHANGE

Everybody has things they don't like about the status quo, but if all you can do is voice grievances, you won't get very far. So, the first step toward creating change is to articulate what you want it to look like, or what Srdja Popović likes to call "defining a vision of tomorrow." Unless you can clearly spell out what you're advocating for, not just what you're against, your movement will be unlikely to grow beyond the angry, the disaffected, and the indignant and will likely turn off everybody else.

Next, you need to identify a keystone change that can help bring that desired future state about. There are three criteria you want to look at:

1. A keystone change needs to be a concrete and tangible goal.
2. A keystone change unites diverse stakeholders in the Spectrum of Allies and the Pillars of Support.
3. A keystone change paves the way for future change.

It's important to note that to say a keystone change is concrete and tangible doesn't mean that it is easy. It took decades for the women's suffrage and LGBT movements to identify their keystone changes of voting and marriage rights, and years more to make them a reality. Other keystone changes we have seen in this book, such as making Alcoa a safer company, transforming factory changeovers at Wyeth Pharmaceuticals, moving Experian's massive digital infrastructure to the cloud, or the Institute for Healthcare Improvement driving the implementation of six life-saving procedures at thousands of hospitals across America, were no mean feats. Still, they were specific, tangible, and led to much greater impacts later on.

I have no doubt that you see things in your world that you would like to change—an injustice in your community, a missed opportunity in your organization, an inefficiency in your industry, or maybe something else. But what is the change you would actually like to see? What does your vision of a better tomorrow actually look like? Once you can articulate that and identify a keystone change as a concrete and tangible goal, you are well on your way to creating a true transformation.

2. MAKE A PLAN

Having an idea for change is only the start. You also need to identify, specifically, *who* you need to win over to bring change about. Power will not fall simply because you oppose it, but it will crumble if you bring those who support it over to your side. So, once you have defined your vision of tomorrow and a keystone change that will help bring it about, you need to devise a plan to get there using the two tools described in Chapter 5: The Spectrum of Allies and the Pillars of Support.

The Spectrum of Allies maps out the terrain on which the battle will be fought by identifying which constituencies you can expect to be active and passive supporters of your vision of tomorrow, who is likely to be neutral, and who will passively and actively oppose your movement. The Pillars of Support identify which institutions you need to pull in to change the status quo. As Clayborne Carson put it, "A social movement that only moves people is merely a revolt. A movement that changes both people and institutions is a revolution."

For any tactic to be effective, it needs to mobilize specific constituencies in the Spectrum of Allies to influence institutions in the Pillars of Support. So it is absolutely essential that you define these things first or you will end up just making noise instead of actually making a difference. In some cases, you can even set your cause back.

3. BUILD A NETWORK OF SMALL GROUPS

Successful movements are rooted in network cascades, and cascades are built upon small world networks. The functional units of these networks are the small groups that link to other small groups. Individually, these clusters mean little, but when they become connected to others and are triggered by an event, they can become immensely powerful.

All too often, we tend to look back at great historical movements through the lens of Gladwell's Law of the Few. So, when we think about Indian independence, we see Gandhi; the civil rights movement, Martin Luther King Jr.; the anti-Apartheid movement, Nelson Mandela, and so on. Yet each were actually just one part of a deep network of groups whose links built up over time. Nobody creates transformational change alone.

The truth is that you can't really create a cascade; you must prepare for it by continuously connecting to others outside your initial base of support. You use the Recruit-Train-Act triangle to build your movement, so that when a trigger opens up a window of opportunity, you are ready to capitalize on it.

4. INDOCTRINATE GENOMES OF VALUES

There are many worthy objectives that you can strive for—narrowing the gap between rich and poor, ending discrimination on the basis of race, gender, or sexual orientation, creating a technology to better the lives of your fellow citizens, or even just striving to serve your customers and other stakeholders more effectively.

Yet shared purpose will soon disintegrate in the face of adversity if there are not shared values. (And remember, values cost something. If not, they are merely platitudes.) Successful movements for change invest tremendous resources in codifying, training for, and enforcing those values. That is often what separates victory and defeat.

Values can be indoctrinated in a variety of ways. Social movements like John Lewis's SNCC and Otpor conducted intensive training for activists and, in a similar way, Facebook created a Bootcamp for its incoming engineers. The Institute for Healthcare Improvement developed "change kits" to help hospitals internalize the values of its movement. Rick Warren of the Saddleback Church writes books and distributes sermons. Lou Gerstner sent companywide e-mails. Yet it doesn't really matter how the values are communicated, but that they are continually reinforced by the behavior and actions of leaders. Values are not optional. They are not "nice to have" or adhered to at some times and not others. They are absolutely critical to making lasting change a reality.

5. CREATE PLATFORMS FOR PARTICIPATION, MOBILIZATION, AND CONNECTION

The reason that nonviolent uprisings deliver better results than violent ones is that they invite far more participation. The goal of a movement is to mobilize, not to administer purity tests. Otpor recognized that it is much more effective to whack a barrel with a bat than it is to sleep in a park night after night. The activists didn't accost passersby or chastise anyone for their lack of commitment. They simply invited people to join in something that was fun, easy, and helped to carry their message.

In much the same way, General Stanley McChrystal transformed the O&I brief from a mere informational exercise into a platform for widening and deepening connections. 100Kin10 organizes conferences so that its members can connect, create common projects, and share best practices. The National Health Service in England designs campaigns to be as easy to adopt as possible. There are nearly limitless possibilities, and every movement for change needs to choose which platforms serve it best, but one commonality is that they must always face outward and pull people in rather than push, shame, or try to coerce them.

Successful movements understand this and are grateful for any help they can get. Unsuccessful movements rally the faithful and demonize those who don't share their ideas or their commitment. They make their point but fail to make a difference.

6. SURVIVE VICTORY

Every movement has an immediate goal, whether it is to promote fundamental rights, to drive implementation of new ideas, methods, and procedures, or simply to return to profitability. That's what drives action. Once those immediate goals are achieved, however, change movements often fall apart. That's what I experienced in Ukraine, and it is incredibly common. The same thing happened in Egypt and many other places. This doesn't just hold true for political movements either. For every CEO like Lou Gerstner or Paul O'Neill who creates lasting, transformative change, there are hundreds that achieved early success and then faltered.

That's why the victory phase of any change movement is always the most dangerous, because the peril lies within. It wasn't Yanukovych who failed the Orange Revolution, it was Yushchenko and Tymoshenko, who quickly fell into infighting and failed to forge a common purpose. It wasn't just the rise of Silicon Valley that led to the demise of the Boston tech firms, but their own rigid way of thinking. Netflix didn't kill Blockbuster, Antioco's successor, Jim Keyes, did.

Successful movements survive victory by staying true to their values even after the initial triumph. Euromaidan succeeded where the Orange Revolution failed because it continued to promote its values after Yanukovych had been removed from office. It wasn't based on any one politician or persona. The turnaround at IBM endured long after Lou Gerstner was gone because it wasn't centered on any particular strategy or technology, but continued to promote the values that made IBM a great company. If Nelson Mandela had looked to take revenge for his many years of suffering after he took power, instead of bringing white Afrikaners into the society he sought to create, he would never have become the revered figure he is today. Values prevail because they are not situational or of the moment, but lasting principles for adaptation.

Most of all, successful movements are able to leave the battle behind, to become, as Srdja Popović put it to me, "mundane and ordinary" and make peace with the fact that victory inevitably leads to the tedious boredom of governance. They do not see that as the price of progress, but its reward.

That's how you win.

NOTES

INTRODUCTION

1. Andy Kroll, "How Occupy Wall Street Really Got Started," *Mother Jones*, October 17, 2011, http://www.motherjones.com/politics/2011/10/occupy-wall-street-international-origins.
2. Mark Engler and Paul Engler, *This Is an Uprising: How Nonviolent Revolt Is Shaping the Twenty-First Century* (Nation Books, 2016).
3. Andrew Fleming, "Adbusters Sparks Wall Street Protest," *Vancouver Courier*, September 27, 2011, http://www.vancourier.com/news/adbusters-sparks-wall-street-protest-1.374299.
4. Matt Sledge, "Reawakening the Radical Imagination: The Origins of Occupy Wall Street," *The Huffington Post*, November 10, 2011, http://www.huffingtonpost.com/2011/11/10/occupy-wall-street-origins_n_1083977.html.
5. https://web.archive.org/web/20111205005640/http://www.france24.com/en/20111015-indignant-protests-go-global-saturday.
6. Micah White, "Occupy and Black Lives Matter Failed. We Can Either Win Wars or Win Elections," *The Guardian*, August 28, 2017, https://www.theguardian.com/commentisfree/2017/aug/29/why-are-our-protests-failing-and-how-can-we-achieve-social-change-today.
7. Tina Rosenberg, "Revolution U: What Egypt Learned from the Students Who Overthrew Milosevic," *Foreign Policy*, February 17, 2011, https://foreignpolicy.com/2011/02/17/revolution-u-2/.
8. Srđa Popović, *Blueprint for Revolution* (Spiegel & Grau, 2015), 11.
9. Ibid., 100–104.
10. Ibid., 12.
11. Tina Rosenberg, *Join the Club* (New York: W. W. Norton & Company, 2011), 226.
12. Gina Keating, *Netflixed: The Epic Battle for America's Eyeballs* (Portfolio Penguin, 2012), 71–74, 110–11. A summary of Antioco's career can also be found at https://www.twst.com/bio/JOHN%20F.%20ANTIOCO.
13. Interview with author.
14. John Antioco described the strategy in an article in the April 2011 issue of *Harvard Business Review*, "How I Did It: Blockbuster's Former CEO on Sparring with an Activist Shareholder," http://hbr.org/2011/04/how-i-did-it-blockbusters-former-ceo-on-sparring-with-an-activist-shareholder/ar/1. It was also described in a *BusinessWeek*

article about Blockbuster's initial public offering, "Why It's Not A Blockbuster IPO," *BusinessWeek*, August 1, 1999, http://www.businessweek.com/stories/1999-08-01/why-its-not-a-blockbuster-ipo.
15. Interview with author.
16. There have been a number of accounts of this meeting and a lot of suggestions about a buyout offer. I haven't been able to substantiate any of them. For his part, Antioco denies that there was any serious discussion at that time.
17. There has been an enormous amount of speculation about this meeting, which is described in Gina Keating's book *Netflixed* (66–67) as well as in a number of accounts online. Perhaps not surprisingly, different people have different recollections. What is clear is that Netflix had not identified a viable business model at the time and was losing lots of money. It had first begun testing its subscription model in September of 1999 and committed to its subscription model in February of 2000, just a few months before the meeting took place (Keating, *Netflixed*, 58–60). When I spoke to John Antioco about the event, he remembers it, but says he wasn't there, although some accounts have him stepping in for a few minutes to shake hands and say hello. He also doesn't remember any serious discussion about an acquisition, for $50 million or any other amount of money, although he says that it might have come up in passing. He did seem to think, at least from what I could gather, that Netflix didn't have anything that Blockbuster couldn't build itself, which seems to be true. Later, after Netflix had identified a sustainable business model, there were serious merger talks, but they didn't get very far because of regulatory concerns. Lawyers on both sides immediately killed the idea.
18. Keating, *Netflixed*, 116–19.
19. Ibid., 172–77, 180–82.
20. Ibid. 214–15.
21. John Antioco, "How I Did It: Blockbuster's Former CEO on Sparring with an Activist Shareholder," *Harvard Business Review*, April 2011, https://hbr.org/2011/04/how-i-did-it-blockbusters-former-ceo-on-sparring-with-an-activist-shareholder.
22. http://www.biography.com/people/stanley-mcchrystal-578710.
23. Stanley McChrystal, et. al., *Team of Teams* (Portfolio/Penguin, 2015), 69.
24. Ibid. 120–22.
25. Ibid., 209.
26. Ibid., 84.
27. Ibid., 174.
28. Ibid., 216.
29. Ibid., 226.
30. Ibid., 218.

31. AnnaLee Saxenian, *Regional Advantage: Culture and Competition in Silicon Valley and Route 128* (Harvard University Press, 1994), 14.
32. Ibid., 15.
33. Ibid., 99.
34. Fox Butterfield, "What You See Is What You Get," *New York Times*, May 1, 1988.
35. Saxenian, *Regional Advantage*, 75.
36. Ibid. 69–73.
37. Ray S. Cline, *A World Power Assessment* (Boulder, CO: Westview Press, 1977). A discussion of Cline's formulation and others can be found in Joseph S. Nye Jr., *The Future of Power* (Perseus, 2011), 3–24.
38. R. H. Coase, "The Nature of the Firm," *Economica* 4, no. 16 (November 1937), 386–405.
39. Michael E. Porter, *Competitive Advantage: Creating and Sustaining Superior Performance* (New York: Free Press, 1985).
40. https://www.businessinsider.com/zuckerbergs-first-book-is-out-of-stock-2015-1.
41. Innosight, *2018 Corporate Longevity Forecast: Creative Destruction is Accelerating*, February 2018, https://www.innosight.com/wp-content/uploads/2017/11/Innosight-Corporate-Longevity-2018.pdf.
42. Perry's analysis can be found at http://www.aei-ideas.org/2011/11/fortune-500-firms-in-1955-vs-2011-87-are-gone/.
43. Moisés Naím, *The End of Power: From Boardrooms to Battlefields and Churches to States, Why Being In Charge Isn't What It Used to Be* (Basic Books, 2013).
44. Ibid., 11.
45. McChrystal et. al., *Team of Teams*, 127.

CHAPTER 1

1. For background on the Orange Revolution, see Anders Åslund and Michael McFaul, eds., *Revolution in Orange* (Washington, D.C.: Carnegie Endowment for International Peace, 2006); Askold Krushelnycky, *An Orange Revolution: A Personal Journey Through Ukrainian History* (Harvill Secker, 2006); Adrian Karatnycky, "Ukraine's Orange Revolution," *Foreign Affairs*, March/April 2005; Timothy Garton Ash and Timothy Snyder, "The Orange Revolution," The New York Review of Books, April 28, 2005.
2. For more information about Holodomor, see Timothy Snyder, *Bloodlands: Europe Between Hitler and Stalin* (Basic Books, 2010); and Anne Applebaum, *Red Famine: Stalin's War on Ukraine* (Penguin Random House, 2017).
3. Anders Åslund and Michael McFaul, eds., *Revolution in Orange* (Washington, D.C.: Carnegie Endowment for International Peace, 2006), 13–14.

4. IMF database.
5. The largest news site was *Korrespondent.*
6. See: Irina Sandul, "Kuchmagate, Two Years On," *Time*, September 26, 2002.
7. "Post Owner Barred From Ukraine," *Kyiv Post*, April 13, 2000.
8. Adrian Karatnycky, "Ukraine's Orange Revolution," *Foreign Affairs*, March/April 2005.
9. Interview with author.
10. Guy Faulconbridge, Anna Dabrowska, and Stephen Grey, "Toppled 'Mafia' President Cost Ukraine up to $100 Billion, Prosecutor Says," Reuters, April 30, 2014, http://www.reuters.com/article/2014/04/30/us-ukraine-crisis-yanukovich-idUSBREA3T0K820140430. https://data.worldbank.org/country/ukraine?view=chart
11. An amazing assortment of incidents can be found in Yuriy Onyshkiv, "Unruly Untouchables," *Kyiv Post*, July 11, 2011, http://www.kyivpost.com/content/ukraine/unruly-untouchables-108662.html; and Mykola Riabchuk, "Like Fathers, Like Sons: Ukraine's Untouchables," Open Democracy, April 12, 2011, https://www.opendemocracy.net/od-russia/mykola-riabchuk/like-fathers-like-sons-ukraine%E2%80%99s-untouchables.
12. Thomas Rid, "Cracks in the Jihad," *The Wilson Quarterly* 34, no. 1 (Winter 2010): 40–48.
13. John Antioco gives his account of the Blockbuster story in "How I Did It: Blockbuster's Former CEO on Sparring with an Activist Shareholder," *Harvard Business Review*, April 2011.

CHAPTER 2

1. Strogatz describes the incident in his book *Sync* (Hyperion, 2004).
2. Duncan Watts, *Six Degrees: The Science of a Connected Age* (W. W. Norton and Company, 2004).
3. Stanley Milgram, "Behavioral Study of Obedience," *The Journal of Abnormal and Social Psychology* 67, no. 4 (October 1963): 371–78.
4. Michael Luo, "Excuse Me. May I Have Your Seat?," *New York Times*, September 14, 2004.
5. Albert-László Barabási, *Linked: How Everything Is Connected to Everything Else and What It Means for Business, Science, and Everyday Life* (Plume, 2003), 27–30.
6. Peter Sheridan Dodds, Roby Muhamadú, and Duncan J. Watts, "An Experimental Study of Search in Global Social Networks," *Science*, August 2003, http://snap.stanford.edu/class/cs224w-readings/dodds03search.pdf.
7. For a more extended discussion of Euler and his creation of graph theory, see Barabási, *Linked*, 9–13.
8. For a fascinating and fabulously entertaining account of Paul Erdős's life, see Paul Hoffman, *The Man Who Loved Only Numbers: The Story of Paul Erdős and the Search for Mathematical Truth* (Hyperion, 1999).

9. Mark Buchanan, *Nexus: Small Worlds and the Groundbreaking Science of Networks* (W. W. Norton and Company, 2002), 34.
10. The formula for potential links is N(N – 1)/2, and the formula for calculating the number of random links needed to connect the whole network is ln(N)/N, where N is the number of nodes in both cases.
11. Many believe that 4Chan played a similar role in promoting memes to benefit Donald Trump in the 2016 election.
12. A full account of Rapoport's life and work can be found in his autobiography: Anatol Rapoport, *Certainties and Doubts* (Black Rose Books, 2000).
13. Watts, *Six Degrees*, 57–59.
14. A. Rapoport and W. J. Horvath, "A Study of a Large Sociogram," *Behavioral Science* 6 (1961): 279–91.
15. Buchanan, *Nexus*, 45–46.
16. Mark Granovetter, *Getting a Job*, 2nd ed. (University of Chicago Press, 1974), 34.
17. Ibid., 53.
18. Mark S. Granovetter, "The Strength of Weak Ties," *American Journal of Sociology* 78, no. 6 (May 1973), 1360–80.
19. Watts, *Six Degrees*, 139.
20. Watts, *Six Degrees*, 49.
21. Ibid, 68.
22. D. J. Watts and S. H. Strogatz, "Collective Dynamics of 'Small-World' Networks," *Nature* 393 (1998).
23. Watts, *Six Degrees*, 20–25.
24. Watts, *Six Degrees*, 236–43. Interested readers might also want to read: Duncan J. Watts, "A Simple Model of Global Cascades on Random Networks," *PNAS* 99, no. 9 (April 30, 2002), 5766–71, https://www.stat.berkeley.edu/~aldous/260-FMIE/Papers/watts.pdf.
25. A full account of Orpheus's management model can be found in, Harvey Seifter and Peter Economy, *Leadership Ensemble* (Times Books, Henry Holt and Company LLC, 2001).
26. Gary Hamel, "First, Let's Fire All the Managers," *Harvard Business Review*, December 2011, https://hbr.org/2011/12/first-lets-fire-all-the-managers.

CHAPTER 3

1. Duncan Watts, *Six Degrees: The Science of a Connected Age* (Vintage, 2004), 206.
2. Duncan Watts wrote that to me in response to a fact check.
3. Malcolm Gladwell, *The Tipping Point* (Little, Brown and Company, 2000), 33.
4. Paul Lazarsfeld, *The People's Choice: How the Voter Makes up His Mind in a Presidential Campaign* (Columbia University Press, 1948).

5. A good summary can be found in Elihu Katz, *The Two-Step Flow of Communication: An Up-to-Date Report on an Hypothesis*, University of Pennsylvania Departmental Papers, 1957.
6. Peter Sheridan Dodds, et al., "An Experimental Study of Search in Global Social Networks," *Science* 301 (2003): 827.
7. Eytan Bakshy, et. al., "Everyone's an Influencer: Quantifying Influence on Twitter," WSDM '11, Proceedings of the Fourth ACM International Conference on Web Search and Data Mining.
8. Duncan Watts in particular emphasized this point. In response to a fact check e-mail, he wrote, "I agree that the mechanisms you describe are closer to the truth of what is happening than 'special individuals' (obviously—after writing two books about it). However, I think there's a big and important difference between describing the nature of the mechanisms at work and being able to say that one particular instance 'worked' and another did not . . . explanations of the sort 'the reason A succeeded and B didn't is because of X' (ex-post) vs. explanations of the sort 'A will succeed and B will fail because of X' (ex-ante). Although both sorts of explanations are common, in principle the latter can be checked for accuracy, whereas the former—benefitting as they do from knowing the answer—cannot. As a result, only ex-ante explanations (i.e. predictions) count for *evaluating* a theory. Put another way, it's fine to use ex-post explanations to generate theories but not to test them."
9. A description of the account can be found in Asch's obituary in the *New York Times*: David Stout, "Solomon Asch Is Dead at 88; A Leading Social Psychologist," *New York Times*, February 29, 1996.
10. Solomon Asch, "Opinions and Social Pressure," *Scientific American*, 1955.
11. Katz, *The Two-Step Flow of Communication.*
12. Mark Granovetter, "Threshold Models of Collective Behavior," *American Journal of Sociology* 83, no. 6 (May 1978): 1420–43.
13. There is an overwhelming amount of literature regarding informational cascades that is too broad to catalog here; however, interested readers can look to Chapter 16 of David Easley and Jon Kleinberg's definitive textbook, *Networks, Crowds, and Markets: Reasoning About a Highly Connected World* (Cambridge University Press, 2010); Suzanne Lohmann's analysis, "The Dynamics of Informational Cascades: The Monday Demonstrations in Leipzig, East Germany, 1989–1991," *World Politics* 47, no. 1 (October 1994); and M. E. J. Newman and D. J. Watts, "Scaling and Percolation in the Small-World Network Model," *Physical Review E* 60, no. 6 (1999): 7332–42.
14. Valuable insights into strategies that lower thresholds can be found in Jonah Berger's excellent book, *Contagious: Why Things Catch On* (Simon & Schuster, 2013).

15. A comprehensive summary of diffusion of innovations research can be found in n Don Stacks and Michael Salwen (Eds) (in press), *An Integrated Approach to Communication Theory and Research* (New York: Routledge), Chapter 27, 418–34.
16. E. M. Rogers, *Diffusion of Innovations* (New York: Free Press, 1962).
17. Stacks and Salwen, 2008, 219.
18. Geoffrey Moore, *Crossing the Chasm: Marketing and Selling Disruptive Products to Mainstream Customers* (Harper Collins, 1991).
19. Duncan Watts, "A Simple Model of Global Cascades on Random Networks," *PNAS* 99, no. 9 (April 30, 2002): 5766–71.
20. See Zeynep Tufecki, *Twitter and Tear Gas* (Yale University Press, 2017), 96–99.
21. Joan Walsh, "The Man Who Blocked John Lewis Speaks," Salon.com, October 13, 2011, https://www.salon.com/2011/10/13/the_man_who_blocked_john_lewis_speaks/.
22. https://www.dailykos.com/stories/2015/10/8/1429460/-Setting-the-record-straight-on-OWS-and-John-Lewis.

CHAPTER 4

1. Peter Ackerman and Christopher Kruegler, *Strategic Nonviolent Conflict: The Dynamics of People Power in the Twentieth Century* (Praeger Publishers, 1994), 169; a full text can also be found here: http://www.indiaofthepast.org/contribute-memories/read-contributions/major-events-pre-1950/283-purna-swaraj-the-demand-for-full-independence-26-january-1930-.
2. Louis Fischer, *Gandhi* (Signet; reprint edition, Penguin Group, 2010), 103.
3. Mark Engler, Paul Engler, *This Is an Uprising: How Nonviolent Revolt Is Shaping the Twenty-First Century* (Nation Books, 2016), 125.
4. Peter Ackerman and Jack DuVall, *A Force More Powerful: A Century of Nonviolent Conflict* (Palgrave Macmillan, 2000), 84.
5. Fischer, *Gandhi*, 5–9.
6. Ibid., 18–19.
7. Mohandas Gandhi, *An Autobiography: The Story of My Experiments with Truth* (Beacon Press, 1993), 105–117.
8. Ibid., 131.
9. Fischer, *Gandhi*, 35.
10. Ackerman and DuVall, *A Force More Powerful*, 65.
11. Gandhi, *An Autobiography*, 148.
12. Fischer, *Gandhi*, 35.
13. Ibid., 30–34.
14. Ibid., 22–23.
15. Fischer, *Gandhi*, 36–49; Ackerman and DuVall, *A Force More Powerful*, 64.

16. Ackerman and DuVall, *A Force More Powerful*, 66–67.
17. Amy Chua, *Political Tribes: Group Instinct and the Fate of Nations* (Penguin Press, 2018), 139–44.
18. Ibid., 72.
19. Fischer, *Gandhi*, 58.
20. Accounts of the Champaran Satyagraha can be found in Fischer, *Gandhi*, 62–65; Gandhi, *An Autobiography*, 405–24; and in Judith Margaret Brown, *Gandhi: Prisoner of Hope* (Yale University Press, 1991), 109–13.
21. Gandhi, *An Autobiography*, 409–10.
22. Ibid., 412.
23. For more on Thurgood Marshal, see Patricia Sullivan, *Lift Every Voice: The NAACP and the Making of the Civil Rights Movement* (The New Press, 2009); Rawn James Jr., *Root and Branch: Charles Hamilton Houston, Thurgood Marshall, and the Struggle to End Segregation* (Bloomsbury Press, 2013); and Gilbert King's thoroughly excellent—and Pulitzer Prize–winning—*Devil in the Grove: Thurgood Marshall, the Groveland Boys and the Dawn of a New America* (Harper, 2012).
24. Fischer, *Gandhi*, 64.
25. Brown, *Gandhi: Prisoner of Hope*, 129–31; Ackerman and Duval, *A Force More Powerful*, 73; Fischer, *Gandhi*, 68–69; Gandhi, *An Autobiography*, 454–62.
26. Fischer, *Gandhi*, 69–71, Ackerman and Duval, *A Force More Powerful*, 73–74.
27. Fischer, 2010, p. 72.
28. Gandhi, 1993, p. 470.
29. Ackerman and Duval, 2000, p. 79.
30. Fischer, *Gandhi*, 106.
31. Ackerman and Duval, *A Force More Powerful*, 86.
32. Ackerman and Christopher, *Strategic Nonviolent Conflict*, 179.
33. Ackerman and Duval, *A Force More Powerful*, 89–90.
34. Ackerman and Christopher, *Strategic Nonviolent Conflict*, 181–83.
35. Ackerman and Duval, *A Force More Powerful*, 99.
36. Ibid., 103–4.
37. Ibid, 108.
38. McChrystal, et al, "Team of Teams."
39. Chris Fussell and C. W. Goodyear, *One Mission: How Leaders Build a Team of Teams* (Portfolio, 2017), 58.
40. Louis V. Gerstner Jr., *Who Says Elephants Can't Dance?* (HarperCollins, 2002), 195–96.
41. Interview with author.
42. Gerstner Jr., *Who Says Elephants Can't Dance?*, 68.
43. Ibid., 163.
44. Charles Duhigg, T*he Power of Habit: Why We Do What We Do in Life and in Business* (Random House Trade Paperbacks, 2014), 97–99.

45. Interview with author.
46. For more on the women's suffrage movement, see Eleanor Flexner and Ellen Fitzpatrick, *A Century of Struggle: The Woman's Rights Movement in the United States* (Harvard University Press, 1959); Sally G. McMillen, *Seneca Falls and the Origins of the Women's Rights Movement* (Oxford University Press, 2008); Jean H. Baker, *Sisters: The Lives of American Suffragists* (Hill and Wang, 2005); and Mary Walton, *A Woman's Crusade: Alice Paul and the Battle for the Ballot* (St. Martin's Press, 2010).
47. For more about the Institute for Healthcare Improvement, see Hayagreeva Rao and Robert Sutton, "The Ergonomics of Innovation," *McKinsey Quarterly*, 2008 no. 4; and David Hoyt, "Institute for Healthcare Improvement: The Campaign to Save 100,000 lives," Stanford Graduate School of Business, Case: L-13, 01/07/2008.
48. Interview with author.
49. Isaac Weinberg, "Wyeth Pharmaceuticals: Changing the Mindsets and Behaviors of 20,000 People . . . One Person at a Time," Stanford Graduate School of Business, Case L-15, September 16, 2009.
50. Satell, "How Experian Embraced the Cloud and Transformed Its Business," Inc.com, November 4, 2018, https://www.inc.com/greg-satell/how-experian-embraced-cloud-transformed-its-business.html?cid=search.
51. Clayborne Carson, *The Autobiography of Martin Luther King, Jr.* (Hachette Book Group, 1998), 60.
52. John Lewis, *Walking with the Wind: A Memoir of the Movement* (Simon Schuster, 1998), 215.
53. Joe Nocera, "Two Days in September," *New York Times*, September 14, 2012.

CHAPTER 5

1. See John Lewis, *Walking with the Wind: A Memoir of the Movement* (Simon & Schuster, 1998), 203; Patricia Sullivan, *Lift Every Voice: The NAACP and the Making of the Civil Rights Movement* (The New Press, 2009), 254–56; Rawn James Jr., *Root and Branch: Charles Hamilton Houston, Thurgood Marshall, and the Struggle to End Segregation* (Bloomsbury Press, 2010), 181–83.
2. Lewis, *Walking with the Wind*, 203–4.
3. Ibid., 207.
4. Ibid., 217.
5. Clayborne Carson, *The Autobiography of Martin Luther King Jr.* (Hachette Book Group, 1998), 224.
6. Ibid., 226.
7. Ibid., 220.
8. https://en.wikipedia.org/wiki/Largest_protests_in_American_history.
9. Interview with author.

10. Louis Fischer, *Gandhi* (Signet Classics, 2010), 49–50.
11. Interview with author.
12. Interview with author.
13. Juan Zarate gives a full and lively account of the evolution and effectiveness of the sanctions in his book *Treasury's War* (PublicAffairs, 2013).
14. I became aware of this as it was happening. On Thursday night before the signing of the agreement between the regime and opposition forces was to take place on Friday, I was chatting with my former colleague Vitaliy Sych, a prominent journalist. When I asked him what he thought of the meeting that was to take place the next day, he told me that the "real meeting" was going on somewhere else. He said that Yanukovych's colleagues in the Party of Regions were through with him. Even for them, he had gone too far.
15. Robert Coram, *Boyd: The Fighter Pilot Who Changed the Art of War* (Back Bay Books, 2004), 363.
16. Bryan Bender, "From the Pentagon to the Private Sector," *Boston Globe*, December 26, 2010, http://archive.boston.com/news/nation/washington/articles/2010/12/26/defense_firms_lure_retired_generals/.
17. Coram, *Boyd*, 349.
18. A full discussion of the Pillars of Support can be found in Robert L. Helvey, *On Strategic Nonviolent Conflict: Thinking About Fundamentals*, 2nd ed. (The Albert Einstein Institution, 2007), 9–19.
19. C. J. Chivers, "How Top Spies in Ukraine Changed the Nation's Path," *New York Times*, January 17, 2005, http://www.nytimes.com/2005/01/17/world/europe/how-top-spies-in-ukraine-changed-the-nations-path.html.
20. Coram, *Boyd*, 365–67.
21. Ibid., 345–59.
22. Ibid., 285–86.
23. Interview with author.
24. https://secure.acce.org/whatisachamber/.
25. U.S. Department of Justice, Bureau of Justice Statistics, https://www.bjs.gov/content/pub/pdf/lpd13ppp.pdf.
26. White House Report, "The Long-Term Decline in Prime-Age Male Labor Force Participation," 2016, https://obamawhitehouse.archives.gov/sites/default/files/page/files/20160620_cea_primeage_male_lfp.pdf.
27. Michael McLaughlin, et al, "The Economic Burden of Incarceration in the U.S.," Institute for Advancing Justice Research and Innovation, October 2016, https://advancingjustice.wustl.edu/SiteCollectionDocuments/The%20Economic%20Burden%20of%20Incarceration%20in%20the%20US.pdf?_ga=2.74271889.2008179901.1526213948-75424379.1526213948.

28. John Meacham, *The Soul of America: The Battle for Our Better Natures* (Random House, 2018), 18.
29. Lewis, *Walking with the Wind*, 74–75; Peter Ackerman and Jack DuVall, *A Force More Powerful: A Century of Nonviolent Conflict* (Palgrave, 2000), 307–8.
30. Lewis, *Walking with the Wind*, 76–86.
31. Ibid., 86.
32. Ibid., 87–89.
33. Ibid., 91–93.
34. Ibid., 94–95.
35. Ibid., 95.
36. Ibid., 95–96.
37. Ibid., 97–98.
38. Ibid., 98.
39. Ibid., 99–100.
40. Ibid., 100-103; Ackerman and Duvall, *A Force More Powerful*, 321–22.
41. Lewis, *Walking with the Wind*, 103.
42. Lewis, *Walking with the Wind*, 103–4; Ackerman and Duvall, *A Force More Powerful*, 322–23.
43. Lewis, *Walking with the Wind*, 104; Ackerman and Duvall, *A Force More Powerful*, 323.
44. Lewis, *Walking with the Wind*, 105–6; Ackerman and Duvall, *A Force More Powerful*, 324–25.
45. Lewis, *Walking with the Wind*, 109–11; Ackerman and Duvall, *A Force More Powerful*, 325–28.

CHAPTER 6

1. For background on Rick Warren and the Saddleback Church, see Charles Duhigg, *The Power of Habit: Why We Do What We Do in Life and in Business* (Random House, 2014), 233–39; Barbara Bradley, "Marketing That New Time Religion," *Los Angeles Times*, December 10, 1995, http://articles.latimes.com/1995-12-10/magazine/tm-12484_1_church-leader/; Alex MacLeod, "A Heart for the Poor," *Presbyterian Record*, January 1, 2008, http://www.presbyterianrecord.ca/2008/01/01/a-heart-for-the-poor/; Malcolm Gladwell, "The Cellular Church," *New Yorker*, September 12, 2005, https://www.newyorker.com/magazine/2005/09/12/the-cellular-church.
2. Gladwell, "The Cellular Church."
3. Duhigg, *The Power of Habit*, 235; Gladwell, "The Cellular Church"; Bradley, "Marketing That New Time Religion"; MacLeod, "A Heart for the Poor."
4. Duhigg, *The Power of Habit*, 235; Gladwell, "The Cellular Church."
5. Duhigg, *The Power of Habit*, 235–37.
6. Ibid., 237.
7. MacLeod, "A Heart for the Poor."

8. AnnaLee Saxenian, "From Brain Drain to Brain Circulation: Transnational Communities and Regional Upgrading in India and China," *Studies in Comparative International Development*, June 2005, https://www.researchgate.net/publication/237827782_From_Brain_Drain_to_Brain_Circulation_Transnational_Communities_and_Regional_Upgrading_in_India_and_China.
9. Interview with author.
10. Joe Nocera, "Two Days in September," *New York Times*, September 14, 2012.
11. Theda Skocpol and Vanessa Williamson, *The Tea Party and the Remaking of Republican Conservatism* (Oxford University Press, 2013), 83–97.
12. Jesse Rhodes, "Broadway's Ten Top Musical Flops," Smithsonian.com, May 10, 2011, http://www.smithsonianmag.com/arts-culture/broadways-top-ten-musical-flops-169390390/.
13. Janice Kaplan, "Bruce Willis Dies Hard on Broadway: When Big Stars Are Big Duds on Stage," *The Daily Beast*, November 16, 2015, http://www.thedailybeast.com/bruce-willis-dies-hard-on-broadway-when-big-stars-are-big-duds-on-stage.
14. Brian Uzzi and Janet Spiro, "Collaboration and Creativity: The Small World Problem," *American Journal of Sociology* 111, no. 2 (September 2005), http://www.kellogg.northwestern.edu/faculty/uzzi/ftp/uzzi%27s_research_papers/0900904.pdf.
15. Robert E. Kelley, "How to Be a Star Engineer," *IEEE Spectrum* 36, no. 10 (October 1999), 51–58, http://vlsicad.ucsd.edu/Research/Advice/star_engineer.pdf.
16. Sandy Pentland, "Beyond the Echo Chamber," *Harvard Business Review*, November 13, 2013, https://hbr.org/2013/11/beyond-the-echo-chamber.
17. Tobias Buchmann and Andreas Pyka, "The Evolution of Innovation Networks: The Case of the German Automotive Industry," University of Hohenheim, Economics Institute, Innovation Economics, November 2012.
18. Anne Marie Slaughter, *The Chessboard and the Web* (Yale University Press, 2017), 168.
19. Valdis E. Krebs, "Mapping Networks of Terrorist Cells," *Connections* 24 (2002): 43–52.
20. Good overviews of measures of network centrality can be found in Slaughter, *The Chessboard and the Web*, 48; and also on the Orgnet website: http://www.orgnet.com/sna.html.
21. Interview with author.
22. Tina Rosenberg, *Join the Club: How Peer Pressure Can Change the World* (W.W. Norton & Company, 2011), 216.
23. Interview with author.
24. Interview with author.

25. Interview with author.
26. Interview with author.
27. Rosenberg, *Join the Club*, 219.
28. Interview with author.
29. Interview with author.
30. Interview with author.
31. Interview with author.
32. Rosenberg, *Join the Club*, 226.
33. E-mail from Srdja Popović.
34. For more on this, see Greg Satell, "The Untold Story Behind the Quest to Train 100,000 STEM Teachers," Inc.com, August 26, 2017.
35. Greg Satell, "Here's Why Your Organization Can't Handle Complexity," Inc.com, October 15, 2017; interview with author.
36. Greg Satell, "IBM Has an Unusual Strategy for Advancing Quantum Computing," Inc.com, June 11, 2017, https://www.inc.com/greg-satell/ibm-has-an-unusual-strategy-for-advancing-quantum-computing.html.
37. Interview with author.
38. David Hoyt, "Institute for Healthcare Improvement: The Campaign to Save 100,000 lives," Stanford Graduate School of Business, Case: L-13, 01/07/2008.
39. Isaac Weinberg, "Wyeth Pharmaceuticals: Changing the Mindsets and Behaviors of 20,000 People . . . One Person at a Time," Stanford Graduate School of Business, Case L-15, 9/16/2009.
40. McChrystal, "Team of Teams," 222–26.
41. Ibid., 244.

CHAPTER 7

1. Background from Mandela's life taken from Nelson Mandela, *Long Walk to Freedom: An Autobiography of Nelson Mandela* (Back Bay Books/Little Brown and Company, 1994).
2. Ibid., 96–100.
3. Ibid., 112.
4. Ibid., 111–12.
5. Ibid., 113–15.
6. Ibid., 116–24.
7. Ibid., 170–76.
8. A full text can be found at https://en.wikipedia.org/wiki/Freedom_Charter.
9. Mandela, *Long Walk to Freedom*, 175.
10. Ibid., 317.
11. Ibid., 238.
12. Ibid., 326.
13. Ibid., 331.
14. Ibid., 332.

15. Ibid., 362–69.
16. Donald Woods, *Biko: The True Story of the Young South African Martyr and his Struggle to Raise Black Consciousness* (Henry Holt & Company, Inc., 1991), 162.
17. Mandela, *Long Walk to Freedom*, 292.
18. Woods, *Biko*, 65.
19. Ibid., 120.
20. Ibid., 120.
21. Jo Becker, *Forcing the Spring: Inside the Fight for Marriage Equality* (Penguin Books, 2015), 28–31.
22. John Lewis, *Walking with the Wind: A Memoir of the Movement* (Simon & Schuster, 1998), 133–34.
23. Interview with author.
24. Robert I. Sutton and Huggy Rao, *Scaling Up Excellence* (Crown Business, 2014), 33–34.
25. Ibid., 37.
26. Canvas Core Curriculum, 236.
27. Ibid., 234.
28. Ibid., 221.
29. Mary Walton, *A Women's Crusade: Alice Paul and the Battle for the Ballot* (St. Martin's Press, 2010), 152–61; also see Jean H. Baker, *Sisters: The Lives of America's Suffragists* (Hill and Wang, 2005), 214–16.
30. Kimberly Chin, "Apple's Privacy Stance Is a Huge 'Competitive Advantage' over Facebook and Google," *Business Insider*, March 21, 2018, https://markets.businessinsider.com/news/stocks/apple-stock-price-competitive-advantage-over-facebook-google-2018-3-1019009278.
31. Carson, *The Autobiography of Martin Luther King Jr.*, 224.
32. Ibid., 281.
33. Duhigg, "The Power of Habit," 116–17.
34. Ibid., 121.

CHAPTER 8

1. Peter Ackerman and Jack DuVall, *A Force More Powerful* (Palgrave, 2000), 116.
2. Ibid., 117.
3. Ibid., 123.
4. Ibid., 125–29.
5. Ibid., 134–35.
6. Ibid., 139.
7. Ibid., 139–41.
8. Ibid., 141–48.
9. Ibid., 148–52.
10. Ibid., 153–65.

11. Ibid., 165–68.
12. Steve Crawshaw and John Jackson, *Small Acts of Resistance* (Sterling Publishing Co. Inc., 2010), 5–6.
13. Erica Chenoweth and Maria J. Stephan, *Why Civil Resistance Works: The Strategic Logic of Nonviolent Conflict* (Columbia University Press, 2011), 6–7.
14. Ibid., 34–38
15. Ibid., 39.
16. David Hoyt, "Institute for Healthcare Improvement: The Campaign to Save 100,000 Lives," Stanford Graduate School of Business, Case: L-13, January 7, 2008.
17. Hayagreeva Rao and Robert Sutton, "The Ergonomics of Innovation," *The McKinsey Quarterly* 2008, no. 4.
18. NHS, "Transforming Community and General Practice Nursing in London—the Art of the Possible," February 9, 2015, https://www.england.nhs.uk/6cs/wp-content/uploads/sites/25/2015/04/change-hour-hb.pdf; also see, Henry Timms and Jeremy Heimans, *New Power: How It's Changing the 21st Century—and Why You Need to Know* (Macmillan, 2018), 155–59.
19. Interview with author.
20. I'm grateful to Srdja Popović for sharing this insight with me.
21. Interview with author.
22. Zeynep Tufekci, *Twitter and Tear Gas: The Power and Fragility of Networked Protests* (Yale University Press, 2017), 39–43.
23. Ibid., 53–60.
24. I'm indebted to Srdja Popović for this insight.
25. Nathaniel Frank, *Awakening: How Gays and Lesbians Brought Marriage Equality to America* (The Belknap Press of Harvard University Press, 2017), 151.
26. Ibid., 151–56.
27. Ibid., 157.
28. Ibid., 156.
29. Ibid., 177–82.
30. Ibid., 188.
31. A lively account of the case can be found in Jo Becker, *Forcing the Spring: Inside the Fight for Marriage Equality* (Penguin Books, 2015).
32. Theodore B. Olson, "The Conservative Case for Gay Marriage," *Newsweek*, January 8, 2010, http://www.newsweek.com/conservative-case-gay-marriage-70923.
33. Martin Luther King Jr. of the Southern Christian Leadership Conference (SCLC); James Farmer of the Congress of Racial Equality (CORE); John Lewis of the Student Nonviolent Coordinating Committee (SNCC); Roy Wilkins of the National Association for the Advancement of Colored People (NAACP); Whitney Young of the National Urban League; and A. Philip Randolph.

34. African National Congress (ANC), South African Communist Party (SACP), South African Congress of Democrats (COD), Coloured People's Congress (CPC), South African Congress of Trade Unions (SACTU), South African Indian Congress (SAIC), and The Federation of South African Women.
35. McChrystal, et. al, *Team of Teams: New Rules of Engagement for a Complex World* (Portfolio, 2015), 178; Fussell and Goodyear, *One Mission: How Leaders Build a Team of Teams* (Portfolio 2017), 198–220.
36. Greg Satell, "This Former Navy SEAL Explains Why You Need to Transform How You Run Meetings," Inc.com, July 15, 2017.
37. Interview with Srdja Popović.
38. Robert Coram, *Boyd: The Fighter Pilot Who Changed the Art of War* (Back Bay Books/Little Brown & Co., 2004), 334–36.
39. Doug McAdam, "Tactical Innovation and the Pace of Insurgency," *American Sociological Review* 48, no. 6 (December 1983), 735–54.
40. I am indebted to Srdja Popović for this insight.

CHAPTER 9

1. Thomas Friedman, "Who Will Influence Whom?," *New York Times*, April 26, 2014, https://www.nytimes.com/2014/04/27/opinion/sunday/friedman-who-will-influence-whom.html.
2. Interview with author.
3. Saul Alinsky, *Rules for Radicals: A Pragmatic Primer for Realistic Radicals* (Vintage Books Edition, 1989), 17–18.
4. Interview with author.
5. Srdja Popović, *Blueprint for a Revolution* (Spiegel & Grau, 2015), 228.
6. Interview with author.
7. Interview with author.
8. Interview with author.
9. Greg Satell, "Breaking Down Silos Is a Myth, Do This Instead," Inc.com, September 9, 2017.
10. Jon Meacham, *The Soul of America: The Battle for Our Better Angels* (Random House, 2018), 272.
11. Interview with author.
12. Interview with author.
13. Greg Satell, "The Beginning of the End for Putin? Real Reform Begins to Take Hold in Ukraine," *Forbes*, April 28, 2015.

INDEX

ABOUT THE AUTHOR

Greg Satell (Gladwyne, PA) is a popular writer, speaker, innovation advisor, and one of today's most recognized experts on transformational change. Previously, as co-CEO of KP Media, a $100 million enterprise, he managed a portfolio of Ukrainian media brands, including *Kyiv Post* and *Korrespondent*, two news organizations that played pivotal roles in the Orange Revolution.